Strategic Foundations of Gene

Dynamic Matching and Barga

The theory of competition has held a central place in economic analysis since Adam Smith. This book, written by one of the most distinguished of contemporary economic theorists, reports on a major research program to provide strategic foundations for the theory of perfect competition.

Beginning with a concise survey of how the theory of competition has evolved, Gale makes extensive and rigorous use of dynamic matching and bargaining models to provide a more complete description of how a competitive equilibrium is achieved. Whereas economists have made use of a macroscopic description of markets in which certain behavioral characteristics, such as price-taking behavior, are taken for granted, Gale uses game theory to re-evaluate this assumption, beginning with individual agents and modeling their strategic interaction. A strategic foundation for competitive equilibrium shows how such interaction leads to competitive, price-taking behavior.

DOUGLAS GALE is Professor of Economics in New York University. A Fellow of the Econometric Society, he has served as assistant editor of *Review of Economic Studies* and co-editor of *Econometrica*. He is currently associate editor of *Journal of Economic Theory*, *Research in Economics* and *Economic Theory* and advisory editor of *Macroeconomic Dynamics*. His research papers have been published in leading journals.

CHURCHILL LECTURES IN ECONOMIC THEORY

On Time
PETER DIAMOND
0 521 46289 4 hardback

Strategic Foundations of General Equilibrium:
Dynamic Matching and Bargaining Games
DOUGLAS GALE
0 521 64330 9 hardback
0 521 64410 0 paperback

Economics and Language
ARIEL RUBINSTEIN
0521 59306 9 hardback
0521 78990 7 paperback

THE CHURCHILL LECTURES IN ECONOMIC THEORY

Strategic Foundations of General Equilibrium

Dynamic Matching and Bargaining Games

DOUGLAS GALE

CAMBRIDGE
UNIVERSITY PRESS

PUBLISHED BY THE PRESS SYNDICATE OF THE UNIVERSITY OF CAMBRIDGE
The Pitt Building, Trumpington Street, Cambridge, United Kingdom

CAMBRIDGE UNIVERSITY PRESS
THE EDINBURGH BUILDING, CAMBRIDGE CB2 2RU, UK
www.cup.cam.ac.uk
40 WEST 20TH STREET, NEW YORK, NY 10011–4211, USA
www.cup.org
10 Stamford Road, Oakleigh, Melbourne 3166, Australia
Ruiz de Alarcón 13, 28014 Madrid, Spain

First published 2000

Printed in the United Kingdom at the University Press, Cambridge

Typeface Trump Medieval System 3B2 [KW]

A catalogue record for this book is available from the British Library

Library of Congress Cataloguing in Publication data

Gale, Douglas.
Strategic foundations of general equilibrium: dynamic matching and
bargaining games/Douglas Gale.
    p. cm. – (Churchill lectures in economic theory)
Includes bibliographical references.
ISBN 0 521 64330 9 hbk 64410 pbk
    1. Competition. 2. Equilibrium (Economics) 3. Game theory. I. Title.
II. Churchill Lectures in Economic Theory
HD41.G35 2000   338.6'048'015193–dc21   99-462249

ISBN 0 521 64330 9   hardback
ISBN 0 521 64410 0   paperback

To my teacher
FRANK H. HAHN

CONTENTS

Contents

ACKNOWLEDGMENTS

This book is based on a series of three lectures delivered in the University of Cambridge in November 1997. Frank Hahn initially invited me to give these lectures. The Master and Fellows of Churchill College provided hospitality while I was in Cambridge. Jayasri Dutta was a charming host. Sudipto Bhattacharya, my discussant, offered a witty and insightful commentary on the lectures. Hamid Sabourian, in probing conversations in Cambridge and New York, made a number of helpful comments, especially on the subject of chapter 3. Robert Rosenthal read chapter 4 and made useful comments. Juan Dubra carefully read an early version of the manuscript and made numerous corrections and suggestions, as did Viral Acharya on a late version of chapter 2. The Cambridge University Press underwrote this lecture series and Patrick McCartan and Ashwin Rattan of the Cambridge University Press handled the publishing. The National Science Foundation and the C.V. Starr Center at New York University provided financial support for the research on which these lectures were based. To all these, I am very grateful.

CHAPTER 1

MARKETS AND GAMES

1.1 Strategic foundations of perfect competition

In these lectures I report on a research program that began in the early 1980s. It is part of a larger effort, underway for a much longer time, to provide strategic foundations for the theory of perfect competition.[1] The theory of competition has held a central place in economic analysis since the time of Adam Smith (1976). By providing strategic foundations for the theory of competition, economists use the principles of game theory to motivate or justify a macroscopic description of markets in which certain behavioral characteristics, such as price-taking behavior, are taken for granted. Game theory begins with individual agents and models their strategic interaction. A strategic foundation for competitive equilibrium must show how strategic interaction by rational agents leads to competitive, price-taking behavior. In practice, this research program includes the following three steps:

1. First, describe a *market or a whole economy*.

    In this step, the economist has to specify the commodities traded, the agents (households and firms) that make up the market or economy, their preferences, their resources, and the available technology.

2. Secondly, define an extensive-form market game describing the behavior of the *agents in the market or economy*.

---

[1] When the context makes the meaning reasonably clear, I adopt the usual practice of writing *competition* or *competitive* when I really mean *perfect competition* and *perfectly competitive*.

Strategic foundations of general equilibrium

In this step, the economist has to specify the players, the information available to each player, the strategies available to them, the outcomes resulting from their choices, and the payoffs received.

3. Thirdly, analyze the market game to show that, under certain conditions, the equilibrium outcome corresponds to a *perfectly competitive equilibrium of the original market or economy.*

There are many ways in which this program can be carried out. I shall be discussing one class of models which I find particularly interesting and fruitful, the class of *dynamic matching and bargaining games* (DMBG). Before getting into the details, however, I want to discuss the motivation for this kind of undertaking.

1.2 Why strategic foundations?

The first question that ought to occur to anyone encountering this kind of work for the first time is "Why?" Why should anyone want to take the time to build strategic foundations for the theory of perfect competition? After all, the theory of competitive equilibrium is well defined and self-contained in its own right. The cornerstones of this theory were laid over a hundred years ago by Alfred Marshall[2] and Léon Walras.[3] The modern axiomatic theory developed by Kenneth Arrow, Gérard Debreu, Lionel McKenzie, and their successors is one of the most complete and definitive constructions that economics has to offer.[4] Instead of pursuing steps 2 and 3, Arrow, Debreu, McKenzie, *et al.*, simply assume that households maxi-

[2] Marshall, A., *Principles of Economics: An Introductory Volume*, 8th edn., London: Macmillan (1920).
[3] Walras, L., *Elements of Pure Economics*, London: Allen & Unwin (1954).
[4] Arrow, K. and G. Debreu, "Existence of Equilibrium for a Competitive Economy," *Econometrica*, 22 (1954), 265–90. McKenzie, L. "On Equilibrium in Graham's Model of World Trade and Other Competitive Systems," *Econometrica*, 22 (1954), 147–61.

2

mize utility subject to a budget constraint, that firms max-imize profits subject to their production technology, and that prices adjust to clear markets. Why do we need more than this? There are three reasons.

Games and markets

The first reason is provided by the rise of game theory. Since the foundations of general equilibrium theory were laid in the nineteenth century, game theory has assumed an increasingly central role in economics. Game theory, as defined by von Neumann and Morgenstern, offers a general and powerful framework with which to analyze interactive decision-making. To the extent that we accept the claim of game theory to be the correct framework for analyzing decision-making by individuals, we should want to use it as a tool for analyzing the behavior of agents in markets. Unfortunately, models of competitive equilibrium are not games in a strict, formal sense. In particular, games have two attractive features that models of market equilibrium do not have:

- In a strategic game, all the endogenous variables are chosen by players in the game.
- In a strategic game, any profile of strategies chosen by the players determines a unique feasible outcome of the game.

A long recognized and embarassing lacuna in the theory of competitive equilibrium is the failure to explain where the prices come from. Sometimes we are reduced to saying that prices are chosen by an "auctioneer," but essentially they are free parameters that are "determined," along with the other endogenous variables, by the market-clearing condition. In other words, unlike strategic games, models of market equilibrium have endogenous variables that are not chosen by the agents.

Another weakness of the classical model of competitive equilibrium is the assumption that agents believe that they can buy and sell as much as they like at the prevailing prices. It is true that agents buy and sell as much as they want in equilibrium, but if an agent deviates from his equilibrium excess demand, he will find that the assumption is violated. Except in the case where agents are literally negligible, any deviation leads to an infeasible set of excess demands. As a result, the market cannot clear and some agent will be disappointed in his attempt to trade. In the language of game theory, there are some strategy profiles to which no feasible outcome corresponds (unless we abandon the assumption that agents can trade as much as they want).

So, by comparison with the framework of game theory, the model of competitive equilibrium has some loose ends when it comes to the treatment of prices and the feasibility of trades.

These loose ends do not mean that the model of competitive equilibrium is a "bad model." On the contrary, it can be regarded as a reduced form of a more complicated model or process that describes the final outcome without giving all the details. One of the advantages of building a strategic foundation for perfect competition is that we will be forced to describe the process completely and explain how the competitive equilibrium outcome is reached. The complete model will, naturally, be an extensive-form game.

When is perfect competition appropriate?

A second reason for wanting a strategic foundation of competitive equilibrium is to provide a theoretical *rationale* for perfect competition. A formal statement of the theory may be aesthetically pleasing, but it does not tell us why or under what circumstances the theory is appropriate. For example, we can define a perfectly competitive equilibrium for an Edgeworth Box economy with two goods and two agents, even though perfect competition is unlikely to be

[5] Ostroy (1980) and Makowski (1983) have characterized competitive equilibrium in terms of the *no-surplus condition*. They have argued that finite economies such as the Edgeworth Box economy sometimes satisfy the no-surplus condition and hence are perfectly competitive. However, the finite economies that satisfy the no-surplus condition are very special, and might be considered pathological.

achieved in a market consisting of only two agents.[5] There is nothing in the formal definition to tell us whether the model applies to economies consisting of two, or a hundred, or a million agents.

One advantage of providing strategic foundations for perfect competition is that we are forced to construct a game in which perfect competition is only one of many possible outcomes. Then we show that under certain conditions competition arises as the unique equilibrium outcome. Deriving perfect competition from a more general framework provides us with a rationale for the competitive equilibrium: it shows under what conditions the model of competitive equilibrium is a good description of rational interaction among economic agents.

This aspect of the research program is illustrated by the distinction between *limit theorems* and *theorems in the limit*. Perfect competition is an idealized state, one which is only more or less imperfectly approximated by reality and then only under certain special conditions. It is a non-trivial task to decide when the theory is a reasonable approximation. Some markets may be approximately perfectly competitive; others are not. How do we know which is which? Consider a sequence of economies, in which the number of agents is growing without bound. In the limit there is a continuum of individually insignificant agents. At what point does the economy become "competitive?" Theorems in the limit characterize the exact conditions under which a perfectly competitive outcome may be expected to occur, whereas limit theorems tell us that, as we approach those conditions, the observed outcome will approach the competitive outcome.

By embedding different accounts of equilibrium behavior in a single theoretical framework, we are able to distinguish and classify the conditions under which different forms of competition arise. So another use for strategic foundations of perfect competition is to understand better the conditions under which perfect competition is an appropriate description of market behavior.

Normative economics

Still another use for strategic foundations of competition comes from the role of the competitive equilibrium as a normative ideal. The classical theorems of welfare economics tell us that, under certain conditions, every perfectly competitive equilibrium allocation is Pareto-efficient and every Pareto-efficient allocation can be decentralized as a perfectly competitive equilibrium with lump-sum transfers. But how is perfect competition brought about? What practical institutions will achieve the desired outcome? In order to use the theory of perfect competition as a practical tool for achieving the efficient allocation of resources, we need more than a definition of a perfectly competitive outcome. We also need a theory of the institutions and conditions under which perfect competition may arise as the result of interactive decision-making by rational agents. In other words, we need a theory of the strategic foundations of perfect competition. Because game-theoretic models describe more completely the institutions that underly the market, they give us insight into the reasons why perfect competition may or may not be achieved. This knowledge may suggest policies to increase the degree of competition and, in the limit, achieve perfect competition. Alternatively, it may convince us that perfect competition is not the optimum in certain circumstances.

1.3 Cooperative market games

Attempts to provide a game-theoretic foundation for competition are almost as old as the theory of competition itself.

In *Mathematical Psychics*, Francis Ysidro Edgeworth (1881) addresses a broad theme, the applicability of mathematics in the social sciences. In particular, he addresses the question of whether the behavior of individuals is "determinate," by which he means "predictable using mathematical models." He argues that social processes, which might be indeterminate when small numbers of economic agents are involved, became determinate, and hence subject to mathematical analysis, when the number of agents is large. As an example, Edgeworth studies trade between two agents in a setting we have since come to call an Edgeworth Box economy. He argues that the outcome of such trade is indeterminate, because only efficiency and individual rationality can be counted on. But as the number of traders increases, the outcome of trade becomes increasingly determinate. The possibilities for recontracting among a large number of agents restrict the possible outcomes and, in the limit, allow for only competitive outcomes.

In *Mathematical Psychics*, Edgeworth follows the three steps of the program listed above. He describes an economy, represents the behavior of the agents by a coalition-forming game and shows that under certain conditions the solution of the game corresponds to a perfectly competitive equilibrium outcome. In modern terminology, he describes a model of an exchange economy consisting of a finite number of economic agents. Each agent has an initial endowment of the commodities available in the economy, a consumption set that specifies the possible commodity bundles the agent can consume, and preferences over his consumption set. The allocation of resources is undertaken by coalitions of agents. Formally, a coalition is any non-empty set of agents. An allocation is attainable for a coalition if the commodity bundle assigned to each agent belongs to his consumption set and the bundles add up to the coalition's total endowment. A coalition can improve on an attainable allocation if there exists an allocation that is attainable for the coalition and makes every member of the coalition better off. Edgeworth introduces the concept of the *contract curve* to describe the outcomes of the recontracting process. The contract curve is what we now call the *core* of the market game. It consists of the set of all attainable allocations that cannot be improved upon by any coalition. Edgeworth shows that as the number of agents grows unboundedly large, the core of the market game shrinks until it contains only the perfectly competitive equilibrium allocations.

This profound result, which stands virtually alone in nineteenth-century contributions to economic theory for its depth and beauty, was re-discovered by Shubik (1959) who showed the equivalence of the core and the contract curve. For the next fifteen years the theory was extended and refined until it reached a more or less definitive state with the publication of Hildenbrand (1974).

Now we have theorems that show that the Shapley value (Aumann and Shapley, 1974), the bargaining set (Mas-Colell, 1989), the set of fair trades (Schmeidler and Vind, 1972), and other solution concepts also shrink to the set of Walras allocations as the number of players becomes very large. The fact that a variety of different solution concepts lead to the same result is a strong argument for the robustness of the competitive equilibrium.

All of these attempts to provide strategic foundations for perfect competition make use of *cooperative* game theory.[6] The cooperative approach to game theory has its limitations. Some of these are peculiar to particular cooperative solution concepts such as the core. Others are common to cooperative games in general.

At the general level, one of the attractions of cooperative game theory is that it provides a criterion for strategic stability that leads directly to a solution of the game, without the tedious business of specifying an extensive-form game. There is no need to specify the strategy set of each player, the order of moves, the information sets, or the players' assumptions about their opponents' behavior. All one needs is a convenient definition of what counts as a plausible outcome of the game.

In particular, there is no need to specify a well defined maximization problem for each individual player. However, this could also be considered a weakness. As

[6] For present purposes we can think of a cooperative game as being defined by a set of players, a specification of the coalitions or non-empty subsets of players that can form, and a specification of the actions or payoffs that can be achieved by each coalition of players. A solution of the game is a set of profiles of actions or payoffs that satisfies some plausible criterion of stability.

Markets and games

John Hicks remarked in his "A Suggestion for Simplifying Monetary Theory" (reprinted in Hicks, 1967), anything seems to go when no one is required to maximize anything. A well defined maximization problem for each agent is one of the characteristic building blocks of modern economics. Cooperative game theory lacks the discipline that comes from having to specify a maximization problem for each agent. As a result, it begs a number of questions.

This can be seen when we look at particular applications of cooperative game theory to market games. Take the core, for example. The formal definition of the core provides a criterion for stability, not a description of the process of coalition formation. An allocation belongs to the core if no coalition can improve on it. The definition suggests that if an allocation does not belong to the core it could never be an "equilibrium" because the improving coalition, whose existence is guaranteed by the definition, would do something to prevent it. Why the improving coalition should do that is not clear. Indeed, it is hard to think about this question without knowing how an allocation comes to be chosen in the first place; but suppose, for the sake of argument, that a non-core allocation has somehow occurred. It is easy to find allocations that (1) do not belong to the core, (2) make some agents better off than they would be in any core allocation, and (3) can be improved on only by coalitions which include the agents who will be worse off at any core allocation. In this case, the improving coalition would be very myopic to veto this allocation if it really believed in the core as a solution concept, because it will certainly be worse off when a core allocation is finally reached. It appears that the core concept requires agents to behave myopically, rushing to join improving coalitions so that they can cut their own throats.

More sophisticated cooperative solution concepts try to eliminate such myopia; but the cooperative framework itself is the obstacle to a consistent theory, because it does not provide each agent with a well defined maximization problem. Without an extensive-form game, many of these problems can never be resolved satisfactorily.

9

For this reason, Nash (1951) proposed that cooperative games should be reduced to non-cooperative games. He interpreted a cooperative game as one in which there is unlimited pre-play communication and binding agreements can be entered into before the game is played. A non-cooperative game is one without pre-play communication or agreements. (This classification is clearly not exhaustive and there are other features that make it less than satisfactory, but the terminology has stuck so I will continue to use it.) The communication and commitment that precede the play of a cooperative game are not explicitly modeled, but they should be regarded as part of the game and analyzed using the same principles as the formal game itself. To do this, we model explicitly the pre-play communication and commitments, and then analyze the behavior of players in this game in the same way as if they were playing a non-cooperative game. This procedure, of reducing the cooperative game to a non-cooperative game by making explicit the informal parts of the cooperative theory, is known as the *Nash Program*.

The *Nash Program* is something that should appeal to economists, because it adopts Hicks' principle that every agent should be given a well defined maximization problem to solve. The use of non-cooperative game theory to provide a strategic foundation for competition is a natural extension of the earlier use of cooperative game theory. Ultimately, a satisfactory foundation for competitive markets requires a non-cooperative (extensive-form) game. This is what I shall be doing here, using non-cooperative game theory to provide a more complete description of what goes on in markets and then deriving the familiar competitive outcomes as an implication of particular conditions and assumptions.

1.4 Non-cooperative market games

The first non-cooperative approach to competition antedates the core by about fifty years. It began with the analysis of duopoly by Antoine Augustin Cournot (1838, 1960). Cournot analyzes the problem of the owners of two mineral springs who want to maximize the profits from marketing their spring water. A duopoly does not satisfy the conditions for perfect competition. The non-cooperative equilibrium of Cournot's model predicts that each supplier will restrict his output of spring water in order to raise the price and increase profits. However, as more and more suppliers are added one can, under certain conditions, show that the non-cooperative equilibrium converges to a competitive equilibrium in the limit as the number of suppliers becomes infinite. More importantly, the Cournot model is a well defined game for any number of players, taking as given the market demand curve faced by the suppliers.

This approach to competitive equilibrium was generalized by Shubik (1973) (see also Shapley and Shubik,1977) with his Cournotian market games. Here is one version of a *Cournot–Shubik Market Game* (CSMG). Start with an exchange economy with a finite number of agents. Each agent has an endowment which he takes to the exchange floor and puts in the center. The agents are given different amounts of a token money which they can use to bid for quantities of the commodities in the center. A strategy for an agent is a vector of non-negative bids, one for each commodity, summing to his endowment of money. Once all the agents have chosen their bids, the commodities are divided in proportion to the bids, that is, an agent receives a fraction of the total endowment of each commodity equal to the ratio of his bid for that commodity to the total of the bids from all agents for that commodity. There are no explicit prices and each agent perceives that his final bundle of commodities depends not only on his own bids but also on the bids of all the other agents. Furthermore, each agent in a finite economy has market power, that is, the ability to change the implicit rate at which goods exchange for money by changing his bid. However, as the number of agents becomes unboundedly large, the Nash equilibrium outcomes of the CSMG converge, under certain regularity conditions, to the Walras allocations.

There are many other variants of these models, with commodity money, credit, bankruptcy, "wash trading," and other complications. The essential point is that the CSMG is a well defined extensive-form game that extends the partial equilibrium story of Cournot to encompass an economy in general equilibrium.

The CSMG provides a strategic foundation for competition and, as such, it is very much in the spirit of the research reported in this book. However, there are some critical features of the CSMG that separate them from the DMBG. The first is that although prices do not enter explicitly into the story, the definition of the CSMG imposes the restriction that all trades in a given commodity take place at the same price. More precisely, each agent gets a fraction of the total endowment of a given commodity and that fraction equals the ratio of his bid to the total bid. Each agent is trading money for the commodity at the same rate, that is, at the same price. In that sense, prices are built into the story in the same way as they were in the original Cournot duopoly model.

A second, more subtle feature is that the institutional structure is highly centralized, again by definition. Every agent is bidding against every other bidder and all the bids are aggregated (added up) in order to determine the final outcome. This is analogous to assuming that everyone trades on a centralized market and that the market mechanism treats every agent symmetrically. Furthermore, we can think of the ratio of the endowment to the total bids as a price. It is only the relaxation of the price-taking assumption that distinguishes this model from the Walrasian model of competitive equilibrium.

So the definition of the CSMG already incorporates some of the features of the Walrasian theory of competitive equilibrium. This is not a criticism of the CSMG as a strategic foundation for competitive equilibrium; however, there may be contexts in which we want to start with more primitive concepts – for example, to allow for decentralized trade or to allow different agents to trade at different prices. In that case, a framework like the DMBG will be needed.

1.5 Dynamic matching and bargaining models

One successful modeling strategy is the class of *dynamic matching and bargaining games* (DMBG). It brings together elements of two branches of economic theory, search theory and bargaining theory. Economic agents are assumed to search at random for trading opportunities and when they meet the terms of trade are determined by bargaining. At one time markets actually worked like this (think of barter in primitive societies or the early stock exchanges). Although most markets have evolved since then, there is still enough realism in this framework to make it relevant. In addition, the flexibility of this framework makes it a good laboratory for "thought experiments," investigating questions about the behavior of actual markets and the design of better ones. In this section I review some of the achievements of the DMBG literature.

The alternating-offers bargaining model

The early 1980s was a period of tremendous activity in the theory of bargaining. The event that sparked this creative surge was the publication of Rubinstein's (1982) paper on the alternating-offers bargaining model. Although the main ideas of the model had been proposed by Stahl (1972) ten years earlier and the analysis of Stahl's model with a finite horizon was already in some textbooks (Moulin, 1986), it was the successful analysis of the *infinite-horizon* bargaining problem by Rubinstein that grabbed the attention of theorists everywhere.

You probably know the elements of the Stahl–Rubinstein model (more general versions can be found in Binmore, Rubinstein and Wolinsky, 1986). Two individuals want to divide a "cake." Without loss of generality we can assume that the cake is worth one dollar and that any division $(x, 1 - x)$ giving a share $x \geq 0$ to player 1 and $1 - x \geq 0$ to player 2 is feasible. The players bargain as follows. First player 1 proposes a division $(x, 1 - x)$ and player 2 accepts or rejects this proposal. If he accepts, the game ends and the two individuals split the cake as agreed. If he rejects, then player 2 proposes a division $(y, 1 - y)$ and player 1 accepts or rejects. The bargaining process continues in this way until an agreement is reached. If agreement is never reached, they both receive nothing.

The individuals are assumed to be impatient and for every period that agreement is delayed, their payoffs are discounted. The discount factor of player i is denoted by $0 < \delta_i < 1$. If the players agree on the division $(x, 1 - x)$ at date t then player 1's payoff is $\delta_1^{t-1}x$ and player 2's payoff is $\delta_2^{t-1}(1 - x)$. This discounting or shrinkage represents the costs of bargaining: other things being equal, the longer it takes to reach agreement, the less "cake" there is for both players.

As you will remember, Edgeworth (1881) thought of the bargaining problem as indeterminate. Nash (1953) himself proposed a simultaneous demand game in which any Pareto-efficient division was an equilibrium outcome. The remarkable result proved by Stahl and Rubinstein is that their bargaining problems are determinate. More precisely, the alternating-offers bargaining game has a unique, *subgame-perfect equilibrium* (SPE)[7] in which the players reach agreement immediately and the division is

$$\left(\frac{1 - \delta_2}{1 - \delta_1\delta_2}, \frac{\delta_2(1 - \delta_1)}{1 - \delta_1\delta_2} \right).$$

The outcome is asymmetric both because the players have different discount rates and because player 1 has a first-mover advantage. If we assume that the players have the same discount rate $\delta_1 = \delta_2 = \delta$ then the equilibrium division is $(1/(1 + \delta), \delta/(1 + \delta))$. Player 1 gets the larger share because he is the first mover.

Now suppose that the bargaining process is "speeded up" by making the time interval between successive rounds smaller and smaller. When the period length becomes van-

---

[7] In a Nash equilibrium each player chooses a best response at each information set that occurs in the equilibrium play of the game. In an SPE each player chooses a best response at every information set, whether or not it occurs in the equilibrium play of the game.

ishingly small, the first-mover advantage disappears. For example, let τ be the period length and then the discount factor δ is given by $e^{-\rho\tau}$, where ρ is the instantaneous rate of time preference. Holding ρ constant, $\delta \to 1$ as $\tau \to 0$. It can easily be seen that the equilibrium division of the cake converges to the symmetric Nash bargaining solution $(1/2, 1/2)$ as δ converges to 1.

The uniqueness result does not survive some simple relaxations of the assumptions presented here. For example, if there are three players then the number of SPEs may be infinite (Shaked, 1994). If the set of possible distributions is discrete rather than continuous then, again, there may be multiple SPEs.

There is a lot more that can be said about this interesting framework (see Osborne and Rubinstein, 1990, for a masterful treatment), but these are the essentials that are needed for what follows.

Marshallian markets

The application of non-cooperative bargaining theory to competitive equilibrium came in a seminal paper by Rubinstein and Wolinsky (1985). Rubinstein and Wolinsky use the alternating-offers bargaining model as a strategic foundation for "competitive" price determination in a Marshallian market.

The model contains a continuum of traders, M buyers and N sellers of an indivisible good. Each buyer wants at most one unit of the good, which he values at one dollar. The sellers each have one unit of the good, which they value at zero dollars. If a buyer and a seller trade, they realize a surplus of one dollar. These gains from trade are the "cake" over which the buyers and sellers will bargain.

In each period, the buyers and sellers are matched at random to form pairs of agents, each consisting of a buyer and a seller. One agent is chosen at random to propose a price at which to trade. The other can accept or reject this price. If an agreement is reached (a price is proposed and accepted), the pair of agents trade and leave the market. Each consumes his share of the surplus after leaving the market. If an agreement is not reached, they remain in the market until the next period. An unmatched agent remains passive until the next period.

A pair of agents can remain together and bargain for several periods, but if one of them is matched with another agent it is assumed that he leaves his former partner and begins bargaining with his new partner.[8] This is the only way that partnerships can be broken up.

Buyers and sellers discount the future using the same discount factor δ. If agreement is reached on a price p after t periods of bargaining, the seller receives $\delta^{t-1}p$ and the buyer receives $\delta^{t-1}(1-p)$.

Whenever an agent leaves the market, he is immediately replaced with an identical agent who has yet to trade, so the number of buyers and sellers is constant over time.

The model described above is not a game in the sense of von Neumann and Morgenstern (1980). In particular, there is no initial node and there is a continuum of players. Rubinstein and Wolinsky study what they call a *quasistationary subgame-perfect equilibrium* which is like a subgame perfect equilibrium in which some possible nodes are not considered. They show that there exists a unique equilibrium in which agents reach agreement as soon as they are matched. The equilibrium division depends on the matching probabilities as well as the discount factor and the identity of the proposer. If a seller meets a new buyer each period with probability $0 < \alpha < 1$ and a buyer meets a new seller each period with probability $0 < \beta < 1$, then the equilibrium price is

---

[8] It is interesting to note that it is optimal for agents to switch whenever they meet a new agent. Since all buyers (resp. sellers) are identical and the equilibrium is stationary, there is no advantage for a seller (resp. buyer) in remaining with his current partner if he has the option of switching. There are other equilibria, however. If agents choose to remain with their current partners regardless of whether they are matched with new partners, this is also optimal. Then the analysis of the model effectively reduces to the examination of series of two-person bargaining problems. The equilibrium payoffs are the same as for the Rubinstein (1982) game.

$$x^* = \frac{2(1 - \delta) + \delta\alpha - \delta(1 - \delta)(1 - \alpha)(1 - \beta)}{2(1 - \delta) + \delta\alpha + \delta\beta}$$

if the seller proposes and

$$y^* = \frac{\delta\alpha + \delta(1 - \delta)(1 - \alpha)(1 - \beta)}{2(1 - \delta) + \delta\alpha + \delta\beta}$$

if the buyer proposes.

The length of a time period in this model represents both the time between successive matches and the time between successive offers by any pair of bargaining agents. Reducing the period length is formally equivalent to reducing the rate at which agents discount the future. As the period length converges to zero, it can be shown that all trade takes place at the same price, that is,

$$\lim_{\delta \to 1} x^* = \lim_{\delta \to 1} y^* = \frac{\alpha}{\alpha + \beta}.$$

The limiting equilibrium price depends only on the matching probabilities since we have assumed that buyers and sellers share a common discount factor. The crucial point is that, for fixed values of α and β, the equilibrium price is bounded away from one and zero, so that both sides of the market get a positive share of the gains from trade.

In the Rubinstein–Wolinsky model, agents have to search for trading partners and search takes time. Because of the time taken to search for trading partners, this is not a "frictionless" market and for that reason alone we might not expect it to be perfectly competitive. Allowing the period length to converge to zero, so that the discount factor converges to one, is a way of reducing the transaction costs or "frictions" so that the market becomes frictionless in the limit. However, Rubinstein and Wolinsky argue that even in the limit, when the market becomes frictionless, their model does not produce the competitive outcome.

Rubinstein and Wolinsky suggest that we take as the perfectly competitive benchmark an auction market with M buyers and N sellers. The demand correspondence $D(p)$ for such a market is defined by

$$D(p) = \begin{cases} M & \text{if } p < 1 \\ [0, M] & \text{if } p = 1 \\ 0 & \text{if } p > 1 \end{cases}$$

and the supply correspondence $S(p)$ is defined by

$$S(p) = \begin{cases} [0, N] & \text{if } p = 0 \\ N & \text{if } p > 0 \end{cases}$$

The unique market-clearing price is $p^* = 0$ if $M < N$ and $p^* = 1$ if $M > N$. In other words, if the number of buyers exceeds the number of sellers, the sellers get all the surplus; if the number of sellers exceeds the number of buyers, the buyers get all the surplus. Only if the number of buyers and sellers is equal can there be a market-clearing price between zero and one.

The interpretation of this result is complicated by the fact that there is, over the infinite history of the market, an infinite number of buyers and sellers. It is not clear how to define a market-clearing price in a market with an infinite number of buyers and sellers. Since every agent eventually gets to trade at the common price, it could be argued that the equilibrium of the Rubinstein–Wolinsky model is "competitive." Although the limiting price $\alpha/(\alpha + \beta)$ does not clear an auction market with M buyers and N sellers, it does clear the market with an infinite number of buyers and sellers flowing through it.

Gale (1987) develops this theme in a paper that analyzes a Marshallian market with many types of buyers and sellers, each of whom wants to trade one unit of the indivisible good. In Gale's model there is a non-atomic continuum of buyers and sellers, with M_i buyers of type $i = 1, \dots, I$ and N_j sellers of type $j = 1, \dots, J$. Buyers of type i value one unit of the good at u_i and sellers of type j value the good at v_j. All agents discount the future using the common factor δ. If a buyer of type i agrees to buy one unit at a price p at date t, his payoff is $\delta^{t-1}(u_i - p)$. Similarly, if a seller of type j agrees to sell one unit of the good at a price p at time t, his payoff is $\delta^{t-1}(p - v_j)$.

Agents are randomly matched in pairs consisting of one buyer and one seller in each period. Matches last exactly one period and the buyer and the seller each have probability 1/2 of being chosen to make a proposal. The proposer names a price and the responder accepts or rejects. If an agreement is reached, a trade is executed at the agreed price and both agents leave the market. Otherwise they wait until the next period, when they will be matched again with new partners, and the bargaining process continues.

The assumption that matches last only one period does not allow for alternating-offers bargaining of the kind that occurs in Rubinstein (1982) and Rubinstein and Wolinsky (1985). This probably does not affect the outcome in a stationary equilibrium, since the buyer (seller) is replaced by an identical agent in the next period. However, the fact that bargaining is brought to an end exogenously does matter, as we saw earlier (see n. 8). Another assumption that is crucial is that agents bargain under complete information. The agents' types are assumed to be common knowledge, so there is no uncertainty about the value of the good to the buyer and seller when they bargain.

In Gale's model, trades may occur at many different prices, depending on the types of buyers and sellers involved as well as the identity of the proposer. However, it can be shown that there is a unique stationary equilibrium of the model and as the discount factor converges to unity the stationary equilibrium prices converge to a common limit – that is, all trades take place at the same price. Furthermore, every agent who wants to trade at this price is able to do so in equilibrium. Since there is no discounting in the limit, each agent gets the payoff he would receive in a competitive equilibrium at this price.

Gale's model is not, strictly speaking, a generalization of the Rubinstein–Wolinsky model because matches are dissolved after one period, but in other respects it is similar. The limiting outcome in this case looks more like a competitive equilibrium because there are many types of agents trading at a single price. However, there exists the same problem of how to interpret the market-clearing condition. Suppose we take as a benchmark an auction market with M_i buyers of type i and N_j sellers of type j. If p is the limiting price, assuming that no one is indifferent to trading, the demand in the auction market is

$$\sum_{\{i:u_i>p\}} M_i$$

and the supply is

$$\sum_{\{j:v_j<p\}} N_j$$

and there is no reason why these two should be equal. So the limiting price p does not correspond to the market-clearing price of an auction market with M_i buyers of type i and N_j sellers of type j. Every agent does get to trade at the limit price p and, since there is no discounting, there is no cost of delay (every agent gets the same utility as if he were able to trade immediately at the price p). It is only by comparison with the static auction market that one is led to question whether the outcome is perfectly competitive.

A peculiarity of the Rubinstein–Wolinsky model is that buyers and sellers are replaced by identical agents whenever they leave the market. This ensures that the stock of agents in the market remains constant over time. Presumably, it is this constancy of the population of agents in the market at any date that suggests the comparison with a static auction market having the same population of agents.

This version of Gale's model adopts the Rubinstein–Wolinsky endogenous replacement assumption. Another way to model entry and exit is to assume a constant flow of potential entrants to the market, in which case a stationary state can be maintained only if the equilibrium price adjusts so that the numbers of buyers and sellers entering the market at each date are equal. If p is the equilibrium price, a buyer of type i will not enter the market if $u_i < p$ and a seller of type j will not enter the market if $v_j > p$. The absence of these types is important because it affects the matching probabilities and hence the equilibrium prices. Furthermore, stationarity requires that equal numbers of buyers and sellers enter the market in each period. Thus, the equilibrium price must equate the flows of buyers and sellers into the market. Assuming that no type is indifferent, stationarity requires that

$$\sum_{\{i:u_i>p\}} M_i = \sum_{\{j:v_j<p\}} N_j,$$

where M_i (resp. N_j) is the flow of potential buyers of type i (resp. potential sellers of type j) into the market at each date. This is exactly the Marshallian notion of equilibrium for an auction market with M_i buyers of type i and N_j sellers of type j.

The long side of the market adjusts so that the equilibrium price satisfies this condition. For example, if more sellers than buyers are entering the market at each date, the sellers will be on the long side. The number of sellers waiting to trade will increase until the price is reduced to the point where the number of sellers entering at each date is just equal to the number of buyers entering. Similarly, if the number of buyers entering the market is greater than the number of sellers, the price will have to rise. Here price is fulfilling its Marshallian role of adjusting to equate the flow of demand and supply, but the price itself is being determined by the relative bargaining power of buyers and sellers, which in turn is influenced by the relative numbers of buyers and sellers in the market.

Walrasian models of exchange

The problems of interpretation that arose in the previous subsection are caused by the stationarity assumption, which implies that an infinite measure of agents flows through the market over time. An economy with an infinite measure of agents does not have a well defined competitive equilibrium to serve as a benchmark. We can avoid this difficulty by working with a finite measure of agents, but this entails analyzing a non-stationary equilibrium.

An example of this approach is found in Gale (1986a, 1986b, 1986c) which take the basic idea of the dynamic matching and bargaining framework from Rubinstein and Wolinsky and apply it to a Walrasian model of exchange.[9]

Begin with an exchange economy consisting of a finite number of types of agents $i = 1, \ldots, I$ and a continuum of each type. All agents have the same consumption set $\mathbf{R}_+^\ell$, where ℓ is the number of commodities, and agents of type i have the same initial endowment e_i and the same utility function $u_i(x)$.

Trade takes place at a sequence of dates. At each date, agents have a probability $0 < \alpha < 1$ of being matched with another agent. Agents are distinguished by their type and by the bundle of commodities they are currently holding, so a typical agent is represented by an ordered pair (i, x) (agents of the same type typically have different commodity bundles). The state of the economy at any date t can then be described by a measure μ_t on the set of ordered pairs (i, x) representing types and current holdings. The probability of being matched with agents belonging to a measurable set A is proportional to the measure $\mu_t(A)$.

Suppose that a pair of agents with current commodity bundles x and y are matched at some date. The two agents' types and commodity bundles are common knowledge when the bargaining begins. Each of them has an equal chance of being chosen as the proposer. Once the proposer has been chosen, he offers a net trade z to the other agent. This net trade must be feasible for both agents. If x is the proposer's commodity bundle and y is the responder's, then feasibility requires that $x + z \geq 0$ and $y - z \geq 0$. The responder can accept or reject the offer or decide to leave the game. If the offer is accepted, then the proposed trades are executed and the agents proceed to the next date with their new bundles $x + z$ and $y - z$, respectively. Otherwise there is no trade.

Matches last for only one period. Agents remain in the market until they choose to exit and they have the option

---

[9] An extension of the simple Rubinstein–Wolinsky framework with a single type of buyer and seller to deal with non-stationary equilibria is found in Binmore and Herrero (1988a, 1988b).

to exit only after they have been matched. Because there is always a positive probability of being unmatched in any period ($\alpha < 1$), there will always be a positive measure of agents who have not yet been matched and so remain in the game.

There is no consumption during the game. After exiting with a commodity bundle x an agent of type i consumes the bundle and receives the payoff $u_i(x)$. Note that there is no discounting. An agent who does not exit is assumed to receive an infinitely negative payoff, so every agent will choose to exit with probability one. Once an agent exits, he cannot re-enter and the game is effectively over for him. Since agents are not replaced, the number of active agents in the DMBG decreases over time. The model is therefore non-stationary, in contrast to the Rubinstein–Wolinsky model.

A number of regularity assumptions, which will not be discussed here, are used in the course of the analysis of this model. Taking these for granted, we can summarize the conclusion of the analysis as follows. A subgame-perfect equilibrium of the DMBG always results in a Walras allocation – that is, each player receives the commodity bundle that he would receive in a Walrasian equilibrium. Conversely, for any Walras allocation there exists a subgame-perfect equilibrium of the DMBG in which almost every agent left the market with the corresponding commodity bundle. In this sense, the dynamic matching and bargaining game implements the Walras allocations.

Recent developments

McLennan and Sonnenschein (1991) provide an elegant extension of Gale's version of this model in which many of the regularity conditions required by Gale were relaxed. The McLennan–Sonnenschein version applies only to stationary environments, in which the population and its characteristics remain constant over time, while traders enter and exit the market. McLennan and Sonnenschein use an approach based on the idea of *fair net trades*. They show that a non-cooperative equilibrium of their model satisfies the fair net trade axioms proposed by Schmeidler and Vind (1972). This implies that the resulting allocation is competitive in the sense that, for some price vector p, every agent behaves as if he were maximizing his utility subject to the usual budget constraint defined by the price vector p. The interpretation of the McLennan–Sonnenschein model presents the same difficulty as the original Rubinstein–Wolinsky model. Since an infinite measure of agents passes through the stationary model, the market-clearing condition is not well defined. In fact, as Dagan, Serrano and Volij (forthcoming) have recently argued, there is something unsatisfactory about the feasibility requirements in their model. They require cumulative trades to be feasible, rather than requiring feasibility period by period. In this case, any allocation is feasible because one can operate Ponzi schemes.

Dagan, Serrano and Volij have further expanded the class of environments in which one can demonstrate the equivalence of DMBG equilibria and Walrasian equilibria, but they do so by dropping one of the key ingredients of the earlier theory. They allow finite coalitions of any size to form. One member is chosen to make a proposal and the rest accept or reject. Although Dagan, Serrano and Volij define a non-cooperative game, it is one that has a strong resemblence to the cooperative notion of the core of an exchange economy insofar as arbitrary finite coalitions are allowed to form and trade among themselves. Finite coalitions can be quite large and large numbers have a "convexifying" effect that explains why many of the restrictive assumptions needed in the analysis of pairwise matching and bargaining are not needed in the analysis of this game.

The recent developments in the theory of DMBG have eliminated many of the technical limitations of the early theory, but there remain a number of important open questions. These questions, to which I turn next, provide the motivation for this book.

1.6 Open questions

The continuum assumption

All of the papers referred to above assume that the economy or market consists of a non-atomic continuum of agents.[10] This *continuum assumption*, as I shall call it, is of course one of the standard assumptions underlying the theory of perfect competition. A competitive market is one in which no firm or consumer has significant market power. Now, this is always an assumption that can at best hold in an approximate sense. In studying economies with a continuum of agents, we hope that the continuum economy is a good approximation to an economy with a large but finite number of agents. To establish the validity of the theory we need to prove limit theorems rather than theorems in the limit. To do this it is necessary to assume the existence of a finite number of agents, let the number increase without bound, and see whether the equilibria of the finite games converge to the appropriate allocation in the limit. (The theory referred to earlier contains a number of limit theorems, of course, but they are limits with respect to the period length or discount factor, not the number of agents.)

The first topic I deal with is the construction of a finite counterpart of the theory based on the continuum assumption. This is done in chapter 2. Dropping the continuum assumption requires us to rebuild the theory in a substantially different way. Some parts of the analysis are straightforward. Others are difficult. The payoff in either case is that one begins to clarify the nature of the arguments and the assumptions that are required to establish competitive limit theorems.

The behavior of Marshallian markets with a finite number of agents has already been investigated by Rubinstein and Wolinsky (1990). The market consists of a finite num-

---

[10] For example, the set of agents can be identified with the points in the unit interval [0,1]. The "number" or "mass" of agents in a set is given by its Lebesgue measure, if this is well defined. In particular, a single agent has measure zero.

ber M of buyers and a single seller. The seller has one unit of the indivisible good to sell which he values at zero. Each of the buyers places a value of one dollar on the good. All agents discount the future using the same discount factor δ. An important difference between this game and the "game" studied in Rubinstein and Wolinsky (1985) is that, instead of having exogenous random matching, the seller can choose the identity of the buyer to whom he wishes to offer the good in each period. Rubinstein and Wolinsky show that for any price $0 \leq p \leq 1$ there exists a subgame-perfect equilibrium in which the good is sold for this price.

The construction of the subgame-perfect equilibria is delicate, but the essential idea is this. Let p be the price at which the good is traded in equilibrium. Obviously, the seller would like to trade at a higher price and the buyers would like to trade at a lower price. To support trade at the price p it is assumed that if the seller asks for a higher price, all of the buyers refuse to trade at that price and offer a lower price instead. The seller has no choice but to accept the lower price. The buyer who initially rejects the seller's offer gets the good at the lower price.

Similarly, if one of the buyers offers a price below p, the seller refuses and sells it to another buyer at a higher price. Since the buyers believe that one of them will always trade with the seller in equilibrium, they have no choice but to accept the higher price.

In this way, any deviator is punished and the agent who supports the punishment strategy by rejecting the deviator's proposal is rewarded. Note that because there is only one good, only one buyer can have the good in equilibrium and the other buyers get a payoff of zero. Thus, the buyers will be at least as well off supporting the punishment strategy as they are along the equilibrium path.

According to a well known "folk theorem," repeated games have many subgame-perfect equilibria.[11] Although

---

[11] For example, if players do not discount the future, then any feasible and strictly individually rational payoff vector can be achieved by some SPE.

DMBG are not repeated games,[12] they have some of the features of repeated games. In particular, if an agent thinks that a deviation from the equilibrium play of the game will trigger a future punishment by his opponents, he may be deterred from deviating. These trigger strategies can then be used to support a large variety of equilibrium behaviors. Some of these equilibria can be eliminated in a model with a continuum of agents. With a continuum of agents, the action of a single agent has no impact on the payoff of the most other agents, so it is natural to assume that agents ignore the actions of any single agent.[13] In effect, agents are anonymous. They are invisible to most other agents, with whom they never come into contact. Anonymity rules out trigger strategies of the kind described above, so an agent can deviate without worrying about the reaction of his future opponents. This fact allows us to eliminate a large number of equilibria. Anonymity is only an assumption, however, and it is one that is not natural in a finite economy, however large. This presents a serious challenge to the development of a theory based on large finite economies.

A finite exchange economy consists of n agents, indexed $i = 1, ..., n$, each characterized by a consumption set $X_i \subset R^\ell$, an endowment of commodities e_i, and a utility function u_i. Trade takes place at a sequence of dates $t = 1, 2, ...$ At each date, a randomly selected ordered pair of agents (i, j) is matched. The first agent i is the proposer and makes an offer in the form of a feasible net trade vector z to the second agent j, which j can accept or reject. In principle, this process can continue indefinitely. There is no discounting, so agents care only about the utility of the commodity bundle they hold after an unlimited number of

[12] Because the allocation of commodities changes over time, a different "game" is being played at each date.

[13] In a DMBG, a single agent's actions will of course be observed by his trading partners, who can hardly be expected to ignore them. However, a single agent will only ever meet a finite number of other agents, and having met him they will never meet him again. So it seems reasonable to assume that agents do not condition their current behavior on the past actions of individual agents.

trading periods has passed. Agent i's payoff is the limiting value of his utility $u_i(x_{it})$ as t goes to infinity, where x_{it} is the bundle of commodities held by agent i at the end of period t. Individual rationality and voluntary trade imply that the equilibrium payoff at each date is greater than or equal to the utility of the currently held commodity bundle $u_i(x_{it})$. Consequently, the limit of $u_i(x_{it})$ exists.

Attention is restricted to *Markov perfect equilibria* (MPE), that is, subgame-perfect equilibria in which the strategies are memoryless (independent of the history of the game). At each date strategies depend only on the current state of the game. One can show that, under certain regularity conditions, the limiting allocation as time goes to infinity must be Pareto-efficient. Pareto-efficiency is a strong result in its own right. In a finite economy each agent has some degree of market power. For the usual reasons, one might expect imperfect competition to lead to distortions in the market as each agent tries to use his market power for his own advantage. In an MPE, however, this is not the case: trade must continue as long as there are unexploited gains from trade. In the limit, all gains from trade are exhausted so the final allocation must be Pareto-efficient. This result has an obvious resemblence to the Coase Conjecture (see Gul, Sonnenschein and Wilson, 1986).

Establishing efficiency is only the first step, albeit an important one, on the road to a competitive limit theorem. There are many Pareto-efficient allocations and, in a finite economy, there is no reason why the limiting allocation should be a Walras allocation.[14] Large numbers of agents are needed to guarantee this. The next step, then, is to analyze the asymptotic properties of MPE as the number of agents increases without bound. Here there is a problem. Since there is no reason to expect the MPE to be unique

---

[14] Under standard convexity conditions, if x is a Pareto-efficient allocation there exists a price vector $p \neq 0$ such that, for every agent i, $p \cdot x_i' > p \cdot x_i$ if $u_i(x_i') > u_i(x_i)$. To ensure that x is a Walras allocation, i.e. that (p, x) is a competitive equilibrium, we need budget balance, i.e. $p \cdot x_i = p \cdot e_i$, for every agent i.

(Walrasian equilibria are not unique and so the MPE of the market game cannot be unique either), there is always the possibility that a small deviation by a single agent might trigger a switch to a very different equilibrium of the continuation game. As a result, even in the limit, individual agents may have non-negligible market power. In fact, to make any progress in such a general setting, it is necessary to impose a *continuity assumption* of the kind introduced in the work of Green (1980, 1984). The appropriate continuity assumption here requires that a small change in a single agent's strategy leads to uniformly (as $n \to \infty$) small changes in the asymptotic (as $t \to \infty$) allocation. Under this assumption, one can show that asymptotic (as $t \to \infty$) equilibrium outcomes converge to Walrasian outcomes as the number of agents becomes unboundedly large.

These results assume that there is no discounting and consumption takes place after the the game is over so only the asymptotic allocation matters to the individual agents. This is in contrast to much of the literature on DMBG, where discounting has played an important role. Recall that in Rubinstein (1982), discounting of future utilities is essential for uniqueness of the SPE. Without discounting, the model collapses to a Nash demand game in which any Pareto-efficient division is a SPE outcome. Discounting has been used to test the robustness of equilibria in many settings. It is also used as a way of representing transaction costs. Search and bargaining are costly because the longer they continue, the more the payoffs are discounted. So an interesting extension of the theory sketched above is to introduce discounting and see whether it significantly changes the results.

Discounting is formally equivalent to introducing a random stopping date for the trading process. Suppose that at each date there is a probability $0 < \gamma < 1$ that the game continues for one more period, given that it has lasted until the present date. As soon as the trading process ends, agents consume their current commodity bundle. The probability that the game stops at date t is given by $\gamma^{t-1}(1 - \gamma)$, that is, the probability γ^{t-1} that it continues at the first $t - 1$ periods multiplied by the probability $1 - \gamma$ that it stops at the tth period. If the game stops at date t the agent's payoff is $u_i(x_{it})$, where x_{it} is the commodity bundle held at the end of date t. To find the expected utility of agent i we simply multiply the probability of stopping at date t by the utility if the game stops at date t and sum over all dates $t = 1, 2, \ldots$ to get

$$(1 - \gamma) \sum_{t=1}^{\infty} \gamma^{t-1} u_i(x_{it}).$$

Here γ plays the role of a discount factor. As the length of a period gets vanishingly short, we assume that the probability of the game continuing for one more period converges to 1, that is, the "discount factor" γ converges to 1 just as in the Rubinstein–Wolinsky model.

In a DMBG, an agent's equilibrium payoff can be expressed as the sum of a current (flow) payoff and the discounted value of the payoff from the continuation game. The conditions for an optimal strategy can be expressed in terms of a recursive equation similar to Bellman's equation in dynamic programing. From this equation it is possible to show that the equilibrium payoffs for each agent form a gradient process. This allows one to establish that the allocation converges to an asymptotic allocation under quite general conditions. Convergence is crucial because, as we already have seen, trade continues in a MPE until all gains from trade have been exhausted. Under certain regularity assumptions the asymptotic equilibrium allocation must be Pareto-efficient.

In a DMBG with discounting, it is important to distinguish between the Pareto-efficiency of the asymptotic allocation and the Pareto-efficiency of the MPE. The presence of discounting (random termination) implies that with probability one the game ends at some finite date t. The asymptotic allocation is reached with probability zero and so becomes irrelevant to the welfare properties of the equilibrium. Even if we let the period length get vanishingly small, so that the continuation probability γ approaches 1, we cannot be sure that the equilibrium payoffs converge to the utility of the asymptotic allocation. The trouble is that the equilibrium path $\{x_t\}_{t=1}^{\infty}$ depends on the value of γ. As γ converges to 1, the rate at which the sequence $\{x_t\}_{t=1}^{\infty}$ converges to the asymptotic allocation may become slower and slower, so that the probability of ending up with an inefficient allocation in the short run remains non-negligible.

To deal with this challenge, we need to show that the sequence of allocations $\{x_t\}_{t=1}^{\infty}$ converges to the asymptotic allocation uniformly quickly for all values of γ. The argument I use is based on bounded rationality (more precisely, bounded complexity of strategies) and shows that if convergence to an efficient allocation occurs it must occur within a bounded number of periods, so that as the period length becomes vanishingly short (the discount rate converges to zero), the time required to reach the efficient limiting allocation converges to zero. In the limit, as the period length becomes vanishingly short, an efficient allocation is reached with probability one.

To sum up the story so far, the theory developed in chapter 2 achieves three things:

- It shows that it is possible to extend the theory of competitive markets to apply to large but finite markets.
- In addition, by separating the conditions needed for efficiency and for budget balance, we gain further insight into the robustness or generality of the two properties.
- Finally, note that at each step, extra assumptions (the Markov property, continuity, bounded rationality) are needed.

This last point is, in some ways, the most interesting. It suggests that a theory of competition cannot be based on the equilibrium properties of the DMBG alone. In addition, we need assumptions about markets, like anonymity and continuity (small agents have small effects), that cannot be derived from the analysis of Nash equilibrium.

If these additional assumptions really are necessary, they need to be justified. This is the subject matter of chapter 3.

Strategic foundations of general equilibrium

Anonymity, continuity, and the Markov assumption

As the number of agents grows without bound, it may be natural to expect that the strategy of a single agent should not matter to the play of the game. As we have seen, this is not a principle of game theory: even when the number of players becomes very large, the actions of a single agent, however insignificant, can trigger a change in the behavior of a large number of the other players, thus making a big difference to the play of the game. Still, it seems that this is not how markets work. Unless there is something special about a distinguished agent – for example, unless he has some private information that is significant for a large number of agents – it just does not seem right that this agent's actions should matter all that much.

Part of the conventional wisdom about markets is that they are anonymous mechanisms. As Hayek (1945) pointed out, one of the wonderful things about markets is the fact that they economize on information. Prices are all that we need to know in order to take the right decisions. It does not matter who trades what: prices are determined by the aggregate of the agents' demands and supplies. So, if a single agent changes his demand by a small amount, that should have only a small effect on prices. Similarly, identities should not matter. Everyone has the same trading opportunities and everyone should be able to execute the same trade at the same price.

While this kind of reasoning sounds plausible, it is hard to demonstrate that markets have these properties in a strategic context. Having accepted the methodological rules of game theory, we are not in a position to abandon them when they make the analysis difficult. If anonymity and continuity are properties of competitive markets, we should be able to find assumptions about the structure of the DMBG that lead to continuous and anonymous equilibria. Otherwise, we are left clinging to the position that there exist economic principles that cannot be deduced from game-theoretic reasoning. This is a bit like saying that there exist economic principles that cannot be deduced from rationality postulates, which is not a position most economists would support. The possibility of demonstrating continuity and anonymity from first principles is an important issue for the strategic foundations of competitive equilibrium.

The Markov assumption essentially says that only the current state of the economy matters and not the history of the game. There are two ways to relax this assumption. For the efficiency results, it turns out that only certain kinds of information have to be excluded from memory, essentially, rejected offers. For the competitive limit result, the state can be defined very broadly and can be expanded to include some elements of history. What is crucial is that the play of the game should respond continuously to the state of the game and that the state should respond continuously to the actions of individual agents. These assumptions seem reasonable but they do not follow strictly from the definition of equilibrium. However, they can be justified in terms of informational limitations. Equilibria in which a non-negligible number of agents remain pivotal as the total number of agents grows without bound are not robust. They require agents to have a great deal of information about what is going on in the economy. Limited communication, bounded rationality (limited computational ability), or limited memory can all be used to justify the Markov assumption.

One way of formalize the property that agents are not pivotal in the limit is by introducing limited recall. As is well known, repeated games have a large number of equilibria supported by various forms of trigger strategies. If a player deviates from the equilibrium path in one of these games, he is punished in the future play of the game by the response of the other players. If an agent's actions are hidden from other players, it becomes impossible to support so many equilibria. Unfortunately, an agent's actions are likely to lead to some observable effect – on payoffs, for example – and this may allow for punishment strategies even if actions are not directly observable. In any case, introducing asymmetric information leads to intractable complications of its own.

An alternative strategy is to limit all agents' ability to recall the past and, hence, their ability to condition future behavior on the history of the game. More precisely, we take a repeated game and turn it into a degenerate type of stochastic game by introducing a set S of *states of the game*. There is a transition probability that maps the current state of the game and the current actions of the players into the next period's state. The strategies of the agents depend only on the current state of the game and not on the history of the game *per se*. So the state of the game serves as a summary of the past play and the current play depends only on this summary, not on the entire history. It is important to note that the state does not affect the payoffs directly. It serves only to condition strategies. In this sense, the state is an extraneous variable, like a "sunspot." The state evolves in response to the play of the game and, in each period, the players' strategies are functions only of the state of the game. This reconfiguration of a repeated game is not by itself restrictive. It merely provides a framework in which it is easy to specify a criterion of robustness. Specifically, I introduce some noise into the evolution of the state to take account of the fact that recall is imperfect and that small changes in the play of the game are likely to be overlooked. Under relatively mild regularity assumptions, it is possible to show that, in the limit, as the number of players grows without bound, the game becomes anonymous. That is, each player comes to have negligible influence on the evolution of the play of the game. This has the additional consequence that in choosing an optimal strategy at each date a player is not influenced by the fear that his choice might trigger some kind of retaliation. This is not quite the same thing as saying that each agent adopts a Markov strategy. In fact, it is possible that the equilibrium play of the game will be non-Markov, but to the extent that this is true, it is because the equilibria of this game may be correlated in the sense of Aumann (1974, 1987) and not because there are trigger strategies in the conventional sense. Although strategies may depend on the past, they depend on the aggregate past and not on the past play of any individual.

The crucial fact is that limited recall in a large game allows agents to ignore the possibility of punishment in the same way that Markov or memoryless strategies allow them to ignore the possibility of punishment.

For the same reason, because strategies depend on the aggregate history and not on individual histories, the effect of an individual agent is small, ensuring continuity in the limit as the number of agents becomes unboundedly large.

In this way, one can argue that the additional properties required to make markets perfectly competitive are, in fact, properties of robust strategic equilibria.

Equilibrium and disequilibrium

A different kind of question relates to the very notion of equilibrium. Why do we assume that economic systems are in equilibrium at all? It is sometimes argued that without an explanation of how the economy gets "into" a state of equilibrium, equilibrium theory is empty. In other words, we need a theory of disequilibrium to justify the use of equilibrium methods of analysis.

Over the years, there have been numerous attempts to explain the disequilibrium behavior of the economy and, in particular, to show that an economy in disequilibrium will eventually approach a state of equilibrium. At one time, the notion of economic equilibrium was considered analogous to the "state of rest" of a physical or mechanical system. This suggests an analogy with statics and dynamics in classical mechanics, where statics are concerned with the determination of states of rest and dynamics are concerned with the processes that lead to states of rest. If equilibrium is a state of rest, then there ought to be a dynamic theory that accounts for how the system is drawn to a state of rest or equilibrium.

The Walrasian theory of the *tâtonnement* (Walras, 1954), Edgeworth's notion of recontracting (Edgeworth, 1881), and the Marshallian dynamics of supply price and demand price (Marshall, 1920) are examples of this kind of dynamic analysis. In the 1950s and 1960s, there grew up a large literature on the stability of equilibrium, including both *tâtonnement* and non-*tâtonnement* processes (see Arrow and Hahn, 1971, for a survey). In the last thirty years, this sort of analysis seems to have fallen out of favor, mainly because the specification of these processes is largely ad hoc, that is, not based on principles of rational behavior.

Instead, equilibrium dynamics has come to dominate economic theory. See Stokey, Lucas and Prescott (1989) for a good example of how this kind of theory has matured. There are plenty of dynamic models, but they are models that are always in equilibrium. The dynamics they portray is the evolution or unfolding of an equilibrium, rather than a process leading to equilibrium.

There is something self-defeating about the rejection of an adjustment process because it is not based on rational behavior. Rational behavior presupposes a kind of equilibrium – at least, an equilibrium of the agent's behavior – so it seems a bit much to require a disequilibrium theory to be based on rational behavior. Taking this argument to its logical conclusion, we would have to give up the search for disequilibrium theory altogether. This kind of argument was made quite convincingly by Hahn (1974), when he described equilibrium behavior as mutually consistent and optimal behavior by a group of agents. This notion of equilibrium applies to any situation in which rational behavior is simultaneously and consistently exhibited by all economic agents, not just to a situation of rest. It effectively disqualifies disequilibrium behavior by refusing to admit that it is economic behavior in any acceptable sense.

In the 1980s, game theorists began to feel the need to explain or justify the use of the Nash equilibrium and its various refinements. This urge may have been inspired partly by the same question that led to the analysis of ad hoc adjustment processes in models of market equilibrium: how do the players get to equilibrium? It was also inspired partly by the vast numbers of equilibria found in many well known games, which made the predictive power of game-theoretic analysis rather weak. The hope was that dynamic analysis might be able to discriminate among equilibria in a way that refinements of equilibrium had failed to do (see, for example, Kandori, Mailath and Rob, 1993; Young, 1993).

The attempt to show how equilibrium is arrived at has taken two paths. One is based on ad hoc theories of learning or adaptation, in which a fixed set of players play a game repeatedly and gradually adjust their strategies in response to experience. An old example of this kind of analysis is the well known model of *fictitious play*. In this model, a one-shot game is infinitely repeated. Each player is endowed with beliefs about the mixed strategies of his opponents and chooses a myopic best response to these beliefs at each date. The players' beliefs are assumed to be the same as the relative frequencies with which strategies were adopted in the past. Under certain conditions, this process can be shown to converge to a Nash equilibrium of the stage game. There are numerous variations on this theme. (For a modern example, see Fudenberg and Kreps, 1998).

Another stream of research comes from *evolutionary game theory* (Weibull, 1995). Originally, this branch of game theory was concerned with the evolution of animal species, but it has been adapted by economists to the human condition. Typically, there is a large population of automata, each of whom is programed to play a single strategy. Pairs of automata are selected at random from the population and play a two-person game with their pre-programed strategies. Then the number of automata using each strategy is changed to reflect the relative success of that strategy. In other words, the number of players using a successful strategy will increase; the number using an unsuccessful strategy will increase less rapidly or will decrease. Different adjustment rules give rise to different dynamics. Again, there are many variations on this theme.

This kind of analysis is subject to the same criticism as the disequilibrium theory based on models of market adjustment processes: it is not solidly based on rational behavior. On the other hand, the cachet of evolutionary theory and widespread interest in learning algorithms and artificial intelligence allows practitioners to claim, with some legitimacy, that they are engaged in a different kind of undertaking, one that has a validity grounded in biology and computer science, whatever economists think of it. Furthermore, the charge of *ad hocery* is not really valid as long as some principles are being used consistently. If one accepts this point of view, then it appears that this kind of analysis provides a (non-economic) foundation for (economic) equilibrium theory, by showing that economic equilibrium is the outcome of an evolutionary or adaptive process.

In chapter 4, I develop a non-maximizing or disequilibrium model of adaptation in a market context. Instead of maximizing expected utility, the behavior of the agents in the market is characterized by rules of thumb. These behavioral rules then define a stochastic process, whose convergence or non-convergence to a market equilibrium is analyzed. This analysis can be used to show that market equilibrium does not make unreasonable demands on the rationality of the agents, because even boundedly rational agents can "learn" to play equilibrium strategies. It can also be used to provide insights into the dynamics of markets without assuming that equilibrium has been reached (yet).

Partial equilibrium, general equilibrium, and the coordination problem

Alfred Marshall, the founder of the Cambridge school of economics, had a very practical approach to the study of economics. In his famous *Principles of Economics* (Marshall, 1920) he defined economics to be "the study of the behavior of men and women in the everyday business of life," a down-to-earth definition that reflected Marshall's hope that economics would be a discipline that would improve the lot of ordinary men and women. It is not surprising, then, that Marshall is mainly associated with partial equilibrium analysis, that amalgam of handy short cuts that allows economists to isolate particular phenomena and study them on the back of a virtual envelope, ignoring the fact that an economy is a complex system in which "everything affects and is affected by everything else." It may not be pure, but it is very practical.

The founder of the Lausanne school, on the other hand, was a man of a different intellectual temperament. Léon Walras evidently loved the systematic element of economics and his great work *Elements of Pure Economics* (Walras, 1954) is devoted to elaborating an elegant theory of general equilibrium in which the interactions of individual agents and individual markets throughout the economy are aggregated to provide a precise account of the equilibrium of the entire economy. It may not be practical, but it is very pure.

An economic theorist today is very glad to have the techniques of both partial equilibrium analysis and general equilibrium analysis in his toolkit. One cannot imagine doing international economics or macroeconomics without a general equilibrium framework, any more than one could imagine industrial organization theory without partial equilibrium analysis. It is perhaps regrettable though that we have come to think of these two very useful forms of economic analysis as separate and distinct, rather than as different aspects of a single theory.

In this book, I am writing about the foundations of the theory of market equilibrium. The theory that has been developed sometimes makes use of a partial equilibrium (Marshallian) framework, and sometimes a general equilibrium (Walrasian) framework. The choice is made for simplicity (or expediency), but it is the same theory that is being developed in either case. This sounds like a good thing, to the extent that it appears to unify the two aspects of the economic analysis of equilibrium. At the same time, there is something a bit worrying about it. Equilibrium in a single market is not the same thing as equilibrium in a vast system of markets. The business of reaching an equilibrium throughout the entire economy is much more complex than the process of reaching equilibrium in a single market, holding the rest of the economy steady. And yet for much of this book I am going to pretend that they are more or less the same thing. In other words, that the Walrasian framework is just a multi-dimensional version of the Marshallian framework. Formally, there is nothing to prevent me from doing so. But economic intuition suggests that this cannot be the whole story and, at the end, I shall want to return to this issue in some detail and question whether the ideas explored here are really a satisfactory account of the foundations of general equilibrium. This will lead to a re-consideration of the work of another great Cambridge economist, John Maynard Keynes.

CHAPTER 2

PERFECT COMPETITION

2.1 Introduction

The objective of this chapter is to provide a complete and precise description of perfect competition as the equilibrium of a non-cooperative game with a large but finite number of players.

For reasons of tractability, all the analysis takes place within the framework of a static pure exchange economy. Ignoring production is a fairly drastic simplification. The justification is that it allows us to focus on price formation and exchange without unnecessary complications. To include production, one would have to answer a number of awkward questions. What is the objective function of the firm? When and how do households receive income from firms? What is the timing of inputs and outputs when production plans have to be feasible? These are questions that deserve to be answered but are outside the scope of the present study.

In a pure exchange economy, competitive equilibrium is characterized by two properties, efficiency and budget balance. The First Theorem of Welfare Economics tells us that competitive equilibrium allocations are efficient. Under the usual convexity assumptions, the Second Theorem tells us that an efficient allocation has a vector of supporting prices $p \neq 0$ at which each agent's consumption bundle minimizes the cost of achieving that level of utility. If x_i is agent i's consumption bundle and another bundle x_i' is preferred to x_i then $p \cdot x_i' > p \cdot x_i$. However, the value of the agent's consumption bundle may not be equal to the value of his endowment at these prices. To ensure that an efficient allocation is a competitive equilibrium,

41

we need to have budget balance: the value of an agent's consumption bundle, determined using the efficiency prices, must be equal to the value of his endowment: $p \cdot x_i = p \cdot e_i$. Thus we can think of a competitive equilibrium allocation as an efficient allocation that satisfies budget balance.

It is convenient to divide the analysis of competition into two parts, one concerned with efficiency and one with budget balance. The conditions needed for efficiency are somewhat weaker than those required for budget balance and the analysis is somewhat more general. In particular, efficiency is a property of strategic equilibrium in finite economies, whereas budget balance requires large numbers of players.

Many of the arguments used in this chapter are familiar. The novel part of the analysis is the assumption of a finite number of players. The earlier literature assumes a non-atomic continuum of players. The continuum assumption is justified by the claim that a continuum of agents is a good approximation to a large but finite number of players. It is important to test the validity of this assumption by proving a competitive limit theorem, showing that as the number of players becomes unboundedly large, the behavior of the finite game is indeed a good approximation to the continuum game.

The vehicle used for the analysis is a *dynamic matching and bargaining game* (DMBG). The DMBG is special and has no particular claim to generality. The important advantage of the DMBG is that it is a playable game, in which all the rules and assumptions are well specified. If we can analyze it convincingly we shall have learned a lot.

The main discovery of this chapter will be that in order to prove a competitive limit theorem we need some assumptions that are not imposed on primitives of the model and are not derived directly from properties of equilibrium. The most important of these concerns the idea that in a competitive market a single agent has a negligible effect on the equilibrium. This idea comes immediately into conflict with the well established principle that, in repeated games, any player can have a large effect because

other players condition their actions on his. The Folk
Theorem of repeated games, which holds for arbitrary
numbers of players, is perhaps the best known example
of this principle. The games under consideration here are
not repeated games, but the same general idea applies. In
choosing a strategy, a player has to consider not just its
direct impact on his payoffs, but also the reaction of the
other players. Because of the possible reactions of other
players, it may be possible to sustain many different outcomes as strategic equilibria. Some of these will depart
from the perfectly competitive outcome, even in a frictionless market with many players.

In this chapter, I am content to point out the restrictions
that must be imposed (somewhat arbitrarily) on equilibrium strategies in order to achieve a competitive limit
theorem. In chapter 3 I attempt to derive such restrictions
endogenously from assumptions about the primitives of
the game.

2.2 Pure exchange economies

We begin by describing a pure exchange economy. In this
economy there is no production. Instead, a finite number of
economic agents has exogenously given endowments of a
finite number of commodities. Because the agents have
different endowments and preferences, there are gains
from trade. The agents exchange commodities in order to
maximize their preferences. To describe a formal model of
an exchange economy, we have to specify the list of commodities, the list of agents, and the agents' preferences and
endowments.

Commodities There is a finite number of commodities,
indexed $h = 1, .., \ell$. Each commodity is assumed to be
homogeneous and perfectly divisible. The quantity of any
commodity h is represented by a real number x_h and we
adopt the usual convention that negative numbers represent "supplies" or "deficits." A *commodity bundle* can
then be represented by a vector $x = (x_1, ..., x_\ell)$, where x_h
represents the quantity of commodity h. The *commodity*

space consisting of all possible commodity bundles is represented by the ℓ-dimensional Euclidean vector space $\mathbf{R}^\ell$.

Agents The economy consists of a finite number of economic agents, indexed $i = 1, .., m$, who can be thought of as "consumers."

Consumption sets A *consumption bundle* is a commodity bundle that is feasible for an agent The set of feasible consumption bundles for agent i is called his *consumption set* and is denoted by $X_i \subset \mathbf{R}^\ell$. For example, the set X_i may consist of non-negative commodity bundles that are compatible with subsistence for agent i. Each consumption set X_i is assumed to be non-empty, closed, convex, and bounded below.

Endowments Each agent has an initial *endowment* of commodities which he wants to exchange for a more preferred bundle Agent i's endowment is denoted by the consumption bundle $e_i \in X_i$. The assumption that e_i is a consumption bundle implies that agent i can survive without trading.

Preferences Agent i's preferences over consumption bundles are represented by the *utility function* $u_i : X_i \to \mathbf{R}$, which assigns the real number $u_i(x_i)$ to each feasible consumption bundle x_i In a pure exchange economy, agents maximize the value of a utility function by exchanging commodities with other agents. The utility function u_i is assumed to be concave, continuous, and increasing.[1] Concavity implies that agents who maximize expected utility are risk averse, as well as having the usual diminishing marginal rate of substitution.

The pure exchange economy is defined by the array $\mathcal{E} = \{(X_i, e_i, u_i)\}_{i=1}^m$.

---

[1] I use the phrase "increasing" to mean increasing. Some writers use the phrase "strictly increasing" for this purpose.

Perfect competition

Pareto- and pairwise-efficiency

The next step is to define two concepts of efficiency and characterize the corresponding sets of efficient allocations.

The allocation of resources in a pure exchange economy is described by a list of the consumption bundles for all the agents in the economy. Formally, an *allocation* is an m-tuple of consumption bundles $x = (x_1, ..., x_m)$ such that $x_i \in X_i$ for each i. An allocation x is *attainable* if aggregate demand equals aggregate supply, that is, the sum of the commodities allocated to the agents is equal to the sum of the endowments:

$$\sum_{i=1}^{m} x_i = \sum_{i=1}^{m} e_i.$$

Let $\hat{X}$ denote the set of attainable allocations. Since each consumption set is closed and bounded below, it is easy to see that the set of attainable allocations is compact.

An attainable allocation x is (strongly) *Pareto-efficient* if there does not exist another attainable allocation x' that makes some agents better off and none worse off, that is, $u_i(x_i') \geq u_i(x_i)$ for any agent i and $u_i(x_i') > u_i(x_i)$ for some agent i. Let $P \subset \hat{X}$ denote the set of Pareto-efficient allocations. The continuity of the utility functions implies that P is closed and hence compact.

An attainable allocation x is *pairwise-efficient* if it is impossible for any two agents i and j to improve their utilities by trading together, that is, there does not exist an attainable allocation x' and a pair of agents (i, j) such that

(i) $x_k' = x_k, \forall k \neq i, j$
(ii) $u_i(x_i') \geq u_i(x_i), u_j(x_j') \geq u_j(x_j)$ with at least one strict inequality.

In addition to the standard assumptions, some non-standard properties will be needed in the sequel. First, it will be assumed that preferences are smooth:

- for any i, u_i can be extended to an open set G_i containing X_i and $u_i: G_i \to \mathbf{R}$ is C^1.

45

This assumption is not strictly necessary, but it simplifies the analysis by allowing us to use the Kuhn–Tucker Theorem to characterize solutions to maximization problems.

The second non-standard property is that the indifference surface through the initial endowment does not intersect the boundary of the consumption set X_i:

• for any i,

$$\{x_i \in G_i | u_i(x_i) \geq u_i(e_i)\} \cap \partial X_i = \emptyset, \qquad (2.1)$$

where ∂X_i denotes the boundary of X_i.

A familiar example that satisfies this assumption is provided by the Cobb–Douglas utility function when the consumption set $X_i = \mathbf{R}_+^\ell$. The importance of the property (2.1) is that it ensures that an allocation that is pairwise-efficient is also Pareto-efficient, as will be shown below.

Because trade is voluntary, we can restrict attention to allocations that are individually rational, that is, allocations x such that $u_i(x_i) \geq u_i(e_i)$ for every i. Under property (2.1) individually rational consumption bundles belong to the interior of the consumption set, not to the boundary. Then we do not need to worry about the boundary of the consumption set when we characterize Pareto-efficient allocations. Without the boundary, there will be no "corner solutions" to worry about and the first-order conditions that characterize efficiency will hold as equations.

Now we are ready to state and prove the promised result, namely, that pairwise-efficiency and Pareto-efficiency are equivalent under the maintained assumptions. The argument is simple. Under condition (2.1), Pareto-efficient allocations are characterized by the condition that all agents have the same marginal rates of subsitution between pairs of commodities. Likewise, pairwise-efficient allocations are characterized by the condition that any two agents have the same marginal rates of substitution between pairs of commodities. These conditions are obviously equivalent so Pareto-efficiency and pairwise efficiency are equivalent.

Perfect competition

In general, there may exist allocations that are pairwise-efficient but not Pareto-efficient. In other words, if condition (2.1) is not satisfied or if the allocation is not individually rational, there may exist allocations that can be improved on by making commodity transfers among three or more agents, but not by making commodity transfers between a single pair of agents.

Proposition 1 *Under the maintained assumptions, an (attainable) and individually rational allocation x is Pareto-efficient if and only if it is pairwise-efficient*

Proof If x is a pairwise-efficient allocation, then it must solve the following maximization problem for each pair of agents (i, j):

$$\max u_i(x_i')$$
$$\text{s.t. } x_i' + x_j' \leq x_i + x_j, u_j(x_j') \geq u_j(x_j),$$

where x_i' and x_j' are restricted to the open sets G_i and G_j. Note that we can dispense with the conditions $x_i' \in X_i$ and $x_j' \in X_j$ since they are guaranteed by the conditions $u_i(x_i') \geq u_i(x_i)$ and $u_j(x_j') \geq u_j(x_j)$. This is the only place that property (2.1) is used.

An application of the "necessity" part of the Kuhn–Tucker Theorem implies that a solution of this problem satisfies the first-order conditions

$$\nabla u_i(x_i) \propto \nabla u_j(x_j), \forall i, j.$$

But according to the "sufficiency" part of the Kuhn–Tucker Theorem, the first-order conditions imply that x solves the problem

$$\max u_i(x_i')$$
$$\text{s.t. } \sum_{j=1}^{m} x_j' \leq \sum_{j=1}^{m} x_j, u_j(x_j') \geq u_j(x_j), \forall j \neq i,$$

where x_i' is restricted to the open set G_i and x_j' is restricted to the open set G_j for every j. In other words, it is impossible to make one agent better off without making some of the others worse off. Since the utility functions are continuous and increasing, this is equivalent to the Pareto-efficiency of x.

Obviously, Pareto-efficiency implies pairwise-efficiency, so the proof of Proposition 1 is complete. ■

In the sequel we study a game in which exchange occurs between *pairs* of agents. This trading process results in a *pairwise*-efficient final allocation. The equivalence of pairwise-efficiency and Pareto-efficiency immediately implies that the final allocation is Pareto-efficient.

As was noted above, without property (2.1) there may exist allocations that are pairwise-efficient but not Pareto-efficient. A simple example will make this clear. Suppose there are three agents $i = 1, 2, 3$ and three goods $h = 1, 2, 3$. Each agent i has an endowment of one unit of good $h = i$ and none of the goods $h \neq i$. The consumption set is assumed to be $\mathbf{R}_+^3$ for each agent and the utility function of agent i is defined by putting

$$u_i(x_i) = \begin{cases} x_{ii} + 2x_{ii+1} & i = 1, 2 \\ x_{ii} + 2x_{i1} & i = 3. \end{cases}$$

Then the allocation $x = (x_1, x_2, x_3) = (e_1, e_2, e_3)$ is pairwise-efficient but not Pareto-efficient. It is not Pareto-efficient because each agent gets a utility of 1 whereas he would get 2 if he gave up his endowment in exchange for one unit of his preferred good. On the other hand, no pair of agents can increase their utility levels because of the lack *of mutual coincidence of wants*. For example, agent 1 would like to give up one unit of good 1 in exchange for one unit of good 2, but agent 2, who has one unit of good 2, does not value good 1. A moment's thought will show that it is crucial for this example that every agent is on the boundary of his consumption set and that the indifference curves intersect the boundary of the consumption set. (The utility functions in this example are not increasing, but the example could easily be adjusted to satisfy this property without changing the result.) (For a more detailed discussion of the relationship between pairwise-, t-wise, and Pareto-efficiency, see Goldman and Starr, 1982.)

2.3 Dynamic matching and bargaining games

The model economy in the preceding subsection describes the agents' environment, but not the restrictions on their behavior. To do that, we need to define an extensive-form game, a set of rules that tells us exactly what actions players are allowed to take and when they are allowed to take them. The rules of the game also tell us exactly what consequences follow from any sequence of actions adopted by the players.

Game theorists take the business of defining a game very seriously. This is not just a matter of mathematical precision. As the Nash Program described in chapter 1 (p. 10) makes clear, the goal in defining a non-cooperative game is to make the assumptions and economic analysis of the game as clear and complete as possible. One criterion of whether we have achieved the goals of the Nash Program is to ask whether the game is "playable." Are the instructions provided complete and clear enough so that someone who was only given these instructions could, in principle, play the game? For example, would an experimental economist be able to go into a laboratory and have subjects play this game or would he have to invent additional rules and conventions himself before the experiment could proceed?

Without a "playable" game in this sense, it is not clear that the object of study is well defined. Imagine that someone gives you an unfamiliar board game as a gift, but the instructions are missing. Without knowing what you are supposed to do, how can you play the game? You don't know what the game is. The same problem confronts a game theorist when he encounters a loosely specified economic environment. Without limiting the actions available to the players and specifying the consequences of these actions, it is difficult to say how the game should be played and what the outcome should be.

The Nash Program requires a non-cooperative game. The fact that a game is non-cooperative in this technical sense does not rule out cooperative behavior. It simply says that if negotiation, pre-play communication, binding agreements, and other elements of cooperation occur, then they must be included in the definition of the game. The Nash Program is a commitment to being explicit about the assumptions and economic analysis of the game, rather than a commitment to a particular kind of game or particular outcomes.

Having adopted these general principles, there remain many different ways of modeling trade among a group of self-interested agents. One model that has proved particularly useful in analyzing decentralized trade is based on pairwise matching and bargaining. Individual agents search for trading opportunities and meet one other individual at a time. When a pair of agents encounter one another (matching), they determine whether and what to trade (bargaining). Bargaining is represented by the "alternating-offers" model of Stahl (1972) and Rubinstein (1982) described in chapter 1.

Even within this framework, there are many choices to be made. How are matches determined? Who meets whom and how often? When agents are matched, how does the bargaining proceed? Are offers made simultaneously or sequentially? How long are offers on the table before they can be withdrawn or amended? When is a match dissolved? Under what circumstances can an agent change his partner? What do agents know about each other and about the previous play of the game?

These details are important because the outcome of the game may depend critically on the details of the modeling. Some people find the sensitivity of the analysis to the details of the modeling disappointing. Since we have limited information about what the "right" specification of the model is, what confidence can we have in the predictions of our theory? Certainly, it would be nice to develop a theory that gives strong, unambiguous predictions under very general conditions; but failing that the best we can do is to understand the reasons for the sensitivity of the results. At the very least, knowing the sensitivity of our results to specific assumptions can teach us to be cautious. Moreover, it provides a starting point for thinking about the kind of data that one might need to make more precise predictions. Finally, although our models are only examples, seeing how the argument is constructed in concrete settings gives us a better understanding of the logic of the argument. This is a useful lesson even if it does not allow us to predict what the world is like from first principles.

With these caveats we are ready to begin the business of describing the game.

Time The pure exchange model is timeless and static. The dynamic matching and bargaining game takes time to play. We assume that time is divided into a countable number of periods or *dates*, indexed $t = 1, 2, \ldots$ The process of matching, bargaining, and exchange occurs at these dates. Consumption occurs after the game is finished (each agent consumes his terminal consumption bundle).

Matching At each date an ordered pair of agents (i_t, j_t) is matched, with $i_t \neq j_t$. It is assumed that for any pair (i, j) with $i \neq j$ there is an infinite number of dates at which the pair (i, j) is matched.

Bargaining Suppose that a pair of agents (i, j) has been chosen (matched) at date t. Agent i is called the *proposer* and j is called the *responder*. The proposer chooses a vector z of feasible net trades. The responder can accept the proposal by saying "Yes," or reject it by saying "No." If the proposal is accepted, the two agents exchange the proposed vector of trades. The proposer gets z and the responder gets $-z$. If the proposal is rejected, no trade takes place and all agents begin the next period with the allocation they had at the beginning of the present period.

It cannot be stressed too often that the game described here is special. Other games would give different results. (I will try to give specific warnings where appropriate.) The point of the exercise is not to claim that this is the unique "true" model, but rather to give an example of the kinds of assumptions and arguments that are needed to ensure a particular outcome, namely, perfect competition in a pure exchange economy.

One particular limitation should be noted immediately. Only one pair of agents is matched at any date and only these agents have an active role at a given date. The other agents remain passive until the next round. The assumption that there is no simultaneous trade is restrictive, but perhaps not as restrictive as it appears. Suppose that we had modeled "time" as a continuous variable, with matches distributed according to a Poisson process. Then the probability that two pairs were formed at the same time would be zero. Here we work with discrete time and retain the assumption that simultaneous matching has a zero probability. Ruling out simultaneous moves simplifies the game. One can only hope that it does not oversimplify.

All pairs of agents meet infinitely often, for each assignment of roles in the bargaining game. This connectedness assumption is important to ensure that the agents function as a single integrated economy.

Weaker assumptions would also suffice. For example, it would be enough to assume that for every pair of agents (i, j) there is some finite sequence of meetings that connects each pair of agents and that this sequence of meetings occurs infinitely often. To ensure this, we would have to assume that for any i and j there exists a sequence $\{i_k\}_{k=0}^{K}$ with $i_0 = i$ and $i_K = j$ and the ordered pair (i_k, i_{k+1}) meets infinitely often for each $k < K$. The stronger assumption is maintained here for simplicity, but the results would still hold with the weaker connectedness assumption.

The play of the game

The play of the game is described by a path. A path is a complete history of the play of the game, a description of everything that happens at every date. Formally, *path* is a sequence $\{a_t\}_{t=1}^{\infty}$ consisting of ordered triples $a_t = (x_t, z_t, r_t)$, where x_t is the allocation that has been reached at the beginning of date t, z_t is the proposal offered by i_t, and r_t is the response made by j_t.

A feasible path must satisfy several conditions. First, x_t must be an attainable allocation at each date t. Secondly, x_t must be consistent with the actions chosen by the agents. Recall that only the proposer and responder are allowed to

Perfect competition

exchange commodities at date t and the actual vector of commodities exchanged is equal to the accepted proposal (if the proposal is rejected there is no trade). Then a feasible path $a = \{a_t\}$ must satisfy

$$x_{it+1} = x_{it} + z_t \text{ if } i = i_t \text{ and } r_t = \text{"yes"}$$
$$x_{it+1} = x_{it} - z_t \text{ if } i = j_t \text{ and } r_t = \text{"yes"}$$
$$x_{it+1} = x_{it} \text{ otherwise,}$$

for every date t. Let A denote the set of feasible paths.

At each date the agents observe the proposal and response. The information available at the beginning of date t consists of the path segment $(a_1, ..., a_{t-1})$. Call this path segment the *history* of the game up until date t and denote it by h_t. At each date t, the proposer moves first and then the responder moves. The proposer knows the history h_t; the responder knows the history h_t and the proposal z_t. So the information set at which the proposer moves has the form (h, x) and the information set at which the responder moves has the form (h, x, z).[2] Let H_i denote the information sets at which agent i controls play.

A strategy for agent i is a decision rule that specifies a feasible action for the player at every information set where he is required to move. If agent i is the proposer at an information set (h, x) then he has to choose a net trade z that is feasible for himself and the responder, that is, $x_i + z \in X_i$ and $x_j - z \in X_j$. If agent i is the responder at an information set (h, x, z) he has to choose "yes" or "no." Formally, a *strategy* for agent i is a function f_i defined on the domain H_i with values in $\mathbf{R}^\ell$ or $\{yes, no\}$ as appropriate. A feasible strategy for i must must satisfy

$$x_{jt} + f_i(h_t, x_t) \in X_j \text{ for } j = i_t$$
$$x_{jt} - f_i(h_t, x_t) \in X_j \text{ for } j = j_t$$

at any information set (h_t, x_t) such that $i = i_t$. The set of feasible strategies for i is denoted by F_i and the set of strategy profiles is denoted by $F = \times_{i=1}^m F_i$.

---

[2] The allocation x is a function of h and to this extent there is some redundancy in this notation for information sets, but there is some advantage in making x explicit since I refer to it often.

For any strategy profile $f \in F$ we can define a unique path $a^f = \{a_t^f\}$ and a unique outcome $\xi(a^f) = \{\xi_t(a^f)\}$. If h_t^f is the history at date t, this determines the attainable allocation x_t uniquely by putting

$$x_{it} = \xi_{it}(a^f) = \begin{cases} x_{it-1} + z_{t-1} & \text{if } i = i_{t-1} \text{ and } r_{t-1} = \text{"yes"} \\ x_{it-1} - z_{t-1} & \text{if } i = j_{t-1} \text{ and } r_{t-1} = \text{"yes"} \\ x_{it-1} & \text{otherwise.} \end{cases}$$

Then the proposal z_t is given by

$$z_t = f_{i_t}(h_t^f, x_t)$$

and the response r_t is given by

$$r_t = f_{j_t}(h_t^f, x_t, z_t).$$

Thus, for any history h_t^f the strategy profile f allows us to define the history $h_{t+1}^f = (h_t^f, a_t^f)$ and by induction we can define the entire path a^f.

Payoffs

The construction of a path for each strategy profile f is crucial in defining the payoffs of the game. Roughly speaking, an agent's payoff is the utility he gets from his terminal consumption, but since the game goes on forever his terminal consumption may not be well defined. For this reason, we calculate the utility he would get if he consumed his commodity bundle at date t and take as his payoff the "lim inf" of this sequence of utilities. For any outcome $\{x_t\}_{t=1}^{\infty}$ we define the payoff to agent i to be the

$$\liminf_{t \to \infty} u_i(x_{it}) = \sup_{T \geq 1}\{\inf\{u_i(x_{it}) | t \geq T\}\}.$$

Note that there is no discounting here and that the use of the lim inf is conservative in the sense that it takes the lowest possible estimate for the limiting value of the agent's utility. In practice, we will be able to show that the sequence of utilities $\{u_i(x_{it})\}$ has a limit and the sequence of allocations has a limit too.

In the same way, the construction of an outcome $\xi(a^f)$ for each strategy profile allows us to define the individual payoff functions $v_i : F \to \mathbf{R}$ by putting the payoff for agent i equal to

$$v_i(f) = \lim_{t \to \infty} \inf u_i(\xi_{it}(a^f))$$

for any strategy profile $f \in F$.

So, finally, we have arrived at a normal form game Γ defined by

- a set of players $\{1, \ldots, m\}$,
- a set of strategy profiles $F = \times_{i=1}^{m} F_i$, and
- a payoff function $v = (v_1, \ldots, v_m)$.

2.4 Equilibrium

Having defined a playable game, the next step in the analysis of the game is to define an equilibrium. The central concept in non-cooperative game theory is the Nash equilibrium, in which each player chooses a strategy that is a best response to the strategy profile chosen by his opponents. In this context, a Nash equilibrium is a strategy profile $f^* \in F$ with the property that for each i the strategy f_i^* maximizes the payoff of agent i given the strategies $f_{-i}^* \equiv (f_1^*, \ldots, f_{i-1}^*, f_{i+1}^*, \ldots, f_m^*)$:

$$v_i(f^*) \geq v_i(f_{-i}^*, f_i), \forall f_i \in F_i.$$

In dynamic games, the Nash equilibrium concept is often found to be too weak to give interesting results. In particular, it does not restrict the behavior of the agents off the equilibrium path. As an example, consider the following strategy profile:

- suppose that every agent i rejects every offer whenever he is in the position of the responder;
- every agent i proposes the no-trade vector $z = 0$ whenever he is in the position of the proposer.

The profile of strategies defined in this way is a Nash equilibrium. Since the proposer anticipates that any offer will be rejected, it is optimal for him to make only the no-trade offer. Since the only offers received in equilibrium are no-trade offers, it is optimal for the responder to reject them.

Thus, each of the strategies is a best response to what the other players are actually doing.

Note, however, that if a proposer were to deviate from the equilibrium strategy and offer a Pareto-improving trade, it would not be optimal for the responder to reject it. This kind of behavior seems unreasonable, but it is compatible with the definition of Nash equilibrium. The problem is that the definition of Nash equilibrium only requires agent i's strategy to be a best response to what the other agents actually do in equilibrium. This does not restrict his behavior at information sets that are not supposed to arise in equilibrium. An equilibrium strategy for agent i may commit him, at some information sets, to take an action that would not be optimal if the information set were reached. This commitment to take a suboptimal action if the information set were reached may be crucial for the equilibrium.

For this reason, we often make use of the stronger requirement of *subgame perfect equilibrium* (SPE) proposed by Selten (1965). SPE is stronger than Nash equilibrium because it requires each player to choose an optimal action in every situation he could conceivably find himself in, and not just those that occur along the equilibrium path. In particular, it rules out empty or non-credible threats, that is, threats which an agent would not be willing to carry out if he found himself in the situation in which he had threatened to take the action. Formally, for any information set $h \in H_i$ let $\Gamma(h)$ denote the subgame that begins at the information set h. For any history h' of $\Gamma(h)$ and any strategy f_i in F_i let $\langle f_i | h \rangle$ denote the strategy defined by putting

$$\langle f_i | h \rangle(h') = f_i(h, h').$$

That is, the strategy $\langle f_i | h \rangle$ tells a player to behave in the new game when he observes the history h' the same as he would have behaved in the original game if he had observed the combined history (h, h'), that is, h followed by h'. Then an SPE of Γ is a strategy profile f^* such that, for any information set $h \in H_i$, $\langle f_i^* | h \rangle$ is a best response to $\langle f_{-i}^* | h \rangle$. Each agent i is required to choose a strategy that satisfies the Nash equilibrium conditions at every possible information set and not just those that are reached along the equilibrium path. In other words, $\langle f^*|h\rangle$ is a Nash equilibrium of $\Gamma(h)$.

Although the concept of SPE restricts the behavior of the agents in ways that may be important, it still leaves open the door for many kinds of behavior as equilibrium phenomena. The reason is well known from the theory of repeated games. As the Folk Theorem for repeated games shows, when players are extremely patient every "individually rational" payoff can be supported as a SPE (Fudenberg and Maskin, 1986). The present game is not a repeated game. A repeated game consists of the repeated play of identical games at successive dates. A DMBG changes over time because the current allocation changes as agents trade. Technically, a DMBG is a *stochastic game* in which the state is the allocation of commodities and the date (recall that the matching process is a function of the date). Since the state changes from period to period, a different game is being played at each date. Nonetheless, the principle of indeterminacy that applies in repeated games can also affect the analysis of this game. An agent's action at date t affects his payoff in two ways. It affects his payoff directly by changing his current commodity bundle and it affects his payoff indirectly by changing the future behavior of his opponents. If a particular action will lead his opponents to adopt a punishment strategy, he can be deterred from choosing that action even if the direct effect on his payoff might be beneficial. In the same way, his opponents' decision to punish him will be motivated by the punishments they anticipate if they fail to punish. In an infinite-horizon game, this never-ending sequence of threats supported by counter-threats supported by counter-counter-threats . . . and so on, may undermine the restrictiveness of SPE altogether. In other words, many threats may become credible if they are supported by further threats *ad infinitum*. The result is a large set of outcomes consistent with SPE behavior.

To avoid this indeterminacy, theorists are sometimes led to restrict their attention to an even smaller set of strategies, namely those which are *memoryless* or *history-independent*. If all agents choose memoryless strategies in equilibrium, the scope for supporting an outcome as an equilibrium is considerably reduced, since an agent knows (when he chooses his action) that it will be forgotten when agents have to make their choices in the future. In the present game, we cannot escape from the effects of memory altogether, since the current allocation is a product of the past and must be known by the agents choosing actions in each period. However, restricting memory as much as possible will be seen to have a crucial effect on the analysis of the game. Formally, a *Markov strategy f* is one in which

- for any information sets $(h, x), (h', x) \in H_i$, where i is the proposer, the strategy chooses the same proposal $z = f(h, x) = f(h', x)$;
- for any information sets $(h, x, z), (h', x, z) \in H_i$, where i is the responder, the strategy chooses the same response $r = f(h, x, z) = f(h', x, z)$.

In other words, a proposer's action at the information set (h, x) depends only on the attainable allocation x and the date t, and not the history h. We have to include t as part of the information because the identity of the proposer i and the responder j are functions of t. Similarly, at the information set (h, x, z) the responder's action depends only on the allocation x, the date t and the proposal z, and not the history h.

The concept of memoryless strategies leads to a further refinement of Nash equilibrium. A *Markov perfect equilibrium* (MPE) is an SPE in which each agent chooses a Markov strategy. Note that we are restricting attention to SPE in which agents choose Markov strategies, which is not the same as restricting an agent's choice to Markov strategies. In a MPE, the agent is allowed to choose any feasible strategy, but it turns out that a Markov strategy is optimal in the set of all strategies.

2.5 The Edgeworth Property

In the 1960s and 1970s economists studied a type of allocation process known as the Edgeworth Process (Uzawa, 1960). An allocation process is a dynamic process in which the state variable is an attainable allocation that evolves according to a deterministic or stochastic law of motion. Corresponding to the allocation process is a utility process defined by the vector of utilities associated with the current allocation at each point in time. The defining property of the *Edgeworth Process* is that the utility process is non-decreasing over time. (See Negishi, 1962, for a more detailed description.)

The Edgeworth Process is like a gradient process, except that it is characterized by a non-decreasing vector of utilities, rather than by a scalar objective function. Under certain regularity conditions it can be shown that an Edgeworth Process converges to a Pareto-efficient allocation (or a set of Pareto-efficient allocations). One difficulty that arises is that there may exist inefficient allocations at which it is impossible to find utility-increasing trades. For example, there may exist Pareto-inefficient allocations that are pairwise-efficient (Madden, 1976). If trade is assumed to take place between pairs of agents and if one of these allocations is reached, the Edgeworth Process may become stuck there and never reach a Pareto-efficient allocation.

The processes generated by the DMBG have a similar property, which I will call the Edgeworth Property. The critical difference between my use of the term here and its use in the earlier literature is that the agents in an Edgeworth Process are assumed to be myopic. They care about the utility of the commodity bundle they currently hold, even though the process is intended to be a *tâtonnement* process in which consumption does not occur until trade stops. In a DMBG, by contrast, agents are far-sighted. They care about the utility of the commodity bundle they receive asymptotically as time goes to infinity. What we can show is that the equilibrium payoff is non-decreasing.

Suppose that f^* is an MPE and that $\{x_t\}$ is the equilibrium outcome. The equilibrium payoff to agent i is given by

$$v_i(f^*) = \lim_{t\to\infty} \inf u_i(x_{it}).$$

At the beginning of date t, before a proposal has been made, the equilibrium payoff is a function of the initial allocation x_t and the date t. Trade is voluntary in the sense that an agent can always guarantee no trade by offering a proposal $z = 0$ whenever he is the proposer and rejecting all offers when he is the responder. At the worst, he can guarantee himself $u_i(x_{it})$, so

$$v_i(f^*) \geq u_i(x_{it})$$

for every agent i and date t. From this it follows immediately that

$$\lim_{t\to\infty} \inf u_i(x_{it}) = v_i(f^*) \geq \lim_{t\to\infty} \sup u_i(x_{it}),$$

which implies that

$$v_i(f^*) = \lim_{t\to\infty} u_i(x_{it}).$$

Proposition 2 *Let f^* be an MPE of Γ and let $\{x(t)\}_{t=1}^{\infty}$ be the equilibrium outcome. Then*

$$v_i(f^*) = \lim_{t\to\infty} u_i(x_{it}), \forall i.$$

Establishing convergence is important. In such a complex game, it is hard to know where to begin to analyze the equilibrium strategies. The fact that payoffs are eventually constant gives us a place to start. As we see in section 2.6, it implies that gains from trade eventually vanish. This allows us to say something about the limiting allocation and then we can work backwards to deduce properties of the entire equilibrium.

2.6 Efficiency

The essential idea developed in this section is that if agents meet repeatedly and bargain over the gains from pairwise trade, the resulting equilibrium allocation must be Pareto-efficient. Stated in this way, the result may sound almost tautological. One of the things to be learned from this analysis is that the result is not trivial and contains some important subtleties.

The intuitive part of the argument is quite easy. Imagine that in the limit as $t \to \infty$ the allocation converges to x. The equilibrium payoff for i is $v_i(f^*) = u_i(x_i)$. As we have already seen, $v_i(f^*) \geq u_i(e_i)$ so x_i is individually rational. Then if x is not Pareto-efficient, it is not pairwise-efficient, according to Proposition 1 (p. 47). This means that two agents – i and j, say – can increase their utility through trade with each other. Sooner or later i and j will meet and one of them can propose to the other a Pareto-improving trade. But this means that they can get more than the equilibrium payoffs, contradicting the conditions for a Nash equilibrium.

There are a couple of technical difficulties in the proof of this result. First, the fact that payoffs and utilities converge along a particular path does not imply convergence of the corresponding allocations. There may be non-negligible trade in the limit even though utilities are not changing. Secondly, the heuristic argument above applies in the limit, whereas we need to show that a contradiction occurs for a large but finite date t when convergence has not yet occurred.

More important than these technical issues is a strategic issue. Without the assumption of MPE, it does not follow that a responder will accept a Pareto-improving offer. Suppose that i and j meet late in the game, when their commodity bundles are x_i and x_j, respectively, and their equilibrium payoffs are $\bar{v}_i$ and $\bar{v}_j$, respectively. Suppose further that i proposes a trade z that is feasible and will give both i and j utilities that are greater than their current equilibrium payoffs, that is,

$$u_i(x_i + z) > \bar{v}_i, u_j(x_j - z) > \bar{v}_j.$$

Should j accept? Not if j thinks that by rejecting i's offer of $-z$ he will get an even higher payoff in the future. But if i anticipates a rejection from j then i has no incentive to make the proposal in the first place. So it may be an equilibrium for the agents not to trade and to receive the payoffs $\bar{v}_i$ and $\bar{v}_j$ in equilibrium. The crucial assumption in this argument is that an offer by i will be remembered in the remainder of the game and used as a signal to the players to change their equilibrium play so that j is rewarded for rejecting i.

In a MPE, a rejected offer is not "remembered" in the continuation game. Strategies depend only on the current state, so the past is "remembered" only to the extent that it has an impact on the current allocation. A rejected offer has no effect on the allocation and so the players in the continuation game cannot distinguish it from a no-trade offer. Since j cannot benefit from rejecting the offer, he must accept the Pareto-improving offer in the example above.

From a purely strategic perspective, the assumption of MPE may seem arbitrary. From a competitive market perspective, it seems more reasonable. In a large market, it is not likely that agents will observe all offers and there is no incentive for third parties to condition their behavior on rejected offers. On the other hand, it could be argued that there are social norms that operate in markets – for example, the notion of a fair price – and that violators will be punished by society at large. This whole question needs to be investigated at length in chapter 3. For the moment it is enough to appreciate the importance of the Markov assumption in establishing this result.

For the proof of Proposition 3, we need to strengthen the assumptions on preferences. Specifically, we assume that:

• Each utility function u_i is strictly concave.

This assumption ensures that allocations converge if utilities converge. If utilities converge but trade does not converge to zero, there must in the limit exist a non-zero trade

Perfect competition

between two agents that leaves utility unchanged. But if two agents can exchange a non-zero commodity bundle that leaves utility unchanged, they can increase utility by trading half as much. The existence of such a trade will be shown to contradict the conditions for an MPE.

The next proposition characterizes the limiting set of allocations on the equilibrium path. It shows first that the allocation converges and secondly that the limiting allocation is Pareto-efficient.

Proposition 3 *The MPE outcome $\{x_t\}$ converges to $x_\infty = \lim_{t\to\infty} x_t \in P$.*

Proof The first step in the proof is to show that $\{x_t\}$ is a Cauchy sequence. The proof is by contradiction. Suppose, contrary to what we want to prove, that for some subsequence (using the same notation) $\|x_t - x_{t+1}\| \geq \varepsilon$ for some $\varepsilon > 0$ and all t. Choose some further subsequence such that $i_t = i$ and $j_t = j$ for all t. It is always possible to choose this subsequence because every ordered pair of agents (i, j) is matched infinitely often. Then choose a further subsequence such that $x_t \to y$ and $x_{it+1} - x_{it} \to z$ along this subsequence. It is possible to choose such a subsequence because the set of attainable allocations is compact. Since

$$\lim_{t\to\infty} u_k(x_{kt}) = \lim_{t\to\infty} u_k(x_{kt+1}) = v_k(f^*),$$

for $k = i, j$, it must be the case that

$$u_i(y_i) = u_i(y_i + z) = v_i(f^*)$$
$$u_j(y_j) = u_j(y_j - z) = v_j(f^*).$$

By strict concavity,

$$u_i(y_i + z/2) > v_i(f^*)$$
$$u_j(y_j - z/2) > v_j(f^*).$$

By continuity,

$$u_i(x_{it} + z/2) > v_i(f^*)$$
$$u_j(x_{jt} - z/2) > v_j(f^*),$$

63

for all t sufficiently large. This contradicts the equilibrium conditions since i can offer j to trade $z/2$ and make them both better off.

This last step is not entirely obvious, since we are considering a deviation from the equilibrium path. We have shown that i can offer j a trade which can make them both better off than they would be along the equilibrium path. However, j may reject this offer if, by doing so, he can achieve an outcome that is better still. Can j do better still? In a Markov equilibrium, the answer is "no." Since strategies are memoryless, if j rejects i's offer the allocation at the beginning of the next period is exactly the same as it was at the beginning of the present period. Since f^* is an MPE, the equilibrium payoff depends only on the next state $(x_t, t+1)$ and can be denoted by $v_j(x_t, t+1)$. On the one hand, since trade is voluntary, $v_j(x_t, t+1)$ must satisfy

$$v_j(x_t, t+1) \leq v_j(f^*);$$

otherwise j could do better than his equilibrium payoff by refusing any offer at date t and this would contradict the equilibrium conditions. On the other hand, if he accepts the offer of z, his payoff must be at least

$$v_j(x', t+1) \geq u_j(x_{jt} - z/2) > v_j(f^*),$$

where the new allocation x' is defined by

$$x'_k = \begin{cases} x_{it} + z/2 & \text{if } k = i \\ x_{jt} - z/2 & \text{if } k = j \\ x_{kt} & \text{otherwise.} \end{cases}$$

So in an MPE agent j must accept the offer of z. Then i can achieve a payoff of at least $u_i(x_{it} + z/2) > v_i(f^*)$ and must deviate.

Note that in order to show that j must accept i's offer it is necessary only to look ahead one period. This is because we are assuming that the strategies f^* constitute an equilibrium. So if j rejects the offer, the resulting payoff is determined by the equilibrium strategies beginning with the current allocation at the next date. Since this payoff is less than he was offered, j's equilibrium strategy must be to accept i's offer.

Perfect competition

So the hypothesis that $\{x_t\}$ is not Cauchy leads to a contradiction of the equilibrium conditions. This contradiction establishes that $\{x_t\}$ is a Cauchy sequence, so $\{x_t\}$ converges to a limit allocation x_∞.

To show that $x_\infty \in P$ we use a similar argument. Suppose that $x_\infty \notin P$. Then x_∞ is not pairwise-efficient, according to Proposition 1, and for some pair (i, j), there exists a feasible trade z such that

$$u_i(x_{i\infty} + z) > u_i(x_{i\infty}) = v_i(f^*)$$
$$u_j(x_{j\infty} - z) > u_j(x_{j\infty}) = v_j(f^*)$$

and by continuity

$$u_i(x_{it} + z) > v_i(f^*)$$
$$u_j(x_{jt} - z) > v_j(f^*),$$

for all t sufficiently large. Since the pair (i, j) is matched infinitely often on ω, we can use the previous argument to show that i must deviate by offering z to j, contradicting the equilibrium conditions. This shows that $x_\infty \in P$. ∎

2.7 Competitive sequences of economies

To get any further with our story, we have to allow the number of agents to grow unboundedly large. There are several ways to do this. One simple way is to assume there is a fixed sequence of agents $i = 1, 2, \ldots$, each characterized by a consumption set X_i, an endowment $e_i \in X_i$ and a utility function $u_i : X_i \to \mathbf{R}$. For each positive integer m, define a pure exchange economy $\mathcal{E}^m$ consisting of the first m agents. Using this economy and a matching probability π^m, one can define a matching and bargaining game Γ^m consisting of the players $I^m = \{1, \ldots, m\}$, the strategy sets $F^m = \times_{i=1}^m F_i^m$, and the payoff functions $\{v_i^m\}_{i=1}^m$ defined in the usual way. The set of Markov perfect equilibria (MPE) corresponding to the game Γ^m is denoted by $MPE(\Gamma^m)$.

The objective of this section is to study the behavior of a sequence of equilibria $\{f^m\}_{m=1}^\infty$, where $f^m \in MPE(\Gamma^m)$ for each m.

For each equilibrium f^m, let $x^m = \{x_t^m\}_{t=1}^\infty$ denote the sequence of attainable allocations observed along the equilibrium path, and let

$$y^m = \lim_{t\to\infty} x_t^m.$$

In other words, y^m is the limit allocation. Since $y^m \in P$ the Second Welfare Theorem and the usual concavity assumptions imply that there exists a supporting price vector p^m such that

$$u_i(y_i) \geq u_i(y_i^m) \text{ and } y_i \neq y_i^m \Longrightarrow p^m \cdot y_i > p^m \cdot y_i^m,$$

for every $i = 1, \ldots, m$. To see this, note that efficiency implies the existence of a common vector p^m proportional to each gradient vector $\nabla u_i(y_i^m)$; strict concavity and the gradient inequality imply the rest.

We can normalize the prices so that $\|p^m\| = 1$ for every m. Since the sequence $\{p^m\}$ is bounded, it possesses a subsequence converging to a limiting price vector p^0. Denote the convergent subsequence by $m \in \mathcal{M}$. This subsequence is the focus of attention in what follows.

Because of the complexity of the sequence of games and corresponding equilibria, two additional assumptions are required in order to characterize equilibria in the limit. One concerns the continuity of the equilibrium play of the game; the other concerns the curvature of the individual utility functions.

Continuity

As the number of agents gets very large, a single individual becomes negligible in terms of his endowment and his potential contribution to the general welfare. However, this does not ensure that his effect on the limit allocation will be negligible, even when the number of agents gets very large. In a dynamic game, the possibility of a large number of agents conditioning their responses on the actions of a single player endogenously generates the possibility that a single player has a non-negligible effect

Perfect competition

in equilibrium. To avoid this possibility, a continuity assumption will be imposed. The essential idea is simple. The continuity assumption requires that a single player have a negligible impact on the limiting allocation.

Before describing the continuity assumption it is worth making several general points about the nature and role of the assumption. First, it is an assumption about endogenous variables. As such it directly restricts the kinds of equilibria that will be considered, rather than the primitives of the model. Such assumptions are often regarded with suspicion because it is not at all clear what is being ruled out. Secondly, it is an assumption about strategies, insofar as it restricts the response of players to deviations from equilibrium play. Thirdly, it is a complex assumption. The situation to which the continuity assumption applies involves two limits, one as time goes to infinity and the other as the number of players grows without bound. Uniform continuity is needed with respect to both limits.

For any strategy profile $f \in F^m$ there is a unique sequence of allocations $\xi(a^f) = \{\xi_t(a^f)\}_{t=1}^{\infty}$, where $\xi_t(a^f)$ is the allocation at date t. Suppose that agent j deviates from the equilibrium by choosing an arbitrary strategy $\hat{f}_j \in F_j$. The resulting path is denoted by $a(f_{-j}, \hat{f}_j)$ and the outcome is $\xi(a(f_{-j}, \hat{f}_j))$. The impact of the deviation on the outcome of the game can be measured by the distance of the current allocation at any date from the equilibrium limit allocation. If y is the equilibrium limit allocation and the current allocation at date t is $\xi_t(a(f_{-j}, \hat{f}_j))$ then the distance between the current and the limit allocations is

$$\frac{1}{m} \sum_{i=1}^{m} \|\xi_{it}(a(f_{-j}, \hat{f}_j)) - y_i\|.$$

Note that we take the average distance. What we need to ensure is that a deviation by a single agent j does not cause a large change in the outcome as measured by this distance.

- Let $\{f^m\}$ be a fixed but arbitrary sequence of MPE. The *continuity assumption* requires that for any $\epsilon > 0$ there exist M and T such that for any agent j and any strategy $f_j \in F_j^m$,

$$\frac{1}{m} \sum_{i=1}^{m} \|\xi_{it}(a(f_{-j}^m, f_j)) - y_i^m\| < \epsilon, \forall m > M, \forall t > T,$$

where it is understood that $m \in \mathcal{M}$.

In other words, any deviation by a single player cannot change the average allocations by a large amount for sufficiently large values of t and m. This does not imply that the deviating player cannot change the consumption bundles of some players, himself included, by a non-negligible amount. What it does imply is that he cannot change the consumption bundles of most players by a non-negligible amount. Also, note that we have bounded this distance *uniformly* in t and m. Uniformity is necessary; otherwise the order of limits would matter.

An assumption of this kind, which restricts the values of endogenous variables, is unfortunately obscure. We do not know what this assumption is ruling out or ruling in in terms of the primitives of the model. We do not know whether the assumption is likely to be satisfied by most MPE or not. For the moment, we have to accept it on the basis of intuitive plausibility and the fact that something like this is needed to make the analysis tractable and to get the result we want. In chapter 3 we investigate the basis for this kind of assumption in more detail.

A similar assumption has been used by Green (1984) to show that the Nash equilibria of an n-person game converge to Nash equilibria of a continuum game as the value of n increases without bound.

An assumption of this kind appears to be needed in order to show that the Nash equilibria of a Cournot oligopoly game converge to competitive equilibria as the number of firms increases without bound. Roberts (1980) provides a counter-example to the competitive limit result. If the equilibrium price correspondence, which maps quantities chosen by firms into equilibrium prices, is multi-valued then a small change in quantity by one firm can lead to a discontinuous change in price. This discontinuous effect of a single firm's action can prevent the achievement of perfect competition in the limit, even though each firm is "small" in terms of its impact on total output.

Curvature

The second assumption requires uniformity in the curvature of the agents' preferences. As we let the number of players grow without bound, the degree of substitutability along an agent's indifference curves may be falling as the index of the agent gets very large. The assumption introduced in this subsection puts a bound on how little substitutability there can be. This assumption is not strictly necessary, for reasons indicated below (p. 73), but it makes life a lot easier.

The first part of the assumption guarantees that the indifference surface has positive curvature, that is, the indifference surface is not kinked. This is guaranteed by the assumption that, for any consumption bundle x_i, there is a ball with positive radius contained in the set of bundles preferred to x_i and tangent to the indifference surface at x_i. The larger this ball is, the flatter the indifference surface must be. For present purposes, it is also necessary to ensure some degree of uniformity in the curvature of the indifference surfaces. This can be done by assuming that for every agent i and every bundle x_i, the ball can be chosen to have a fixed minimum radius $r > 0$. The rest of this section deals with details that can be skipped by the non-technical reader.

For any agent i and consumption bundle $x_i \in X_i$, let

$$H_i(x_i) \equiv \{x_i' \in X_i | u_i(x_i') \geq u_i(x_i)\}$$

denote the set of consumption bundles that are at least as good as x_i. Define the normal function $g_i : X_i \to \mathbf{R}^\ell$ by putting

$$g_i(x_i) = -\nabla u_i(x_i)/\|\nabla u_i(x_i)\|.$$

Then we note that for any $\alpha > 0$, the point $x_i - \alpha g_i(x_i)$ belongs to $H_i(x_i)$ and lies at a distance α from the point x_i. Let

$$B(x, r) = \{y \in \mathbf{R}^\ell \mid \|x - y\| \leq r\}$$

denote the ball with center x and radius r.

- Our *curvature assumption* is that for some $\alpha > 0$, for any i and for any $x_i \in X_i$,

$$B(x_i - \alpha g_i(x_i), \alpha) \subseteq H_i(x_i),$$

that is, every point in the ball with radius α and center $x_i - \alpha g_i(x_i)$ is weakly preferred to x_i.

As before, we could restrict this assumption to hold only for individually rational bundles x_i such that $u_i(x_i) \geq u_i(e_i)$.

Note that the strength of this assumption comes from the fact that α is chosen independently of i and the consumption bundle x_i. This means that there is a uniform bound on the curvature of the indifference curves of every agent at every point in his consumption set.

Linearity

The preceding subsections have introduced two special assumptions that are needed to continue the development of a competitive limit theorem. The next step is to show that budget balance is satisfied. More precisely, it will be proved that any net trade lying in the competitive budget set $\{z \in \mathbf{R}^\ell \mid p^0 \cdot z \leq 0\}$ is achievable in an asymptotically pure MPE for m sufficiently large. In other words, we shall have demonstrated that each agent can achieve the same utility that he would obtain in a competitive equilibrium with price vector p^0.

The strategy of the proof, which is an adaptation of the proof used in Gale (1986) and Osborne and Rubinstein (1990), consists of a number of steps. First, we note that since the limiting allocation is efficient and has a supporting price vector, for any net trade z such that $p^0 \cdot z < 0$ we can find a number n such that $-z/n$ is a preferred trade for any agent j holding the limiting bundle y_j^m. This follows from the curvature assumption. Then we claim that the following strategy must allow agent i to achieve the net trade z. Simply offer to trade z/n whenever the opportunity arises and refuse all other trades. Repeat this pattern until the trade z/n has been executed n times. Any agent j must be willing to trade $-z/n$ for t sufficiently large because as t gets large the agent's current bundle converges to y_j^m so $-z/n$ is a preferred trade. Since agent i has an infinite number of opportunities to make these trades, with probability one, he will surely achieve the net trade z.

A number of assumptions are needed to make this argument go through, however. We have already mentioned the curvature assumption. Another is the continuity assumption. It is crucial that the agent's deviation does not change the limit allocation, by very much, for most players. If it did, the supporting prices p^0 and the set of preferred trades z would be altered, so we could not be sure that anyone would accept $-z/n$. Finally, the Markov assumption is important, as it was in the proof of efficiency, because it ensures that if an agent j refuses to trade $-z/n$ with agent i he is not going to be rewarded for that refusal in the continuation game.

Lemma 4 *Let $\{f^m\}$ be a competitive sequence of MPE satisfying the maintained assumptions. For any i and z such that $e_i + z \in X_i$ and $p^0 \cdot z < 0$, $v_i^m(f^m) \geq u_i(e_i + z)$ for all $m \in \mathcal{M}$ sufficiently large.*

Proof Fix i and choose z such that $p^0 \cdot z < 0$. Choose M so that $p^m \cdot z < 0$ for all $m > M$ and then choose $0 < \lambda \leq 1$ and $\epsilon > 0$ so that for all $j \leq m$ and $m > M$, the ball with radius ϵ and center $y_j^m - \lambda z$ is contained in the ball with radius α and center $y_j^m + \alpha p^m$ and hence contained in $H_i(y_j^m)$. The possibility of this construction is guaranteed by the curvature assumption.

Now consider the following strategy f_i for some fixed but arbitrary m. Choose a number $n > 1/\lambda$ and have agent i offer to trade z/n at every opportunity until he has made the aggregate trade z. In other words, put

$$f_i(h) = \begin{cases} z/n & \text{if } i \text{ is the proposer and he has traded} \\ & kz/n \text{ for } k < n; \\ 0 & \text{if } i \text{ is the proposer and he has traded} \\ & \text{something other than } kz/n \text{ for } k < n; \\ \text{"No"} & \text{if } i \text{ is the responder.} \end{cases}$$

The exact pattern of trades depends on the order of play, but agent i will meet every agent $j \neq i$ an infinite number of times. The continuity assumption implies that there exist numbers M and T such that for all $m > M$ and $t > T$,

$$\frac{1}{m} \sum_{j=1}^{m} \|\xi_{jt}(f^m_{-i}, f_i) - y^m_j\| < \epsilon/2.$$

This implies that for at least half the agents,

$$\|\xi_{jt}(f^m_{-i}, f_i) - y^m_j)\| < \epsilon. \tag{2.2}$$

Let J denote the set of agents satisfying the inequality (2.2). Then for all j belonging to this set and for $m > M$ and $t > T$,

$$u_j(\xi_{jt}(f^m_{-i}, f_i) - z/n) > u_j(\xi_{jt}(f^m)).$$

This follows from the fact that $\xi_{jt}(f^m_{-i}, f_i) - z/n$ belongs to the ball with center $y^m_j - z/n$ and radius ϵ and $u_j(\xi_{jt}(f^m))$ converges to $u_j(y^m_j)$ as $t \to \infty$.

Then the Markov property implies that an agent $j \in J$ must accept an offer of z/n for $t > T$ sufficiently large if he has not already done so.

Thus, agent i can in the limit carry out the trade z for almost every realization ω and so $\xi_{it}(f^m_{-i}, f_i) \to e_i + z$ as $t \to \infty$. ■

Lemma 4 shows that, in the limit, the outcome of an MPE of the game maximizes each agent's utility subject to a linear budget constraint. This brings us to the conclusion of our argument that, in the limit as the number of agents gets very large, the dynamic matching and bargaining game achieves a competitive equilibrium allocation. The allocations are always attainable and Lemma 4 shows that the terminal consumption bundle of each agent gives him a utility equal to the competitive equilibrium indirect utility $v_i(p^0, p^0 \cdot e_i)$ at prices p^0 with the wealth $p^0 \cdot e_i$.

A counter-example with limited substitution

It is now clear why uniform curvature was needed for the preceding argument. We want to show that an agent can trade any vector z such that $p \cdot z < 0$ by breaking z up into n pieces z/n and trading each of these pieces with a different agent. If the agents do not have uniform curvature, there may not be n of them for whom $-z/n$ is a preferred trade. Of course, there could be other ways of achieving the net trade z. One could find a sequence $\{\rho_i\}$ of positive numbers summing to one and make a sequence of trades $\{\rho_i z\}$. If the numbers $\rho_i \to 0$ were chosen appropriately it might be possible to make the desired trade without assuming uniform curvature. Clearly, the agents who have limited substitutability would be offered the smallest trades. However, even if this approach were adopted, some bound on substitutability would be needed to ensure that the trade z could be achieved. To see how lack of uniform curvature can prevent convergence to a competitive equilibrium allocation, consider what would happen if most agents' preferences had no curvature at all.

Suppose that there are two commodities $\ell = 2$ and two agents $m = 2$. Agent 1 has Cobb–Douglas preferences

$$u_1(x_1) = \log_e x_{11} + \log_e x_{12}$$

and agent 2 has Leontief preferences

$$u_2(x_2) = \min\{x_{21}, x_{22}\}.$$

Suppose that the initial endowment is given by $e_1 = (3, 2)$ and $e_2 = (2, 3)$. There is a unique competitive equilibrium in which each agent consumes $(2.5, 2.5)$ but this is not the only limiting equilibrium allocation of the DMBG. For example, the allocation in which agent 1 gets $(2.5 - \varepsilon, 2.5 - \varepsilon)$ and agent 2 gets $(2.5 + \varepsilon, 2.5 + \varepsilon)$, for sufficiently small $\varepsilon > 0$, can be supported as an equilibrium of the DMBG, as is shown in section 2.11.

It is no surprise that competition fails with two agents, but the same kind of allocation can be achieved as an MPE of a DMBG with any number of agents. Suppose that, in addition to agents 1 and 2 there are a large number of additional agents with Leontief preferences and endowments $(1, 1)$. The same bundles for agents 1 and 2 are still attainable. Furthermore, the presence of the additional agents does not affect the equilibrium play of the game. There is no possibility of trade between agent 1 and agents $i > 2$, so they might as well not be there.

By contrast, if the additional agents had Cobb–Douglas preferences identical to agent 1's and endowments equal to $(1, 1)$ then the argument of Lemma 4 would apply. By making small offers to trade a small vector $z/n = (-0.5, 0.5)/n$ to n different agents, agent 1 could achieve his competitive trade z.

The competitive limit theorem

The preceding analysis can be summed up in a *competitive limit theorem*. Take an infinite sequence of agents $i = 1, 2, \ldots$ and define the exchange economy $\mathcal{E}^m$ to comprise the first m agents $i = 1, 2, \ldots, m$, for every finite number m. Then define the game Γ^m by specifying an order of play $\pi^m = \{(i_t^m, j_t^m)\}$. The sequence $\{\Gamma^m\}$ is called a *competitive sequence of games* if the following assumptions are satisfied for every i:

- $X_i \subset \mathbf{R}^\ell$ is non-empty, and $X_i \equiv \{x_i \in G_i | u_i(x_i) \geq c_i\}$ for some constant c_i (hence X_i is closed);
- $e_i \in X_i$;
- $u_i : X_i \to \mathbf{R}$ is strictly concave, increasing, and C^1 on an open superset of X_i;

and the sequence satisfies

- the curvature assumption introduced above (p. 70);
- the sets $\{X_i\}$ are uniformly bounded below and the mean endowments $m^{-1} \sum_{i=1}^m e_i$ are uniformly bounded above.

74

Perfect competition

The last assumption is the only new one. It guarantees that the resources available to agents do not grow on average as the size of the economy expands without limit.

Now let $\{f^m\}$ be a sequence of equilibrium strategy profiles such that $f^m \in MPE(\Gamma^m)$ for each m. A subsequence $m \in \mathcal{M}$ is called a *competitive sequence of equilibria* if the following properties are satisfied:

- for every m, f^m is an MPE and $x_t^m \to y^m$ for almost every ω;
- for every $m \in \mathcal{M}$ there exists a price vector p^m such that $\|p^m\| = 1$ and $u_i(x_i) > u_i(y_i^m)$ implies $p^m \cdot x_i > p^m \cdot y_i^m$, for $i = 1, \dots, m$;
- $\lim_{m \in \mathcal{M}} y_i^m = y_i^0$ and $\lim_{m \in \mathcal{M}} p^m = p^0$; and
- the subsequence satisfies the continuity assumption introduced above on p. 68.

Call (y^0, p^0) a *competitive limit equilibrium* if, for every i,

$$y_i^0 \in \arg\max\{u_i(x_i)| \ x_i \in X_i, p^0 \cdot x_i \leq p^0 \cdot e_i\}.$$

In other words, at the limiting allocation y^0 each agent is maximizing his utility subject to a budget constraint defined by the limiting price system p^0. This property is guaranteed by Lemma 4.

Although the limit allocation (with respect to time) $y^m = (y_1^m, \dots, y_m^m)$ is attainable in the sense that $\sum_{i=1}^m (y_i^m - e_i) = 0$, there is no guarantee that the limit allocation (with respect to numbers of agents) $y^0 = (y_1^0, y_2^0, \dots)$ will be *attainable* in the sense that

$$m^{-1} \sum_{i=1}^m (y_i^0 - e_i) \to 0. \tag{2.3}$$

The reason y^0 may not be attainable is that the convergence of $\{y_i^m\}_{m=1}^\infty$ to y_i^0 may not be uniform with respect to i. Of course, if we assume uniform convergence then we can be sure that the limiting allocation y^0 will be attainable. For any $\varepsilon > 0$ and all m sufficiently large, uniform convergence implies that $\|y_i^0 - y_i^m\| \leq \varepsilon$ for $i = 1, \dots, m$. From this it easily follows that

$$m^{-1}\|\sum_{i=1}^{m}(y_i^0 - e_i)\| = m^{-1}\|\sum_{i=1}^{m}(y_i^0 - y_i^m + y_i^m - e_i)\|$$

$$= m^{-1}\|\sum_{i=1}^{m}y_i^0 - y_i^m\|$$

$$\leq m^{-1}\sum_{i=1}^{m}\|y_i^0 - y_i^m\| \leq \varepsilon$$

for all m sufficiently large. Thus,

$$\lim_{m\to\infty}m^{-1}\|\sum_{i=1}^{m}(y_i^0 - e_i)\| \leq \varepsilon.$$

Since the choice of ε was arbitrary, the limit is in fact zero.

Call (y^0, p^0) a *strong competitive limit equilibrium* if it is a competitive limit equilibrium and y^0 is attainable in the sense of condition (2.3).

Theorem 5 *Let $\{\Gamma^m\}$ be a competitive sequence of games, let $\{f^m\}_{m\in\mathcal{M}}$ be a corresponding competitive sequence of equilibria and let y^0 and p^0 be the limiting allocation and price system. Under the maintained assumptions (y^0, p^0) is a competitive limit equilibrium and if the convergence of $\{y_i^m\}$ to y^0 is uniform then (y^0, p^0) is a strong competitive equilibrium.*

This brings us to the end of our first attempt to characterize the MPE of the dynamic matching and bargaining game. As we have seen, some strong assumptions are needed to carry through the program of providing strategic foundations for the theory of competitive equilibrium. These will be investigated in more detail in chapter 3. In the remainder of this chapter, I explore some other aspects of the theory, beginning with existence.

2.8 Existence

So far, we have focused on the characterization of MPE without worrying too much about the restrictiveness of the Markov property. Do MPE even exist? A complete characterization of existence is not available in general, but in a special case we can say quite a lot. It turns out that MPE do exist for a rich class of economic environments. Furthermore, they have a nice structure that makes them natural objects to study and allows us to pursue a constructive approach to existence.

The strategy for proving that an MPE exists is quite simple. In the theory of repeated games and DMBGs with a continuum of agents (for example, Gale, 1986c), one constructs an equilibrium by guessing the equilibrium outcome and then proving that it can be supported as an MPE by appropriate strategies. Here too the proof is constructive. I assume that the outcome of the MPE converges to a competitive equilibrium allocation for the economy. The first step is to find trading rules that will allow agents to trade commodities to get from their initial endowments to their competitive equilibrium consumption bundles while keeping the value of their current bundles constant. These trading rules can be used as the basis of the equilibrium strategies: whatever allocation has been reached, the agents take as their target a competitive equilibrium relative to that allocation and use the trading rules to trade towards their target. The difficult step is to show that these strategies constitute an MPE, that they prevent anyone from doing better than his equilibrium payoff. In fact this can be shown only in special cases, so it is necessary to make some special assumptions. This should not be surprising, given the fact that in a finite economy each of the agents has some "market power." In general, we should expect the competitive equilibrium to be the outcome of an MPE when the number of agents is unboundedly large.

Let $\mathcal{E} = \{(X_i, u_i, e_i)\}_{i=1}^m$ be a fixed but arbitrary economy and for any attainable allocation $x \in \hat{X}$ let $\mathcal{E}(x)$ denote the exchange economy formed by taking x as the initial endowment, that is, $\mathcal{E}(x) = \{(X_i, u_i, x_i)\}_{i=1}^m$. Let $W(\mathcal{E}(x))$ denote the set of Walras allocations of $\mathcal{E}(x)$, that is, the set of allocations x^* such that for some price system p^* the ordered pair (p^*, x^*) is a competitive equilibrium of $\mathcal{E}(x)$. Under certain conditions, it can be shown that there exists an MPE of Γ that implements the Walras allocations of $\mathcal{E}$. This ensures that the discussion of the preceding sections has not been vacuous. More interestingly, it shows that the competitive equilibrium can be implemented by an MPE even for finite games. This conclusion would not be too surprising if we considered SPEs rather than MPE, because SPEs allow for the use of trigger strategies. For this reason, the set of SPEs may be much larger than the set of MPEs. In any case, the proof of existence of MPE is not without difficulty.

Under the maintained assumptions, every efficient allocation $x \in P$ has associated with it an essentially unique vector of supporting prices. Let $\Delta = \{p \in \mathbf{R}_+^\ell \mid \sum_{h=1}^\ell p_h = 1\}$ denote the $(\ell - 1)$-dimensional simplex. For any Pareto-efficient allocation $x \in P$, let $\pi(x)$ denote the unique price vector in Δ such that

$$p \propto \frac{\partial u_i(x_i)}{\partial x_i}, \forall i = 1, \ldots, m.$$

By Proposition 1 we know that the gradients of the utility functions are proportional. So the price vector exists and is positive under the maintained assumptions and the normalization ensures that it is unique.

For any Pareto-efficient allocation x, let $H(x)$ denote the hyperplane through x defined by

$$H(x) = \{x' \in \mathbf{R}^{\ell m} \mid \pi(x) \cdot x_i' = \pi(x) \cdot x_i, i = 1, \ldots, m\}$$

and let $B(x)$ denote the set of attainable allocations in $H(x)$, that is, $B(x) = H(x) \cap \hat{X}$. The importance of the set $B(x)$ is that starting from an initial endowment in $B(x)$, the allocation x is a Walras allocation.

Proposition 6 *Suppose that x is a Pareto-efficient allocation and $x' \in B(x)$. Then x is a Walras allocation of $\mathcal{E}(x')$, that is, $x \in W(\mathcal{E}(x'))$.*

Proof By construction and the gradient inequality, for every agent i, $u_i(x_i'') > u_i(x_i)$ implies that $\pi(x) \cdot x_i'' > \pi(x) \cdot x_i = \pi(x) \cdot x_i'$. Thus,

Perfect competition

$$x_i \in \arg\max\{u_i(x_i'')|x_i'' \in X_i, \pi(x) \cdot x_i'' \leq \pi(x) \cdot x_i'\},$$
$$\forall i = 1, \ldots, m,$$

and $(\pi(x), x)$ is a competitive equilibrium for $\mathcal{E}(x')$. ∎

The second fact that we need is that the sets $\{B(x)|x \in P\}$ form a partition of the set of attainable allocations, that is, each attainable allocation belongs to one and only one set in $\{B(x)|x \in P\}$. To ensure this we need to assume that the competitive equilibrium allocation of $\mathcal{E}(x)$ is unique for every attainable x.

Uniqueness Assumption For any attainable allocation x, the set of Walras allocations $W(\mathcal{E}(x))$ is a singleton.

There are well known conditions such as gross substitutability that can guarantee uniqueness. There is no need to pursue the details here.

Now note that if

$$x'' \in B(x) \cap B(x')$$

for two Pareto-efficient allocations $x \neq x'$, then x and x' are both Walras allocations for the exchange economy $\mathcal{E}(x'')$, contradicting our assumption. Thus, uniqueness of equilibrium implies that the sets $\{B(x) : x \in P\}$ are non-intersecting. Secondly, any attainable allocation x' must belong to $B(x)$ for some Pareto-efficient allocation x. This is because under the maintained assumptions, each exchange economy $\mathcal{E}(x')$ has a Walras allocation x and every Walras allocation is Pareto-efficient. Thus, we have the following result.

Proposition 7 *The set of attainable allocations $\hat{X}$ is partitioned by $\{B(x) : x \in P\}$.*

With these two propositions established, we are ready to define an equilibrium strategy for Γ. Define the function $\phi : \hat{X} \to P$ by putting

$$\phi(x) = B^{-1}(x)$$

for any attainable allocation x. In the equilibrium we are going to construct, $\phi(x)$ will be the target allocation once the current allocation x has been achieved. In other words, for any attainable allocation x that is reached during the play of the game, the MPE will implement a Walras allocation $\phi(x) \in W(\mathcal{E}(x))$ in the continuation game. To see exactly how this will be done, it is necessary to specify a *trading rule*. Intuitively, when agents i and j meet, the trading rule maximizes a measure of their trade subject to a number of constraints.

Let x be the current allocation and (i, j) be the matched pair during the current period. Let $z = \zeta(x, i, j)$ denote the proposal made by agent i, where $\zeta(x, i, j)$ is defined by putting

$$\zeta(x, i, j) = \arg\max \sum_{h=2}^{\ell} -\exp\{z_h\}$$

$$\text{s.t. } |z_h| \leq |\phi_{kh}(x) - x_{kh}|, k = i, j; h = 2, \ldots, \ell;$$
$$sign\{z_h\} = sign\{\phi_{ih}(x) - x_{ih}\} = -sign\{\phi_{jh}(x) - x_{jh}\},$$
$$\text{for } k = i, j, h = 2, \ldots, \ell;$$
$$\pi(x) \cdot z = 0;$$
$$x_i + z \in X_i, x_j - z \in X_j.$$

Since $\phi(x)$ is a Walras allocation relative to the initial endowment x, we can think of $\phi(x) - x$ as the vector of agents' excess demands. The first constraint says that the absolute value of the trade in commodities $h = 2, \ldots, \ell$ cannot exceed the absolute value of the excess demands of agents i and j for the corresponding commodity. The second constraint says that the trade in commodities $h = 2, \ldots, \ell$ must have the same sign as the agents' excess demands. The final constraint says that the trade must respect the agents' budget constraints at the equilibrium prices $\pi(x)$. Note the special role of commodity 1. It acts as a means of payment and agents may be forced to trade in a direction that increases or changes the sign of their excess demands in order to balance the budget constraint.

Now the trading rule ϕ can be used to define an equilibrium strategy profile $f = (f_1, \ldots, f_m)$ as follows. For any attainable allocation x and ordered pair (i, j), put

$$f_i(x, i, j) = \zeta(x, i, j) \tag{2.4}$$

and for any net trade z put

$$f_j(x, i, j, z) = \begin{cases} \text{"yes"} & \text{if } \pi(x) \cdot z \le 0, x_j - z \in X_j \\ \text{"no"} & \text{otherwise.} \end{cases} \quad (2.5)$$

The first step in establishing that f is an MPE is to show that f leads to an outcome $\phi(x)$ starting from any initial allocation x. The only obstacle to this outcome is the possibility that the process will get stuck because of an inadequate amount of the numeraire good. To avoid this possibility, we make the following assumption.

Interiority Assumption   For each i and any attainable allocation x we assume that either (i) $\phi_i(x) = x_i$ or (ii) for some $\varepsilon > 0$, $\phi(x) - (\varepsilon, 0, \dots, 0) \in X_i$

There will exist efficient allocations on the boundary of X where condition (ii) cannot be satisfied, but in that case we assume that no trade is optimal, so that agent i effectively does not participate in the trading process. Note that if the allocation $\phi(x)$ is individually rational relative to the initial endowment e then $\phi(x)$ belongs to the interior of X anyway, but since we have to define a continuation equilibrium for every possible subgame – i.e. for every possible allocation x – we cannot rely on individual rationality relative to e to ensure the trading process does not get stuck.

Under the interiority assumption, if all agents adopt the strategies in f then the allocation will converge to the Walras allocation $\phi(x)$.

Proposition 8   *For any initial allocation x let $\{z_t\}$ denote the sequence of excess demands generated along the equilibrium path by the strategy profile f. Then $\{z_t\}$ converges to 0.*

Proof   By construction, the absolute values of the excess demands for commodities $h = 2, \dots, \ell$ are monotonically non-decreasing. Thus, they must converge. Suppose the excess demands z_t converge to some limit z_∞, say.

If $z_\infty = 0$ then there is nothing to prove, so suppose that $z_\infty \ne 0$. Then there are two cases to be considered. Either (i) every agent has achieved his demand for commodity 1 and hence can afford to give up a small amount of commodity 1 in exchange for other commodities or (ii) some agent i has an excess supply of commodity 1. In case (i) market-clearing (attainability) and the budget constraints imply that there exist at least two agents i and j and some commodity $h \geq 2$ such that $z_{ih} < 0$ and $z_{jh} > 0$. By construction, $\zeta(x, i, j)$ is bounded away from 0 for any $x \in B(x^*)$ close to the limit value $x^* - z_\infty$, where $x^* = \phi(x)$ is the Walras allocation. Since (i, j) are matched infinitely often we have a contradiction of the assumption of convergence. In case (ii), $z_{i1}^0 < 0$ for agent i and the budget constraint implies that $z_{ih\infty} > 0$ for some commodity h. Then market clearing implies that there is some agent j such that $z_{jh\infty} < 0$ and by construction, $\zeta(x, i, j)$ is bounded away from 0 for any $x \in B(x^*)$ close to the limit value $x^* - z_\infty$. Since i and j meet infinitely often this contradicts the convergence assumption. This establishes that $z_\infty = 0$. ∎

For any attainable allocation x, Proposition 8 shows that agent i's equilibrium payoff in the continuation game beginning at x is given by

$$v_i(x) = u_i(\phi_i(x)), \forall i = 1, \ldots, m.$$

To show that f is an MPE we need to show that the strategies defined by (2.4) and (2.5) are best responses at every information set. A sufficient condition for this is the following:

Independence Assumption The competitive equilibrium price vector is independent of the attainable allocation x, that is, $\pi(x) = p$ for all x.

This assumption is quite strong. It would be satisfied, for example, in a representative agent economy, where all agents had identical, homothetic preferences. The independence assumption would also be satisfied if agents had transferable utility. Strictly speaking, transferable utility is not consistent with other assumptions we have made, though the results would probably continue to hold without them.

To show that the proposer's strategy is optimal, suppose that the current allocation is x, the pair (i, j) is matched, and the vector z is traded. That is, agent i receives the bundle $x_i + z$ and agent j receives the bundle $x_j - z$. Let x' denote the new allocation and let $p = \pi(x) = \pi(x')$. If $p \cdot z < 0$, then

$$p \cdot \phi_i(x') = p \cdot x_i'$$
$$< p \cdot x_i$$
$$= p \cdot \phi_i(x)$$

which implies that $v_i(x) = u_i(\phi_i(x)) > v_i(x') = u_i(\phi_i(x'))$, so that agent i is worse off. On the other hand, the responder will not accept any vector z such that $p \cdot z > 0$. Thus, the only possibility for i to increase his payoff is to offer a trade z such that $p \cdot z = 0$. But we know from the definition of f that any such z leads to $\phi(x)$ and so does not increase the ultimate payoff. Thus, offering $\zeta(x, i, j)$ is weakly optimal for the proposer.

Now we can show that the responder's strategy is optimal. The responder accepts any vector z such that $p \cdot z \leq 0$. By the preceding argument we can show that any trade z such that $p \cdot z > 0$ makes j worse off, so it is optimal to reject such offers, and any trade z such that $p \cdot z = 0$ leads to the same outcome so it is weakly optimal to accept such offers. On the other hand, if $p \cdot z < 0$ then

$$v_j(x') = u_j(\phi(x'))$$
$$\geq \max\{u_j(\hat{x}_j) | \hat{x}_j \in X_j, p \cdot \hat{x}_j \leq p \cdot x_j'\}$$
$$> \max\{u_j(\hat{x}_j) | \hat{x}_j \in X_j, p \cdot \hat{x}_j \leq p \cdot x_j\}$$
$$= u_j(\phi_j(x)) = v_j(x),$$

so it is optimal to accept such offers. This completes the proof of the desired result.

Theorem 9 *If the Uniqueness, Interiority and Independence Assumptions are satisfied, then the strategy profile f defined in (2.4) and (2.5) is an MPE and the equilibrium outcome $\{x_t\}$ converges to the asymptotic allocation $x^* = \phi(e)$.*

The key elements of the argument presented above seem to be the Uniqueness Assumption, which ensures that the strategy f is Markov, and the Independence Assumption, which ensures that value-increasing (value-reducing) trades are payoff-increasing (payoff-reducing). An interesting question is whether and how the Independence Assumption can be weakened.

The Independence Assumption is clearly not a necessary condition. As long as the effect of price changes is not too great a similar argument would hold. For example, for any efficient allocation x let

$$B_i(x) = \{x_i' \in X_i | \pi(x) \cdot x_i' = \pi(x) \cdot x_i\}.$$

Then the following assumption, which looks like a strengthening of the Uniqueness Assumption, will do the trick.

Non-Intersection Property For any $x, x' \in P$ and any agent i, either $B_i(x) \cap B_i(x') = \emptyset$ or $B_i(x) = B_i(x')$.

The Non-Intersection Property is clearly implied by the Uniqueness and Independence Assumptions. It implies uniqueness, but it is weaker than independence because it allows for the supporting prices $\pi(x)$ to vary with x.

Corollary 10 *If the Non-Intersection Property and the Interiority Assumption are satisfied, then the strategy profile f defined in (2.4) and (2.5) is an MPE and the equilibrium outcome $\{x_t\}$ converges to the asymptotic allocation $x^* = \phi(e)$.*

Proof Suppose as in the proof of Theorem 9 that two agents i and j have met and made a trade that changes the allocation from x to x'. If $\pi(x) \cdot \phi_i(x') > (\geq)\pi(x) \cdot \phi_i(x)$ and $\pi(x) \cdot \phi_j(x') \geq (>)\pi(x) \cdot \phi_j(x)$ then the Non-Intersection Property implies that $\pi(x) \cdot x_i' > (\geq)\pi(x) \cdot x_i$ and $\pi(x) \cdot x_j' \geq (>)\pi(x) \cdot x_j$. But this is impossible since $x_i + x_j = x_i' + x_j'$. Hence, one of the agents can be made better off only if the other is made worse off and this prevents any payoff-increasing deviation from the strategy f. ∎

In general, we should not expect to achieve a competitive equilibrium relative to the initial endowments e when there is a small number of agents. Even with a large but finite number of agents, the market power possessed by individual agents may lead to distortions that prevent the attainment of the competitive equilibrium. But the market power of agents should get smaller as the number of agents gets larger and this may allow the attainment of an approximate competitive equilibrium as an MPE of the DMBG. Alternatively, the competitive equilibrium may be an ε-equilibrium for a sufficiently large number of agents m. For example, if we could show that for any allocation x that occurs on the equilibrium path and any trade that is possible for agents i and j, it is impossible for them to increase their utilities by more than ε by deviating from the equilibrium path, then the competitive equilibrium could be achieved as an ε-MPE. Whatever trades these agents can make, the equilibrium prices will not change by very much if the number of agents is very large, and consequently they cannot change their payoffs very much by distorting the prices. Note however that the notion of ε-MPE used here is applied to each information set separately. In calculating the increase in payoff from a deviation, an agent assumes that in the future play the other agents will follow the equilibrium strategies and hence he cannot make any payoff-increasing deviations in the future. A sequence of successful deviations might increase his payoff by more than ε but this is not taken into consideration because each of them in isolation is unable to increase payoffs by more than ε and hence will not be made.

2.9 Efficiency with discounting

Up until now we have assumed that agents do not discount future utilities. In this section, the analysis is extended to include the possibility of discounting.

There are two reasons for wanting to include discounting. The first reason is that time matters. If convergence to an efficient or Walrasian allocation takes a very long time, then even a small amount of discounting will have a large effect on the payoffs. The assumption that agents do not care whether they consume early or late will not be a good approximation. By introducing discounting, we can test the robustness of the efficiency results when the time taken to converge matters. Of course, introducing a cost of time will change the results somewhat, since convergence will always take some time and discounting will reduce the eventual payoffs. For that reason, we concentrate on the case where the discount rate is small (the period length is short) and ask whether we obtain approximately the same results as in the case with no discounting.

The second reason for the interest in discounting is that it has played a crucial role in the bargaining literature, where it has been shown to yield determinate outcomes under certain circumstances. Beginning with the Stahl–Rubinstein theory, it has been shown that discounting forces agents to reach a determinate agreement, whereas the bargaining problem has an infinite number of solutions in the absence of discounting. So it is an interesting question whether discounting makes a difference in the present context.

In the bargaining literature, there are two interpretations of discounting. One is the usual interpretation that individuals prefer early consumption to late consumption and that their time preferences can be represented by geometrically discounting the utility of future consumption. If the (constant) rate of time preference is ρ, the discount factor applied to future utilities is defined to be $\gamma = (1 + \rho)^{-1}$. An agreement reached at date t giving the agent an (undiscounted) utility w is worth $\gamma^{t-1}w$ in terms of present utility.

The second interpretation assumes that there is a positive probability that the bargaining process will be stopped before an agreement is reached. If no agreement is reached, the agents both receive zero, so the equilibrium payoff is equal to the sum over all t of the probability that the game does not end before t times the utility of the agreement reached at t. The probability that the game continues until date $t+1$, conditional on the game lasting until date t, is a constant $0 < \gamma < 1$, so the probability that the game reaches date t is γ^{t-1}. Let w_t denote the equilibrium payoff if agreement is reached at date t. Then the expected payoff is $\sum_{t=1}^{\infty} \gamma^{t-1} w_t$.

So, the two approaches produce the same payoff functions and are formally equivalent. (See Binmore, Rubinstein and Wolinsky, 1986, for a subtle analysis of the differences between the two interpretations.)

In the present context, the second interpretation is easier to use. We can simply assume that when the game stops at date t every individual consumes the bundle that he is currently holding. If the game stops at date t and agent i is holding the bundle x_{it} then he receives the utility $u_i(x_{it})$. Since the probability that the game stops at date t is $\gamma^{t-1}(1 - \gamma)$, the expected utility of agent i from the outcome $\{x_t\}$ is

$$(1 - \gamma) \sum_{t=1}^{\infty} \gamma^{t-1} u_i(x_{it}).$$

This interpretation has a number of advantages over the time-preference interpretation. First, under the time-preference interpretation it is not clear exactly when consumption takes place. It could take place any time after trading stops, but trading may continue for different lengths of time for different agents and forever for some. In any case, it is not clear how to apply time-preference discounting. Secondly, when the future is discounted, there may be an incentive for some agents to drop out of the trading process and consume their bundles immediately, if the gains from future trade are sufficiently small. Or there may be an incentive to begin consuming before trade has finished. Both of these possibilities – voluntary exit and continuous consumption – introduce complications that are beyond the scope of the present treatment.

The equilibrium path

If f^* is an MPE and $\{x_t\}$ is the equilibrium outcome, then the equilibrium payoff of agent i at the beginning of date t, before a proposal has been made, is a function of the attainable allocation x_t and the date t. Let $v_i(x_t, t)$ denote the equilibrium payoff of player i at date t when the initial allocation at that date is x_t. As in the case without discounting, we can show that the utilities $u_i(x_{it})$ converge to the equilibrium payoffs $v_i(x_t, t)$, but the argument is slightly different with discounting.

The no-trade strategy is always available to the agent, so at any date an agent can ensure that he holds his current bundle until the game stops. Since the game stops with probability one, his equilibrium payoff must be at least as great as the utility from his current bundle. Thus, at each date t and for each agent i,

$$v_i(x_t, t) \geq u_i(x_{it}). \tag{2.6}$$

Suppose now that the game has continued until date t. With probability $(1 - \gamma)$ the game stops at date t and the agent is forced to consume his current bundle x_{it}. With probability γ the game continues at least one more period and he begins date $t + 1$ with a continuation-game payoff of $v_i(x_{t+1}, t + 1)$. Then the equilibrium payoffs must satisfy the recursive relation

$$v_i(x_t, t) = (1 - \gamma)u_i(x_{it}) + \gamma v_i(x_{t+1}, t + 1). \tag{2.7}$$

These two relationships (2.6) and (2.7) imply that the equilibrium payoffs are non-decreasing,

$$v_i(x_t, t) \leq v_i(x_{t+1}, t + 1), \tag{2.8}$$

for every t.

From the definition of the payoffs, we know that

$$v_i(x_t, t) = (1 - \gamma) \sum_{s=t}^{\infty} \gamma^{s-t-1} u_i(x_{is}).$$

Consequently,

$$v_i(x_t, t) - \gamma v_i(x_{t+1}, t+1)$$

$$= (1 - \gamma) \sum_{s=t}^{\infty} \gamma^{s-t-1} u_i(x_{is}) - \sum_{s=t+1}^{\infty} \gamma^{s-t} u_i(x_{is})$$

$$= (1 - \gamma) u_i(x_{it}), \tag{2.9}$$

Taking limits in (2.9) and dividing by $(1 - \gamma)$ implies that

$$\lim_{t \to \infty} v_i(x_t, t) = \lim_{t \to \infty} u_i(x_{it}).$$

Hence we have the following result:

Proposition 11 *Let f^* be an MPE of Γ, let $\{x_t\}_{t=1}^{\infty}$ be the equilibrium outcome and let $\{v_i(x_t, t)\}_{t=1}^{\infty}$ be the equilibrium payoffs. Then*

$$\lim_t u_i(x_i(t)) = \lim_t v_i(x_t, t)$$

and $v_i(x_t, t) \le \lim_{t \to \infty} v_i(x_t, t)$ for every t.

Asymptotic efficiency

Proposition 11 can be used to prove the asymptotic efficiency of the equilibrium allocations. The proof is the same as in the case without discounting and will not be proved here.

Proposition 12 *There exists an attainable allocation x_∞ such that*

$$\lim_{t \to \infty} x_t = x_\infty \in P.$$

Pareto-efficiency

Although this proposition parallels the efficiency theorem derived for the game without discounting, it is in fact weaker. Asymptotic efficiency implies nothing about the equilibrium payoffs of the game, viewed from the initial date, because the game terminates in finite time with probability one. The natural case to look at is the one in which $\gamma \to 1$, which one hopes will approximate the "frictionless" case $\gamma = 1$. Here there is a problem. If the convergence of the sequence $\{x_t\}$ is sufficiently fast, then a small risk of termination should not matter too much. But what happens if the rate of convergence is slow? More precisely, suppose that for each value of γ, f^γ is an MPE of $\Gamma(\gamma)$ and let $\{x_t^\gamma\}$ denote the corresponding sequence of attainable allocations along the equilibrium path. In general, one would expect $v_i(f^\gamma) < u_i(x_{i\infty}^\gamma)$, where x_∞^γ is the limit of $\{x_t^\gamma\}$ as $t \to \infty$. If the rate of convergence of $\{x_t^\gamma\}$ to x_∞^γ becomes slower as $\gamma \to 1$, then there is no reason to expect that the desired result

$$\lim_{\gamma \to 1}[u_i(x_{i\infty}^\gamma) - v_i(f^\gamma)] = 0$$

holds.

Some bound on the rate of convergence to the asymptotic allocation is needed to ensure that the effect of discounting disappears in the limit as $\gamma \to 1$. It is very difficult to obtain such a bound in general because the strategies can be very complex. There are too many possibilities that cannot, in our present state of knowledge, be ruled out.

Instead of dealing with the complexity of the current game, we can simplify it by assuming that the game has a finite number of states. Then the Markov property and the finiteness of the state space immediately ensure that convergence in utility occurs in finite time. Since utility is non-decreasing and there are only a finite number of states, the utilities cannot keep changing indefinitely.

There are several possible motivations for the assumption of finiteness:

- *Indivisibility can be motivated by realism.* In practice, most commodities have an irreducible minimum quantity that can be traded. All trades have to be made in multiples of this unit. As a result, the set of attainable allocations is finite.
- The concept of a *perfectly divisible commodity* is an idealization of a commodity with a small but finite minimum unit. The introduction of a small minimum unit for each commodity can be thought of as a test of robust-

ness of the model with perfectly divisible commodities. If the introduction of an indivisible unit makes a big change to the results, the perfectly divisible commodity is not a good approximation.

- A continuous strategy space allows for *very complex strategies*, which may be extremely sensitive to small changes in the state of the game. Imposing finiteness is a way of bounding complexity and thus building in an element of bounded rationality.

For any $\eta > 0$, let X_i^η denote the subset of X_i consisting of bundles consisting of integral multiples of η^{-1} of each commodity:

$$X_i^\eta \equiv \{x_i \in X_i | x_{ih} = m_h \eta^{-1}, \forall h, \exists m_h \in \{0, 1, \ldots, \ell\}\}.$$

The game with this consumption set substituted for X_i is denoted by $\Gamma(\gamma, \eta)$.

Let $f^{\gamma, \eta}$ denote a Markov perfect equilibrium of $\Gamma(\gamma, \eta)$ and $\{x_t^{\gamma, \eta}\}$ the corresponding outcome. Convergence in utilities is proved in exactly the same way as before (divisibility played no role in the proof) and it must occur in a finite number of steps since there is only a finite number of values that $v_i(x_t, t)$ can attain. Let $N^{\gamma, \eta}$ denote the minimum number of periods before every agent i reaches the limiting payoff $v_i^{\gamma, \eta}$ of the equilibrium $f^{\gamma, \eta}$. Finally, let P^ε denote the ε-Pareto-optimal set of the economy, that is, the set of attainable allocations x such that there does not exist an attainable allocation x' such that $u_i(x_i') > u_i(x_i) + \varepsilon$.

The previous arguments can be adapted to show that if $x_\infty^{\gamma, \eta}$ is a limit point of the sequence $\{x_t^{\gamma, \eta}\}$ as $t \to \infty$, then for any $\varepsilon > 0$ and all $\eta > \eta(\varepsilon)$, $x_\infty^{\gamma, \eta}$ must belong to P^ε. If not, then for some fixed $\varepsilon > 0$ we can find arbitrarily large values of η such that $x_\infty^{\gamma, \eta} \notin P^\varepsilon$. Let x_∞^γ be a limit point of $x_\infty^{\gamma, \eta}$ as this subsequence of values of $\eta \to \infty$. Clearly, $x_\infty^\gamma \notin P^\varepsilon$ and this implies that there exists an ordered pair (i, j) who meet infinitely often and a trade z such that $u_i(x_{i\infty}^\gamma + z) > u_i(x_{i\infty}^\gamma)$ and $u_j(x_{j\infty}^\gamma - z) > u_j(x_{j\infty}^\gamma)$. Then, by continuity, for sufficiently large values of η we can find a trade $z^{\gamma, \eta}$ such that $z^{\gamma, \eta}$ is a feasible trade and

$u_i(x_{i\infty}^{\gamma,\eta} + z^{\gamma,\eta}) > u_i(x_{j\infty}^{\gamma,\eta})$ and $u_j(x_{j\infty}^{\gamma,\eta} - z^{\gamma,\eta}) > u_j(x_{j\infty}^{\gamma,\eta})$. By previous arguments we can show that

$$v_k^{\gamma,\eta}(x_t^{\gamma,\eta}, t) \leq \lim_{t\to\infty} v_k^{\gamma,\eta}(x_t^{\gamma,\eta}, t) = u_k(x_{k\infty}^{\gamma,\eta})$$

for $k = i, j$ and this allows us to generate a contradiction of the equilibrium conditions for the game $\Gamma(\gamma, \eta)$ for sufficiently large η and t, since agents i and j can make an improving trade and get a payoff better than $v_i(x_t^{\gamma,\eta}, t)$ and $v_j(x_t^{\gamma,\eta}, t)$, respectively. This contradiction proves the following result.

Lemma 13 *Let $f^{\gamma,\eta}$ be an MPE of $\Gamma(\gamma, \eta)$. For any $\varepsilon > 0$ there exists a number $\eta(\varepsilon)$ such that for all $\eta > \eta(\varepsilon)$, if $x_\infty^{\gamma,\eta}$ is the limit of the equilibrium allocations $\{x_t^{\gamma,\eta}\}$ then $x_\infty^{\gamma,\eta} \in P^\varepsilon$.*

Clearly, for some fixed value of $\eta > \eta(\varepsilon)$ the vector of equilibrium payoffs $v(f^{\gamma,\eta})$ will be ε-Pareto-efficient in the limit as $\gamma \to \infty$. In this sense, we can say that $f^{\gamma,\eta}$ is approximately efficient as $\gamma \to 1$ and $\eta \to 0$ in that order.

Theorem 14 *Let $f^{\gamma,\eta}$ be an MPE of $\Gamma(\gamma, \eta)$ for every value of (γ, η). For any $\varepsilon > 0$ there exist numbers $\eta(\varepsilon)$ and $\gamma(\varepsilon)$ such that for all $\eta > \eta(\varepsilon)$ and $\gamma > \gamma(\varepsilon)$, $f^{\gamma,\eta}$ is ε-Pareto-optimal, that is, there does not exist an attainable allocation x such that $u_i(x_i) > v_i(f^{\gamma,\eta}) + \varepsilon$ for every i.*

2.10 Random matching

In many bargaining models, the alternating-offers assumption is replaced by the assumption that proposers and responders are chosen at random. This assumption makes the model symmetric and hence allows for the possibility of stationary equilibria. Similarly, in a DMBG, random matching at each date imposes symmetry on the model and allows for stationary equilibria. In the model with a fixed order of play, the structure of the game depends on the date because the identity of the proposers and responders is a function of the date. There is a more compelling reason than this for being interested in random matching, however. Random matching ensures that the outcome of the DMBG is, in principle, random even if the agents are using pure strategies and this randomness raises a number of interesting issues. First, various convergence properties that require only elementary analysis in the deterministic case become much more subtle and require more powerful tools in the stochastic case. Secondly, because agents are risk averse, randomness becomes a source of inefficiency itself and hence can prevent the attainment of the competitive equilibrium.

In place of the deterministic order of play we adopt the following assumption:

Matching At each date an ordered pair of agents (i, j) is chosen at random. Let π_{ij} be the probability that (i, j) is chosen. We assume that $\pi_{ij} > 0$ for all (i, j) such that $i \neq j$ and $\pi_{ii} = 0$, and $\sum_i \sum_j \pi_{ij} = 1$. The matching probabilities are the same at each date and independent across dates.

The assumption that all ordered pairs (i, j) are formed with positive probability at each date implies that all ordered pairs (i, j) are formed an infinite number of times with probability one. This ensures that the agents are all connected and form a single, integrated economy.

The rest of the model is defined as in section 2.3 and the definition of MPE is the same as in section 2.4. Because the outcome of the game is stochastic, it is no longer possible to restrict attention to individually rational allocations. Although an equilibrium must be individually rational *ex ante*, the outcome need not be individually rational *ex post*. So the assumption (2.1) has to be strengthened: instead, it is assumed that X_i coincides with one of the upper contour sets of u_i:

- for any i, for some constant c_i,

$$X_i \equiv \{x_i \in G_i | u_i(x_i) \geq c_i\} \qquad (2.10)$$

The property (2.10) ensures that pairwise-efficiency is equivalent to Pareto-efficiency. Weaker conditions would also suffice for this result. For example, if we could ensure that indifference surfaces were tangent to the boundary of the consumption set at each point on the boundary, the same result would hold.

We begin the analysis of equilibrium by giving a more precise description of the equilibrium path. Because the matching process is random, the equilibrium path is a stochastic process even if pure strategies are chosen in equilibrium. Let $(\Omega, \mathcal{F}, P)$ denote the underlying probability space, where Ω is the set of states of nature, $\mathcal{F}$ is the σ-field of measurable subsets of Ω, and P is a probability measure on $(\Omega, \mathcal{F})$. All of the random variables that define the equilibrium path are assumed to be defined on this underlying probability space. For example, we can take Ω to be the set of sequences $\{(i_t, j_t)\}_{t=1}^{\infty}$, $\mathcal{F}$ the σ-field generated by the cylinder sets of Ω, and P the probability measure determined by the kernel π. Then we can regard $x(t, \omega)$, $i(t, \omega)$, $j(t, \omega)$, $z(t, \omega)$, and $r(t, \omega)$ as stochastic processes defined on $(\Omega, \mathcal{F}, P)$.

The information available at the beginning of date t is represented by a sub-σ-field of $\mathcal{F}$, which is denoted by $\mathcal{F}_t \subset \mathcal{F}$. The elements of $\mathcal{F}_t$ are the observable events at the beginning of date t. They correspond to the possible histories h_t. The random variables determined at date t are not necessarily measurable with respect to $\mathcal{F}_t$ because they depend on information that becomes available only at date t and is therefore not included in $\mathcal{F}_t$. For example, the identity of the responder j_t is not known at the beginning of date t.

Convergence

Now suppose that f^* is an MPE. The equilibrium payoff to a player at the beginning of date t, before the random choice of proposer and responder has been made, is a function of the attainable allocation $x(t)$ and the date t. Recall that $x(t)$ can be determined by looking at the history h_t and hence is measurable with respect to $\mathcal{F}_t$. The equilibrium payoff of player i is denoted by $v_i(f^*)$ and the payoff conditional on date t and the state of nature ω can be denoted by

$v_i(f^*|x(t, \omega), t)$. Since the context normally makes the equilibrium strategy clear, we suppress the reference to f^* and write $v_i(x(t, \omega), t)$ for the payoff at date t in state of nature ω.

Since there is no discounting, the equilibrium payoff at the beginning of date t must be equal to the expected value of the equilibrium payoff at the beginning of date $t+1$, conditional on the information available at the beginning of date t. Thus,

$$E[v_i(x(t, \omega), t)|\mathcal{F}_t] = E[v_i(x(t+1, \omega), t)|\mathcal{F}_t], \forall t. \qquad (2.11)$$

We can define a stochastic process $\{V_i(t)\}$ by putting $V_i(t)$ equal to the equilibrium payoff at date t

$$V_i(t) = v_i(x(t), t)$$

and (2.11) implies that $\{V_i(t)\}$ is a *martingale* with respect to the filtration $\{\mathcal{F}_t\}_{t=1}^{\infty}$ (Karlin and Taylor, 1975, chapter 6).

The next step is to show that equilibrium payoffs are bounded. Trade is voluntary so the no-trade strategy is available. It follows immediately that in equilibrium,

$$v_i(x(t, \omega), t) \geq u_i(x_i(t, \omega)), \forall t. \qquad (2.12)$$

This proves that $\{V_i(t)\}$ is bounded below. Also, since $x(t) \in \hat{X}$ and $\hat{X}$ is compact,

$$v_i(x(t, \omega), t) \leq \sup_{x \in \hat{X}} u_i(x_i) < \infty, \forall \omega,$$

so $\{V_i(t)\}$ is bounded above.

The Martingale Convergence Theorem tells us that a bounded martingale converges to a constant with probability one (Karlin and Taylor, 1975, theorem 5.1, p. 278). In this case, there exists a random variable V_i^{∞} such that, for almost every ω, the sequence $\{V_i(\omega, t)\}$ converges to the constant $V_i^{\infty}(\omega)$. This is not the same as saying that there exists a constant c and that $\{V_i(t)\}$ converges almost surely to c. Every sample path becomes constant in the limit, but different sample paths may have different limiting values. The Martingale Convergence Theorem also tells us that the mean is preserved in the limit, so

$$E[V_i(t)|\mathcal{F}_t] = E[V_i^{\infty}|\mathcal{F}_t]. \qquad (2.13)$$

The Martingale Convergence Theorem is a powerful tool. It tells us that equilibrium payoffs must converge and it allows us to draw this conclusion with very little information about the nature of the game or the equilibrium strategies.

Once we know that the equilibrium payoffs converge, we can show that the same must be true for the utility associated with the limiting allocations. To see this, recall that agent i's payoff is defined to be the expected value of the lim inf of the utility of his commodity bundle:

$$v_i(f^*) = E[\lim_{t \to \infty} \inf u_i(\xi_{it}(a^{f^*}))].$$

Thus, the expected payoff conditional on the information available at the beginning of date t must satisfy

$$E[V_i(t)|\mathcal{F}_t] = E[\liminf_s u_i(x_i(s))|\mathcal{F}_t].$$

Since the mean is preserved in the limit, according to (2.13), we have,

$$E[V_i^\infty|\mathcal{F}_t] = E[\liminf_s u_i(x_i(s))|\mathcal{F}_t]. \tag{2.14}$$

On the other hand, from the individual rationality condition, (2.12) we can see that

$$\limsup_t u_i(x_i(t)) \le \limsup_t V_i(t) \tag{2.15}$$
$$= V_t^\infty,$$

so, putting (2.14) and (2.15) together, we have that for almost every ω,

$$\lim_t u_i(x_i(t)) = V_i^\infty.$$

In other words, the utility of the commodity bundle held by agent i converges almost surely [a.s.] to a constant. Putting all of these results together, we have the following proposition.

Proposition 15 *Let f^* be an MPE of Γ, let $\{x(t)\}_{t=1}^\infty$ be the equilibrium outcome and let $\{V_i(t)\}_{t=1}^\infty$ be the equilibrium payoffs. Then*

Perfect competition

$$\lim_t u_i(x_i(t)) = \lim_t V_i(t) = V_i^\infty \quad a.s.$$

and $E[V_i(t)|\mathcal{F}_t] = E[V_i^\infty|\mathcal{F}_t]$.

As before, we can use this convergence result to show that the limiting allocation must be pairwise- and hence Pareto-efficient.

Efficiency

The essential idea is the same as in the non-stochastic case, trade continues until all gains from trade are exhausted and the resulting equilibrium allocation must be Pareto-efficient. The additional complication in this case is that the limiting payoffs may be random and depend on the realization of ω, so each sample path has to be considered separately.

For the proof of Proposition 3, we needed to strengthen the assumptions on preferences. Specifically, we assumed that:

• Each utility function u_i is strictly concave.

This assumption is needed here too to show that allocations converge if utilities converge. The next proposition characterizes the limiting set of allocations on the equilibrium path. It shows first that the current allocation converges to a constant and secondly that the limiting allocation is Pareto-efficient. But note that the limiting allocation may be a random variable, that is, it depends on the particular realization of the equilibrium path.

Proposition 16 *There exists a random variable x^∞ on Ω such that*

$$\lim_{t \to \infty} x(t) = x^\infty \in P$$

almost surely.

Proof Let Ω^* denote the set of states such that for every $\omega \in \Omega$, each pair (i, j) is matched infinitely often and the equilibrium conditions are satisfied on the sequence

97

Strategic foundations of general equilibrium

$\{a(t, \omega)\}_{t=1}^{\infty}$. Clearly, Ω^* is a set of full measure. The first step in the proof is to show that for any fixed ω in Ω^*, $\{x(t, \omega)\}$ is a Cauchy sequence. The proof is by contradiction. Suppose, contrary to what we want to prove, that for some subsequence (using the same notation) $\|x(t, \omega) - x(t+1, \omega)\| \geq \varepsilon$ for some $\varepsilon > 0$ and all t. Choose some further subsequence such that $i(t, \omega) = i$ and $j(t, \omega) = j$ for all t. It is always possible to choose this subsequence because the assumptions on the matching probabilities $[\pi_{ij}]$ guarantee that every ordered pair of agents (i, j) is matched infinitely often for almost every state ω. Then choose a further subsequence such that $x(t, \omega) \to y$ and $x_i(t+1, \omega) - x_i(t, \omega) \to z$ along this subsequence. It is possible to choose such a subsequence because the set of attainable allocations is compact. Since

$$\lim_{t \to \infty} u_k(t, \omega) = \lim_{t \to \infty} u_k(t+1, \omega) = V_k^{\infty}(\omega),$$

for $k = i, j$, it must be the case that

$$u_i(y_i) = u_i(y_i + z) = V_i^{\infty}(\omega)$$
$$u_j(y_j) = u_j(y_j - z) = V_j^{\infty}(\omega).$$

By strict concavity,

$$u_i(y_i + z/2) > V_i^{\infty}(\omega)$$
$$u_j(y_j - z/2) > V_j^{\infty}(\omega).$$

By continuity,

$$u_i(x_i(t, \omega) + z/2) > V_i(t, \omega)$$
$$u_j(x_j(t, \omega) - z/2) > V_j(t, \omega),$$

for all t sufficiently large. This contradicts the equilibrium conditions since i can offer j to trade $z/2$ and make them both better off. This last step follows from the Markov Property. The argument is the same as the one used in the proof of Proposition 3 for the deterministic case.

So the hypothesis that $\{x(t, \omega)\}$ is not Cauchy leads to a contradiction of the equilibrium conditions. This contradiction establishes that $\{x(t, \omega)\}$ is a Cauchy sequence, so $\{x(t)\}$ converges to a random variable x^{∞} almost surely.

Perfect competition

To show that $x^\infty(\omega) \in P$ almost surely we use a similar argument. Suppose that for some ω in Ω^*, $x^\infty(\omega) \notin P$. Then $x^\infty(\omega)$ is not pairwise-efficient, according to Proposition 1, and for some pair (i, j), there exists a feasible trade z such that

$$u_i(x_i^\infty(\omega) + z) > V_i^\infty(\omega)$$
$$u_j(x_j^\infty(\omega) - z) > V_j^\infty(\omega)$$

and by continuity

$$u_i(x_i(t, \omega) + z) > V_i(t, \omega)$$
$$u_j(x_j(t, \omega) - z) > V_j(t, \omega),$$

for all t sufficiently large. Since the pair (i, j) is matched infinitely often on ω, we can use the previous argument to show that i must deviate by offering z to j, contradicting the equilibrium conditions. This shows that $x^\infty(\omega) \in P$ for all $\omega \in \Omega^*$. ∎

Proposition 16 shows that the limit allocation is Pareto-efficient with probability one, but this is not the same thing as showing that the equilibrium is Pareto-efficient. The limit allocation is a random vector x^∞ that belongs to the efficient set P almost surely. Since agents are risk averse, Jensen's Inequality implies that

$$E[u_i(x_i^\infty)] \le u_i(E[x_i^\infty]),$$

with strict inequality if $u_i(\cdot)$ is strictly concave and x_i^∞ is non-degenerate. Agents would rather have the expected value of the limiting allocation. The set of attainable allocations $\hat{X}$ is convex so $x^\infty \in \hat{X}$ implies that $E[x^\infty] \in \hat{X}$. To ensure Pareto-efficiency *ex ante* we would have to assume that x^∞ is degenerate, that is, almost surely equal to a constant allocation y.

Call an MPE *asymptotically pure* if the allocations on the equilibrium path converge to a single allocation almost surely, that is, for some constant $y \in \hat{X}$

$$x(t, \omega) \to y$$

for almost every ω. This is stronger than restricting attention to pure-strategy equilibria, because even with pure strategies the randomness associated with the matching process might lead to a random allocation in the limit. On the other hand, even if the MPE is asymptotically pure, it does not mean that the equilibrium is non-stochastic. Random matching may still have an effect along the equilibrium path leading to y and there may be randomness off the equilibrium path.

The assumption that an MPE is asymptotically pure is strong. Furthermore, it restricts endogenous variables so it is not entirely clear what it might require in the way of restrictions on the primitives of the model to ensure that the equilibrium is asymptotically pure. An example of an MPE that is not asymptotically pure is given in section 2.11.

Restricting attention to MPE that are asymptotically pure, one can define a competitive sequence of economies and equilibria and show that in the limit as $m \to \infty$ the asymptotic allocations (as $t \to \infty$) converge to a Walras allocation for the limit economy. The proof is essentially the same as for the non-stochastic case and will not be repeated here.

Existence

The proof of existence given in section 2.8 can easily be adapted to the case of random matching. The strategies are essentially the same and as long as all pairs (i, j) are matched infinitely often with probability one, the trading rules defined there guarantee convergence to a competitive equilibrium allocation with probability one. The proof that this is an equilibrium is the same as in the non-stochastic case because the asymptotic allocation is independent of the realized matches as long as all pairs are formed infinitely often.

Discounting

It is also possible to rework the analysis of the DMBG with discounting for the assumption of random matching.

As before, the equilibrium path can be described as a stochastic process defined on the underlying probability space $(\Omega, \mathcal{F}, P)$. In addition to the random variables $x(t)$, $i(t)$, $j(t)$, $z(t)$, and $r(t)$ we have to define the Markov stopping time $\tau(\omega)$ at which the game stops.

If f^* is an MPE, then the equilibrium payoff to a player at the beginning of date t, before the random choice of proposer and responder has occurred, is a function of the attainable allocation $x(t)$ and the date t. Let $v_i(x(t, \omega), t)$ denote the equilibrium payoff of player i at date t in the state of nature ω. The no-trade strategy is always available to the agent, so at any date an agent can ensure that he holds his current bundle until the game stops. Since the game stops with probability one, his equilibrium payoff must be at least as great as the utility from his current bundle. Thus, at each date t and for each agent i,

$$v_i(x(t), t) \geq u_i(x_i(t)), \tag{2.16}$$

with probability one.

Suppose now that the game has continued until date t. With probability $(1 - \gamma)$ the game stops at date t and the agent is forced to consume his current bundle $x_i(t)$. With probability γ the game continues at least one more period and he begins date $t + 1$ with a continuation-game payoff of $v_i(x(t + 1), t + 1)$. Then the equilibrium payoffs must satisfy the recursive relation

$$v_i(x(t), t) = (1 - \gamma)u_i(x_i(t)) + \gamma E[v_i(x(t + 1), t + 1)|\mathcal{F}_t], \tag{2.17}$$

where this equation is understood to hold with probability one. These two relationships (2.16) and (2.17) imply that the equilibrium payoffs form a *submartingale*, that is,

$$v_i(x(t), t) \leq E[v_i(x(t + 1), t + 1)|\mathcal{F}_t], \tag{2.18}$$

for every t (Karlin and Taylor, 1975, p. 248). To see this, suppose to the contrary that for some non-null set $S \in \mathcal{F}_t$,

$$\int_S v_i(x(t, \omega), t)P(d\omega) > \int_S v_i(x(t + 1, \omega), t + 1)P(d\omega). \tag{2.19}$$

Then, since $\gamma > 0$, we can use the recursive relations (2.17) and (2.19) to conclude that

$$\int_S v_i(x(t, \omega), t)P(d\omega) = \gamma \int_S u_i(x_i(t, \omega))P(d\omega)+$$

$$(1 - \gamma) \int_S v_i(x(t+1, \omega), t+1)$$

$$P(d\omega) < \gamma \int_S u_i(x_i(t, \omega))P(d\omega)+$$

$$(1 - \gamma) \int_S u_i(x_i(t, \omega))P(d\omega)$$

$$= \int_S u_i(x_i(t, \omega))P(d\omega),$$

which contradicts (2.16). This contradiction demonstrates (2.18) and proves that the payoffs are a submartingale.

As in the model without discounting, we define a stochastic process $\{V(t)\}$ consisting of the equilibrium payoffs by putting $V_i(t, \omega) = v_i(x(t, \omega), t)$ for every i and t. We have shown that $\{V(t)\}$ is a submartingale with respect to $\{\mathcal{F}_t\}$ and it is straightforward to show that $\{V(t)\}$ is bounded. Then the Martingale Convergence Theorem implies that $\{V_i(t)\}$ converges almost surely to a variable V_i^∞ and $E[V_i(t)|\mathcal{F}_t] \le E[V_i^\infty|\mathcal{F}_t]$ (Karlin and Taylor, 1975, p. 278).

From the definition of the payoffs, we know that

$$E[V_i(t)|\mathcal{F}_t] = (1 - \gamma)E\left[\sum_{s=t}^\infty \gamma^{s-t-1} u_i(x_i(s))|\mathcal{F}_t\right].$$

Consequently,

$$E[V_i(t)|\mathcal{F}_t] - \gamma E[V_i(t+1)|\mathcal{F}_t]$$

$$= (1 - \gamma)E[\sum_{s=t}^\infty \gamma^{s-t-1} u_i(x_i(s))|\mathcal{F}_t]$$

$$- E\left[\sum_{s=t+1}^\infty \gamma^{s-t} u_i(x_i(s))|\mathcal{F}_t\right]$$

$$= (1 - \gamma)E[u_i(x_i(t))|\mathcal{F}_t] = (1 - \gamma)u_i(x_i(t)), \quad (2.20)$$

where the expectation operation $E[\cdot|\mathcal{F}_t]$ can be eliminated in the last line because $x_i(t)$ is $\mathcal{F}_t$-measurable. Taking limits in (2.20) and dividing by $(1 - \gamma)$ implies that

$$V_i^\infty = \lim_{t\to\infty} u_i(x_i(t)) \text{ a.s.}$$

Hence we have the following result:

Proposition 17 *Let f^* be an MPE of Γ, let $\{x(t)\}_{t=1}^{\infty}$ be the equilibrium allocations and let $\{V_i(t)\}_{t=1}^{\infty}$ be the equilibrium payoffs. Then*

$$\lim_t u_i(x_i(t)) = \lim_t V_i(t) = V_i^{\infty} \ a.s.$$

and $E[V_i(t)|\mathcal{F}_t] \le E[V_i^{\infty}|\mathcal{F}_t]$.

Asymptotic efficiency

Proposition 17 can be used to prove the asymptotic efficiency of the equilibrium allocations. The proof is the same as in the case without discounting and will not be given here.

Proposition 18 *There exists a random variable x^{∞} on Ω such that*

$$\lim_{t \to \infty} x(t) = x^{\infty} \in P$$

almost surely.

Pareto-efficiency

As in the model with a non-stochastic order of play (deterministic matching), the asymptotic efficiency result implies nothing about the efficiency of equilibrium, because the game ends in finite time with probability one. So in addition to the need to assume the MPE is asymptotically pure, one also needs to bound the time taken for convergence of the trading process. This can be done as on p. 91 by using a finite set of allocations to approximate the original game. The details are similar to those on pp. 91–2 and will not be repeated here.

Competitive sequences of equilibria

Once efficiency has been established, one can analyze competitive sequences of equilibria in the usual way.

2.11 Mixed equilibria

In the analysis of the model with random matching we focused on asymptotically pure MPE. There can be mixed equilibria as well. In fact, it is hard to rule out mixed equilibria. The essence of the problem arises from the fact that the set of Walras allocations is generically finite but not a singleton (Debreu, 1970). We have seen that, under certain special conditions, any deterministic equilibrium path leads to a Walras allocation. Furthermore, the number of MPE may be as large as the number of different Walras allocations. Mixed equilibria can be generated by randomizing over the MPE. For example, the Walras allocation that is eventually reached can be conditioned on some random element of the allocation process, which acts like a "sunspot." If such an equilibrium exists, the final outcome will be a probability distribution over Walras allocations. If consumers are risk averse, a probability distribution over Walras allocations need not be Pareto-efficient, since there are no markets for trading this uncertainty. *Ex ante*, the game does not implement a Walras allocation even though *ex post* it will result in one of a finite number of Walras allocations.

To construct a mixed equilibrium with a random outcome, we first consider an exchange economy $\mathcal{E}$ that has multiple competitive equilibria. Then we show that each of these competitive allocations can be attained as the asymptotic outcome of an MPE. We can then construct a mixed equilibrium by using some random move by Nature to select one of the asymptotically pure MPE.

The construction is based on a two-person Edgeworth Box economy $\mathcal{E} = \{(X_i, u_i, e_i)\}_{i=1}^2$. For simplicity, no discounting is assumed. Since $\mathcal{E}$ has multiple competitive equilibria we cannot use the results from section 2.8. However, when there are only two agents, any competitive equilibrium can be attained asymptotically as the outcome of an MPE. The first step is to give an explicit proof of this proposition.

Suppose that (p^*, x^*) is a competitive equilibrium for $\mathcal{E}$. Let ϕ be a function from $\hat{X}$, the set of attainable allocations,

Perfect competition

to the set P of Pareto-efficient allocations that satisfies the individual rationality condition:

$$u_i(\phi_i(x)) \geq u_i(x_i), i = 1, 2,$$

and is consistent with x^*:

$$\phi(e) = x^*.$$

We can think of $\phi(x)$ as the target allocation once x has been reached. Note that strict quasi-concavity of u_i implies that $\phi(x)$ is the unique Pareto-efficient allocation that is as good as $\phi(x)$, so

$$\phi(\phi(x)) = \phi(x).$$

Similarly, the payoff to player i conditional on reaching the allocation x is $v_i(x) = u_i(\phi_i(x))$.

Let $f = (f_1, f_2)$ denote an asymptotically pure MPE that implements (p^*, x^*) and define the strategy profile f as follows. If x is an attainable allocation and (i, j) a pair of matched agents such that $i \neq j$, then put

$$f_i(x, i, j) = \phi_i(x) - x_i$$
$$= x_j - \phi_j(x)$$

and

$$f_j(x, i, j, z) = \begin{cases} \text{"yes"} & \text{if } z = \phi_i(x) - x_i \text{ or } v_j(x - z) > v_j(x) \\ \text{"no"} & \text{otherwise.} \end{cases}$$

In words, the proposer always makes an offer that, if accepted, will bring the pair to the target allocation $\phi(x)$; the responder accepts that offer or one that is strictly preferred and rejects all others.

The strategy profile f clearly implements the competitive allocation (p^*, x^*) in the sense that the final allocation will be x^* if these strategies are followed. To see that this is an asymptotically pure MPE, we need to show that the agents are choosing best responses at every information set. Suppose that the current allocation at the beginning of some period is x and that the pair (i, j) has been chosen by Nature. The equilibrium proposal is $z = f_i(x, i, j)$. The proposer cannot do any better because the proposal $z = \phi_i(x) - x_i$ is individually rational and the responder will reject any other offer unless it satisfies $v_j(x - z) > v_j(x)$. Since $\phi(x)$ is Pareto-efficient, this last inequality implies that $v_i(x - z) < v_i(x)$, so the proposer cannot do better than to offer z.

Similarly, the responder cannot do better than to follow this strategy along the equilibrium path because the proposal z is individually rational and if he rejects the offer, with probability one he will end up with the same allocation in the future. Off the equilibrium path, it is optimal to accept any proposal z that satisfies $v_j(x - z) > v_j(x)$ and weakly optimal to reject any proposal z that satisfies $v_j(x - z) \leq v_j(x)$, so again f_j is optimal for the responder.

This completes the proof of the following proposition.

Proposition 19 *Let (p^*, x^*) be a competitive equilibrium for the two-person economy $\mathcal{E}$. Then there exists an asymptotically pure MPE f of Γ such that the asymptotic allocation under f is x^*.*

Now suppose that the economy has two competitive equilibria (p^A, x^A) and (p^B, x^B). As shown above, there exist asymptotically pure MPE corresponding to each of the competitive equilibria – call them f^A and f^B, respectively. Using these MPE strategy profiles, there is no difficulty in constructing a *subgame*-perfect equilibrium (SPE) in which the outcome is a probability distribution over the two Walrasian outcomes (p^A, x^A) and (p^B, x^B). Simply condition the choice of strategy on who is first chosen to be the proposer.

- If $i = 1$ is chosen to be the proposer at date 1 then have both players adopt the strategies f^A corresponding to the MPE that leads to (p^A, x^A).
- If $i = 2$ is chosen to be the proposer at date 1 then have both players adopt the strategies f^B corresponding to the MPE that leads to (p^B, x^B).

It is clear that the strategies defined in this way constitute an SPE and that the outcome produces x^A with probability $1/2$ and x^B with probability $1/2$. Since the agents are risk averse, this random allocation is not Pareto-efficient –

they would both prefer to receive $\frac{1}{2}(x^A + x^B)$ for sure – so it cannot be a Walrasian outcome. The equilibrium is not an MPE, as I have defined it, because the strategies depend on the move of Nature at the first date.

Theorem 20 *Suppose that the two-person economy $\mathcal{E}$ has two equilibria (p^A, x^A) and (p^B, x^B) with $x^A \neq x^B$. Then there exists an SPE such that with probability $1/2$ the asymptotic allocation is x^A and with probability $1/2$ the asymptotic allocation is x^B.*

The arguments we have used in previous subsections cannot be used to eliminate the possibility of this equilibrium. Once the game begins with a move by Nature at date 1, it is already too late. The conditioning of the strategies on this random move prevents the achievement of the competitive equilibrium before anyone has a chance to move. The remaining play of the game satisfies all the conditions we could hope for, so equilibrium arguments cannot undo the conditioning.

Note that this conditioning of the play of the game on an initial move by Nature produces a correlated equilibrium in the sense of Aumann (1974), with a probability distribution over pure equilibria. The initial move by Nature plays the role of a "sunspot" or correlation device.

The structure of the equilibrium is very special and it could be argued that we are in a sense implementing the competitive equilibria. From date 1 onwards it appears that the game implements a single, non-stochastic competitive equilibrium relative to the initial endowments. However, there may be other, more complicated equilibria, that do not have this property. For example, there may be SPEs in which the limit allocation is not a Walras allocation relative to the original endowments. Or there may be SPEs in which, for any finite date t the limit allocation is not a Walras allocation relative to the current allocation at date t. We simply do not know.

If it turns out that randomness is an intractable obstacle to the implementation of competitive equilibria, then the theory would appear to be rather fragile. Random matching is a common ingredient in search models. It is included on the grounds of both realism and the simplicity it offers in many settings. At the very least we should want to include this kind of randomness.

One possible way of preserving the competitive theory in settings with random matching is to appeal again to large numbers, this time to get rid of aggregate uncertainty. Of course, if there is aggregate uncertainty in the world, then perhaps the definition of competitive equilibrium should be expanded to allow for conditioning on this uncertainty. The problem for the theory is small amounts of uncertainty that nonetheless matter a lot. But if there are large numbers of individuals and lots of randomness in the matching process, we might assume that overall it will not matter too much because the distribution of matches will not differ too much across realizations of the process. Of course, showing this may not be easy; but it is not implausible that for well behaved cases we can ignore the effect of this kind of uncertainty on the equilibrium outcome.

2.12 A summing up

This completes my attempt to develop a competitive theory based on dynamic matching and bargaining games with a finite number of agents. It has been a bumpy road. Strong assumptions have been required, assumptions imposed not on the primitives of the model, but rather on endogenous variables.

- Attention is restricted to Markov perfect equilibria (although, as has been pointed out, it is only a small amount of information that needs to be ignored in order to prove the competitive limit theorem).
- The continuity assumption imposed on competitive sequences of equilibria says that individual agents have a negligible effect (relative to the entire economy).
- Equilibria are assumed to be asymptotically pure.
- A finite-state approximation to the original DMBG is required to ensure that, in the case of discounting, the

time taken for convergence is not too long. Otherwise, the effect of discounting does not necessarily disappear as the discount factor γ converges to 1.

Furthermore, the implications of these assumptions are obscure. It is not clear what restrictions on the primitives of the model would be necessary to ensure these properties hold in equilibrium.

Nonetheless, the assumptions themselves are not implausible. The ideas that small agents have little impact on equilibrium, that strategies are Markov, that agents are anonymous, are ideas that economists are quite comfortable with. They seem to accord with our intuitive understanding of large economies and with at least some of the "facts" we know about competitive markets.

One possible conclusion is that competitive theory requires fundamental properties which, for some reason, cannot be derived from game-theoretic analysis. This is an intriguing idea, but one that does not give us much to say in terms of traditional game theory.

Another view is that the model needs to be changed. A richer model may give us more structure and allow us to actually simplify the equilibrium analysis. This approach is explored in chapter 3.

CHAPTER 3

CONTINUITY AND ANONYMITY

Chapter 2 presented a theory of dynamic matching and bargaining games (DMBG) with a finite number of agents. This theory is more difficult than the corresponding theory for a continuum economy, chiefly because of the strategic problems that arise in finite games. The theory of bargaining deals with small numbers of players, usually only two, and strategic issues arising in these sorts of bargaining problems have been exhaustively studied. Bargaining in markets with a large but finite number of agents is still relatively unexplored territory, however. One of the few papers dealing with this topic is the innovative and imaginative paper of Rubinstein and Wolinsky (1990). It is well worth reviewing the results in this paper because they reinforce the lessons drawn from chapter 2 about the importance of Markov strategies, anonymity, and continuity.

3.1 Rubinstein and Wolinsky (1990)

Rubinstein and Wolinsky (1990, hereafter RW) contains a rich array of models, illustrating the importance of different informational and institutional assumptions in the analysis of DMBG. As a benchmark, RW begins with a model in which the matching process is exogenous. There are S sellers and $B > S$ buyers in the market. Each seller has one unit of an indivisible good which is worth nothing to him. Each buyer wants to buy at most one unit of the indivisible good, which is worth one dollar to him. Time is divided into discrete dates $t = 1, 2, \ldots$ At each date, the agents are randomly matched in pairs consisting of one seller and one buyer (each feasible configuration of pairwise matches has equal probability). One member of the pair is randomly chosen to be the proposer and the other is the responder. Each member has probability $1/2$ of being chosen as proposer. The proposer chooses a price $p \in [0, 1]$. The responder accepts or rejects the offer.

At each date, the agents are randomly rematched. Unmatched buyers are forced to remain inactive for the period.

When agreement is reached on a price p, the buyer receives a payoff $1 - p$ and the seller receives a payoff p. There is no discounting. Agents exit the market as soon as an agreement is reached.

Agents have complete information about the past play of the game, but at the moment when they choose their actions they do not know what actions are being simultaneously chosen by other agents.

The central result that RW obtains for this model is the following theorem.

Theorem 1   *For every price p^* between 0 and 1 and for every one to one function β from the set of sellers to the set of buyers there exists a sequential equilibrium in which seller s sells his unit to buyer $\beta(s)$ for a price of p^*.*

In other words, a continuum of outcomes can be supported by sequential equilibria of the game (sequential equilibria are needed here because it is a game of imperfect information). The intuition of the proof was described in chapter 1 for the case where there is one seller $S = 1$ and many buyers $b = 1, \ldots, B$ (p. 26). One buyer b^* is identified as the intended recipient of the good at the price p^*. The equilibrium strategies require the seller to offer the good at a price of $p = 1$ whenever he is the proposer and is matched with a buyer $b \neq b^*$. Every buyer $b \neq b^*$ rejects the offer. Whenever buyer $b \neq b^*$ is the proposer he offers to buy the good at a price of $p = 0$ and the seller rejects. When the seller meets buyer b^*, whichever is chosen as the proposer offers a price $p = p^*$ and the responder accepts. These strategies clearly produce the required outcome and the payoffs of the seller and buyer b^* are p^* and $1 - p^*$, respectively, because there is no discounting.

To prevent a deviation, we make use of the following subgame equilibrium strategies. Suppose that the seller has deviated by proposing a price $p \neq p^*$. The responder rejects this offer and the game then moves into a subgame in which the formerly rejecting buyer b^{**} becomes the intended recipient of the good and the selling price becomes $p^{**} = 0$. The strategies are the same as those given earlier with the price p^{**} in place of p^* and the buyer b^{**} in place of buyer b^*.

If one of the buyers deviates by offering a price $p \neq p^*$ then the seller rejects, another buyer is chosen to be the intended recipient b^{**}, and the price at which the unit is traded changes to $p^{**} = 1$. The strategies are defined in the usual way.

Deviations from these punishment strategies can be treated in an exactly similar way.

It is easy to see that the initial deviator is no better off and may be worse off in the punishment phase that is triggered by his deviation. Furthermore, the responder is always at least as well off following the punishment as he would be if he accepted the proposed deviation. It can also be seen, by inspection of the strategies, that a responder who is called upon to reject an offer can never be better off accepting it. Also, a responder who is supposed to accept and rejects instead does not make himself better off if we assume that the game continues as before after a deviating rejection.

These strategies are ultimately quite complicated, in the sense that there is no limit to the number of potential deviations and each additional deviation requires a tailor-made response that makes the play of the game more complicated. As RW points out, one can think of this construction as requiring a large amount of information for the players to execute the equilibrium strategies. For the purposes of comparison, they consider an alternative model in which the amount of information available to the agents is limited. Specifically, the game satisfies the following anonymity assumption:

Continuity and anonymity

At the beginning of each date t, all that the buyers and sellers know about the previous play of the game is the number of buyers B_t and the number of sellers S_t remaining in the game.

Under this assumption, the proposer's strategy is a function of the number of buyers and sellers (B_t, S_t) and the date t. The responder's strategy is a function of the numbers of agents (B_t, S_t), the date t and the proposal p. RW show that, under the anonymity assumption, the only equilibrium outcome is the competitive one.

Theorem 2 *If each player's information consists only of B_t, S_t, and t, the unique sequential equilibrium outcome is such that the good is sold for a price of 1.*

Two points are worth noting. First, the anonymity assumption is identical to the strong Markov assumption, which requires strategies to be functions of a minimal set of payoff-relevant variables at each date: strategies are not allowed to be conditioned on variables that do not directly affect the future payoffs of the game.[1] Secondly, the assumption of anonymity has the immediate effect of preventing the agents from punishing a deviator, because deviations are not remembered after they occur.

To see how anonymity works, suppose there is one seller and two buyers. The game stops as soon as trade occurs, so $(B_t, S_t) \equiv (2, 1)$ as long as the game continues. The anonymity assumption implies that the proposals by each agent depend at most on the date t and the responses depend at most on the date t and the proposal p. Of course, different agents can have different strategies.

Let $1 - \alpha$ be the infimum of the seller's payoff over all subgame-perfect equilibria (SPEs) of the game (SPE suffices here because there is only one match per period). Because there are two buyers, they cannot both get the good and the

---

[1] In chapter 2 the Markov property was used in a weaker sense: equilibrium strategies were allowed to depend on the date as well as a minimal set of payoff-relevant variables.

sum of their payoffs at any point in the game must be less than or equal to $\alpha \leq 1$. Then one of the buyers must be expecting to get no more than $\alpha/2$ and if the seller gets a chance to make a proposal to this buyer he can ask for anything up to $1 - \alpha/2$ and be sure of getting it. Call this buyer the "Loser." The existence of a Loser puts a lower bound on the seller's payoff. With probability $1/4$ the seller is matched with the Loser and the seller is chosen to make the proposal. In that case the seller gets $1 - \alpha/2$. With probability $3/4$ he cannot get less than $1 - \alpha$. So his payoff must be at least

$$\tfrac{1}{4}(1 - \alpha/2) + \tfrac{3}{4}((1 - \alpha)) = 1 - \tfrac{7}{8}\alpha \geq 1 - \alpha.$$

The last inequality is strict, which contradicts the definition of $1 - \alpha$ as the infimum of the seller's payoffs, unless $\alpha = 0$. But $\alpha = 0$ means that the good is always traded at a price $p = 1$.

The crucial point in this argument is that each of the buyers has a future payoff that is independent of the offers made by the seller in the current period. In the heuristic proof of Theorem 1, any deviation by the seller was "remembered" by other players and resulted in a reward for the buyer who rejected the deviating proposal. In the anonymous game, by contrast, the buyer's reservation utility is independent of the proposal and this fact allows the seller to exploit the buyer's weakness, demanding the maximum price that is consistent with the buyer's reservation level.

The absence of discounting is also important. What makes Theorem 1 "work" is the creation of relationships among buyers and sellers. At any moment, each unit of the good is dedicated to a particular buyer at a particular price. Each deviation from the equilibrium strategies leads to the creation of a new relationship to punish the deviator. Because the matching process is random and there may be a large number of buyers and sellers, it can take a long time for the designated buyers and sellers to meet one another and consummate the trade. The agents do not care how long it takes for the designated buyer and seller to find each other because there is no discounting.

Continuity and anonymity

However, if agents discount the future, these relationships can be quite costly to maintain. By the time trade takes place the surplus generated may be heavily discounted. If a seller (buyer) could trade with the first buyer (seller) he meets, he would be much better off, other things being equal. For this reason discounting makes it suboptimal to carry out the punishment strategies that are needed to support the equilibria in Theorem 1. In fact, discounting eliminates large numbers of sequential equilibria altogether. To see this, suppose the model is amended to allow for a common discount factor $0 < \delta < 1$. Then it can be shown that there is a unique equilibrium in the case of a single seller. Let $x(B)$ and $y(B)$ be defined as the (x, y) solution of the system of equations

$$y = \frac{\delta(x + y)}{2}$$
$$1 - x = \frac{\delta(1 - x + 1 - y)}{2B}.$$

Theorem 3 *Suppose that $S = 1$ and that all agents discount the future using the common factor $0 < \delta < 1$. Then there is a unique SPE in which trade takes place immediately and the price is $x(B)$ or $y(B)$ depending on whether the buyer or seller was chosen to propose.*

Interestingly, this result has not been established for $S > 1$.[2]

Note that for fixed values of B and $0 < \delta < 1$, the surplus is shared between the two sides of the market; but as $B \to$

---

[2] Suppose that there were a unique equilibrium for $S > 1$. What would it look like? If all trade occurs at the first date, then we can use Theorem 3 to calculate the equilibrium payoffs. If a buyer and seller fail to reach agreement at date t then they anticipate that there will be exactly one seller still active at date $t + 1$ and the payoffs in that continuation game will be uniquely determined by Theorem 3. Then in the bargaining at date t we know that the SPE payoffs will be determined in the usual way: the proposal will offer a price that makes the responder indifferent between accepting that price and rejecting it in favor of the payoff from the continuation game. In this equilibrium, the payoffs are determined not by the number of buyers and sellers but rather by the payoffs in the

∞ the equilibrium price converges to 1. A large number of buyers makes the equilibrium of Theorem 1, in which one buyer is designated as the good's recipient, extremely inefficient. The exorbitant cost of maintaining relationships in the limit leads to the same outcome as the assumption of anonymity in Theorem 2. An important point to note, however, is that letting $B \to \infty$ is increasing the number of buyers relative to the number of sellers, since we are holding $S = 1$. This is not the same thing as allowing the size of the market to increase by replication, for example.

Less obvious, but also true, is the fact that as $\delta \to 1$, $x(\delta, B) \to 1$ and $y(\delta, B) \to 1$ so that again the seller obtains the maximal price of 1. There is a simple intuition for this result. When $\delta < 1$ the buyers have some bargaining power because they can threaten to delay agreement. This allows them to "hold up" the seller and get some of the surplus. When $\delta \to 1$ this power disappears and the seller is able to exploit fully his monopoly of the good, specifically the power to determine which buyer gets the good.

We can interpret Theorem 3 as showing that the multiple equilibria of Theorem 1 are not robust. There appears to be a close analogy with the role of discounting in the Stahl–Rubinstein alternating-offers model. In the alternating-offers game with no discounting, any Pareto-efficient outcome (division of the cake) can be supported by an SPE; with a positive amount of discounting, however small, there is a unique SPE outcome. So we treat the game with no discounting as a limiting case of the game with discounting and argue that all but one of the equilibrium outcomes in the limit are pathological. In the same way, we can argue that the indeterminacy of equilibrium shown

continued

continuation game with $B - S$ buyers and one seller. Whether this is the only equilibrium is not known. If this is the unique equilibrium, it suggests once again that the effect of large numbers is strongly dependent on the details of the extensive-form game. No matter how large B and S are, it is the difference $B - S$ that appears to be critical in determining the equilibrium payoffs.

in Theorem 1 is pathological, since it disappears once an arbitrarily small amount of discounting is introduced.

RW has a clever comeback to that charge. It points out that the power of discounting to increase the cost of maintaining relationships depends on the assumption that both the formation and the termination of matches are random and exogenous. If the choice of partner were *endogenous*, it ought to be possible to show the existence of multiple equilibria in the presence of discounting. To support this claim, RW considers a model in which there is a single seller and the seller can choose, at the beginning of each period, which buyer he wants to bargain with in that period.

Theorem 4 *If $S = 1$ and the seller can choose in each period the buyer with whom he wishes to bargain, there is a continuum of SPE outcomes: for each buyer b and each price $x(1) \leq p \leq 1$, where $x(B)$ is defined in Theorem 3, there is an SPE in which buyer b receives the good and the price is either p or $\delta p/(2 - \delta)$, according to whether the seller or buyer b is the proposer in the first meeting between them.*

Thus, indeterminacy survives discounting.

The indeterminacy found in this model has a family resemblance to an indeterminacy that arises in the Rubinstein–Wolinsky (1985) model described in chapter 1. In the original paper, it is assumed that a pair of agents separates whenever one of them is matched with a new agent. This behavior is optimal, given that each agent expects all the others to follow the same rule. Since all buyers are identical and all sellers are identical, an agent is indifferent between switching to a new partner and remaining with the old, and if there is a positive probability that his current partner will go off with someone new, the agent strictly prefers to play it safe by hooking up with a new partner himself. However, by a similar reasoning, it would also be optimal for an agent to remain with his current partner and ignore the new matches, if that is what he believes all other agents will do. In that case, two agents, once matched, will stay together until an agreement is reached. The existence of a large number of buyers and sellers becomes immaterial and the equilibrium outcome will be the same as in the two-person bargaining game.

The same two kinds of equilibria exist in the voluntary-matching game described in Theorem 4. In one, the seller bargains with a single buyer, ignoring the existence of the other buyers. This equilibrium sets a lower bound to the equilibrium price – namely, $x(1)$, the price determined in the two-person bargaining game. In the other, competition among the buyers is allowed full force and the equilibrium price is $p = 1$. Once we have two equilibria in the model, it is easy to support more. Other equilibria can be supported by making the decision to separate depend on the agents' behavior.

Although there exists a continuum of equilibrium outcomes in the voluntary-matching model (Theorem 4), the degree of indeterminacy depends on the number of buyers B and the discount factor δ. Just as in the case of exogenous matching with discounting (Theorem 3), the interval of equilibrium prices collapses to $p = 1$ if either (1) the number of buyers grows unboundedly large, or (2) the discount factor approaches 1.

In the end, one could use these results to argue either against or in favor of the competitive outcome, depending on which set of assumptions one finds most attractive. The value of the results is really that it shows the importance of the fine details of the model in determining the outcome. Further it clarifies the role of anonymity, continuity, and the Markov property in supporting competitive outcomes.

- Anonymity and other informational restrictions, which RW treats in a way that is equivalent to the Markov property, are used to rule out complex strategies that are required to support indeterminacy in models with large but finite numbers of agents.
- The particular strategies that are used in the proof of Theorem 1 ensure that a single agent may have a large

impact on the subsequent play of the game, even when the number of players is large.

- Discounting restores "uniqueness" when matching is exogenous (Theorem 3), but not when it is endogenous (Theorem 4). However, in the voluntary-matching game with discounting, non-Markov strategies are required to support indeterminacy.

It is perhaps also worth noting that another factor that makes it difficult to interpret these results as supporting or contradicting the competitive theory is the fact that the competitive outcome is the same as the monopolistic outcome.

3.2 Bounded rationality and uniqueness

In the RW game, strategies are sequences of functions mapping histories into actions. If we think of the complexity of a strategy as being measured by the number of variables on which an agent's action can be conditioned, then the strategies available in some versions of the RW game are unboundedly complex. More precisely, since there is no bound on the length of a history, there is no bound on the complexity of the strategy that may be adopted. In this section we explore a restriction on agents' strategies that is less restrictive than the Markov property, but nonetheless allows for some bound on the ability of the agents to condition their behavior on the history of the game. Whereas RW interprets its restrictions on strategies in terms of the information available to agents, the restrictions considered here are interpreted as a form of *bounded rationality*: there is a limit on the amount of information about past play of the game that an agent can retain and process in determining the future play of the game. For the purpose of this discussion, I retain the assumptions that appear to be most amenable to indeterminacy – namely, voluntary matching and no discounting. Also, only the case with a single seller and finite number n of buyers is considered.

Strategic foundations of general equilibrium

Bounded memory states

The Markov assumption eliminates the use of any information from the past to condition the future play of the game. In fact, the assumption that strategies are memoryless is the most restrictive assumption that is consistent with existence of an equilibrium. At the other extreme, the entire history of the game can be remembered and used to condition the future play of the game. In this section, we take an intermediate course, by allowing agents to remember a limited amount of what happened in the past. By placing a bound on the agents' memory we put a bound on the complexity of their strategies.

An agent's memory is represented by a set of *memory states*, each of which represents an admissible amount of information that can be retained from the past. Let S denote the set of memory states and note that S is common to all agents. The seller makes offers and chooses the buyer to whom the offer is made at each date. A strategy for the seller is a function $f : S \to I \times [0, 1]$ that maps a memory state s into an ordered pair (i, p), with the interpretation that the seller offers buyer i the object for a price of p. A strategy for a buyer i is a function $g_i : S \times [0, 1] \to \{Y, N\}$ that maps an ordered pair (s, p), representing an offer of the object to agent i at price p, into a response Y or N. These strategies apply only if the object has not already been sold, of course. Given a memory state s, the strategy profile $(f, g) = (f, g_1, \ldots, g_n)$ determines a unique action $a = (i, p, r)$ according to the equations

$$(i, p) = f(s) \tag{3.1}$$

and

$$r = g_i(s, p). \tag{3.2}$$

The memory state evolves according to an exogenously given rule ϕ. This rule represents the agent's ability to encode new information that he receives in the language of the memory states. Formally, ϕ maps the current memory state and the actions chosen in the current period into the future memory state. If s_t is the current memory state,

120

a_t the joint action at date t, and s_{t+1} the memory state at date $t + 1$, then the law of motion is written

$$s_{t+1} = \phi(s_t, a_t) \qquad (3.3)$$

where $a_t = (i_t, p_t, r_t)$, $(i_t, p_t) = f(s_t)$, and $r_t = g_{i_t}(s_t, p_t)$. For any strategy profile (f, g) and initial state s_0, there is a unique path determined by (3.1), (3.2), and (3.3). With this set of strategies and this path we can associate a unique payoff function for the players. Let $U(f, g, s_0)$ (resp. $V_i(f, g, s_0)$) denote the seller's (resp. buyer i's) payoff from the strategy profile (f, g) and initial state s_0.

If the set of memory states is rich enough, this way of describing strategies does not restrict the game at all. For example, if S is the set of all possible histories H and $\phi : H \times A \to H$ is defined by

$$\phi(h, a) \equiv (h, a),$$

then the game in which strategies are defined on memory states is strategically equivalent to the RW game in which strategies are defined on complete histories. The point of this formalism is to allow for flexibility in choosing restrictions on the set of strategies. If we take the set S to be a singleton, then we are restricted to the Markov strategies.[3] Assuming S to be a finite set allows for a richer set of strategies, but one that limits complexity when n is large. Restricting the set S to be finite, we can show that there is an essentially unique outcome, in which the seller gets all the surplus, when the number of players is sufficiently large.

Theorem 5 *If (f, g) is an SPE of the game with a fixed set of memory states S and $|S| < n$, then the seller offers the object to one of the buyers at a price $p = 1$ and the buyer accepts.*

Proof The equilibrium payoff for the seller (resp. buyer i) in state s is denoted by $u(s) = U(f, g, s)$ (resp. $v_i(s) = V_i(f, g, s)$). It depends only on the state s because, for a given strategy profile (f, g), the future play of the game is a function of the current state. Feasibility requires that

---

[3] The game continues only if there has been no trade, so there is only one payoff-relevant state in which the game continues.

$$0 \leq \sum_{i=1}^{n} v_i(s) \leq 1 \qquad (3.4)$$

for all states s. This implies that there exists a buyer i such that

$$v_i(s) \leq \tfrac{1}{2}, \forall s. \qquad (3.5)$$

Otherwise, for each buyer i there exists a state s_i such that $v_i(s) > 1/2$. Since $|S| < n$, $s_i = s_j$ for some pair of agents $i \neq j$. In other words, there exists a state s such that $v_i(s) > 1/2$ for at least two buyers, contradicting the feasibility condition (3.4). This contradiction proves that (3.5) must hold for some $i = k$, say.

The condition (3.5) allows us to place a lower bound on the equilibrium payoff of the seller. Given any state s, the seller knows that agent k cannot expect a payoff higher than $1/2$ from the continuation of the game. Therefore agent k should accept any price offer $p < 1/2$. But this means that the seller can get a payoff of $1/2 - \varepsilon$ by offering a price $p - 1/2 - \varepsilon$ to buyer k. Since ε is arbitrary, the seller must get $1/2$ in equilibrium:

$$u(s) \geq \tfrac{1}{2}, \forall s. \qquad (3.6)$$

Condition (3.6) and feasibility imply a new bound on the sum of buyers' payoffs

$$0 \leq \sum_{i=1}^{n} v_i(s) \leq \tfrac{1}{2}, \forall s$$

and this implies by the previous argument that for some agent i

$$v_i(s) \leq \tfrac{1}{4}, \forall s.$$

Continuing in this way, we can see that, in the limit, we must have $v_i(s) = 0$ for all s and i and $u(s) = 1$ for all i. ∎

The proof of Theorem 5 uses induction. An alternative proof, which is less heuristic but more efficient, does not require induction: if we let

$$\alpha = \min_i \max_s \{v_i(s)\}$$

then we can see that $u(s) \geq 1 - \alpha$ and, by the usual argument, this implies that $\alpha \leq \alpha/2$ and hence $\alpha = 0$. By choosing to deal with the weakest buyer i, for whom $\max_s\{v_i(s)\} = 0$, the seller can guarantee himself the maximum payoff.

It is obvious that trade must take place in equilibrium or the payoffs in Theorem 5 cannot be achieved. However, trade does not have to take place at the first date. Although the agents' strategies do not change over time the state s can change over time and this allows us to introduce delay in the equilibrium strategies. For example, let $S = \{1, 2, \ldots, T\}$ and $s_0 = 1$ and suppose that for any action profile a the evolution of the memory state is

$$\phi(s, a) = \begin{cases} s + 1 & \text{if } s < T \\ s & \text{if } s = T \end{cases}.$$

Then the memory state is essentially counting time and we can use it to code the date at which trade takes place. For example, at any $s < T$ the seller offers the object at a price $p = 1$ to buyer i and buyer i rejects the offer. At $s = T$ the seller offers the object at a price $p = 1$ to buyer i and i accepts. Since there is no discounting, both agents are indifferent among the T dates at which trade could take place.

The argument in the proof of Theorem 5 is similar to the argument in the heuristic proof of Theorem 2. In the anonymous equilibrium, there is a single memory state (the Markov case) and there are two buyers, so the number of buyers is greater than the number of memory states. For the proof of Theorem 5, it is necessary only to extend the argument to an arbitrary finite number of memory states and a (larger) finite number of buyers. What makes both arguments work is the fact that there is only one unit of surplus available to reward all the buyers for punishing the seller. In the proof of Theorem 1, this one unit of surplus is cleverly used to reward the agent who reponds to a deviant proposal: by rejecting the deviating offer the responder gets all the surplus, and that is enough to discourage him from accepting any deviation from the equilibrium path. The assumption that the set of states is less than the number of buyers prevents the set of strategies from being rich enough to implement this scheme of punishment and reward. There will always be one buyer who is a "Loser", that is, gets less than one unit of surplus no matter what the seller does. The seller can target this buyer and extract the maximal amount of surplus. The Loser is the weak link in the chain. The existence of one Loser ensures that all the buyers are Losers and ultimately they all end up with nothing.

The interpretation of the outcome of this game as "competitive" may not be entirely convincing. It is well known in bargaining games with discounting that allowing one agent to make all the offers typically allows that agent to capture all the surplus. Since the monopolistic outcome is the same as the competitive outcome, the fact that the seller captures all the surplus could be interpreted, quite naturally, as a monopolistic outcome. However, the same outcome can be obtained in a model in which the proposer is chosen randomly. For example, suppose that the seller chooses the buyer i with whom to bargain and then the proposer is chosen with equal probability to be the seller or buyer i. Since there is no discounting and the seller will be chosen as proposer infinitely often, the argument above can be used to prove that the seller can force an outcome in which he gets all the surplus.

Imperfect memory

The bounded memory assumption clarifies one sense in which bounded rationality, or bounded complexity of strategies, can select the competitive outcome from a large, possibly infinite set of equilibria. At the same time, it is a rather strong assumption. Another approach to this problem does not restrict the number of memory states in relation to the number of players. Instead, it introduces a "small" amount of randomness to mimic the effects of imperfect memory. Specifically, for some fixed value of $\varepsilon > 0$ we assume that, with probability $1 - \varepsilon$, the transition is determined by (3.3) and with probability ε the new state is uniformly distributed on S:

$$s_{t+1} = \begin{cases} \phi(s_t, a_t) & \text{w. pr. } 1 - \varepsilon + \varepsilon/|S| \\ s \neq \phi(s_t, a_t) & \text{w. pr. } \varepsilon/|S|. \end{cases}$$

The random element in the transition is like a "trembling hand" in the play of the game. It ensures that there is always a small probability that the players in the continuation game are following the "wrong" strategy, for example, rewarding the wrong player.

This element of bounded rationality in the game leads to the same outcome as before. Intuitively, the small amount of randomness prevents any one buyer from being awarded the entire surplus. This ensures that the seller can guarantee himself a positive amount of the surplus in any state. This in turn reduces the maximum that the buyers as a group can hope to get and the small amount of randomness ensures that any buyer must get less than this new, lower maximum. Then the seller can guarantee himself even more. Pursuing this argument to its logical conclusion shows that, in equilibrium, the seller must get the entire surplus.

Theorem 6 *If (f, g) is an SPE of the game with imperfect memory and $n > 2$, then the seller offers the object to one of the buyers at a price $p = 1$ at the first date and the buyer accepts.*

Proof As before, let (f, g) be a fixed SPE and put $u(s) = U(f, g, s)$ and $v_i(s) = V_i(f, g, s)$ for $i = 1, \ldots, n$. Let $1 - \alpha$ be the minimum payoff to the seller, that is,

$$1 - \alpha = \min\{u(s) : s \in S\}.$$

Then feasibility implies that

$$\sum_{i=1}^{n} v_i(s) \leq \alpha, \forall s. \tag{3.7}$$

From the feasibility constraint (3.7) it follows that, for some buyer i, $v_i(s) \leq \alpha/2$ for at least a fraction $(n - 1)/n$ of the states. To see this, let

$$S_i = \{s \in S | v_i(s) > \alpha/2\}.$$

125

By the definition of S_i and the feasibility condition (3.7) it is clear that $S_i \cap S_j = \emptyset$ for $i \neq j$ so there must exist an agent i such that

$$|S_i| \leq \min_{j=1,\dots,n} |S_j| \leq \frac{|S|}{n}.$$

For this agent i, $|S \backslash S_i| \geq \frac{n-1}{n} |S|$ as claimed.

Now consider the expected payoff of agent i for any memory state s_t and action $a_t = (i, p)$:

$$
\begin{aligned}
E[v_i(s_{t+1})|(s_t, a_t)] &\leq (1 - \varepsilon)\alpha + \varepsilon\left(\frac{1}{n}\alpha + \frac{n-1}{n}\frac{\alpha}{2}\right) \\
&= \left[\frac{\varepsilon}{2}\left(\frac{n+1}{n}\right) + (1 - \varepsilon)\right]\alpha \\
&= \alpha - \varepsilon\alpha\left(1 - \frac{n+1}{2n}\right).
\end{aligned}
$$

As long as $n > 2$, the preceding inequality shows that $v_i(s) < 3\alpha/4$ for every s and, in an SPE, this means that agent i must accept any offer $p < 1 - \alpha(1 - \varepsilon/2)$. Then the seller can guarantee himself a payoff arbitrarily close to $1 - \alpha(1 - \varepsilon/2)$. This contradicts the definition of $1 - \alpha$ unless $\alpha = 0$. ∎

The requirements for Theorem 6 are weaker than for Theorem 5: Theorem 6 requires only the existence of what we might call an ε-Loser, that is, someone who receives less than $(1 - \varepsilon)\alpha$ in every state, and $\varepsilon > 0$ can be arbitrarily small. In the same terminology, Theorem 5 requires the existence of a 1/2-Loser.

The assumptions made in Theorem 6 are in one respect stronger than necessary. The argument never refers to the number of elements in S. In fact, looking at the details of the proof, it appears that the same argument applies to an arbitrary measurable space S, for example, a compact metric space endowed with the Borel sets $\mathcal{B}(S)$ and a non-atomic probability measure P.

What both theorems teach us is that it is not necessary to assume completely memoryless strategies in order to rule out all non-competitive behavior. Strategies can be conditioned on a large amount of information about the past, as long as the complexity of the strategies is restricted so as to prevent the kinds of complicated punishments needed to support the continuum of equilibria described in Theorem 1.

Following a different approach, Chatterjee and Sabourian (1998) have analyzed bargaining games between finite automata. The idea of requiring strategies to be played by finite automata (finite-state machines) is intended to impose some bound on the complexity of play. The automaton is designed to play a best response, but it has the minimal number of states needed along the equilibrium path. This assumption does not eliminate non-uniqueness, but it does limit the amount of delay that can occur in equilibrium.

3.3 The Limit Principle

Non-cooperative models of oligopoly have long been used to provide a strategic foundation for competitive equilibrium (see the discussion in chapter 1, p. 10). The earliest and best known approach is based on the well known Cournot model of oligopoly. In this model, there are n identical firms, each of which simultaneously chooses the quantity of output it wants to produce. An inverse demand function, representing the behavior of the consumers in the market, determines the market-clearing price as a function of the aggregate output. The profit of each firm is determined by the price and the firm's output, so we have a well defined game in which the payoff of each firm is a function of the n-tuple of quantities chosen. The outcome is described by a Nash equilibrium of this game.

When the number of firms in the market is finite, the static Cournot oligopoly game predicts that competition will be imperfect, and the price will be higher and output lower than in the competitive, price-taking equilibrium. However, as the number of firms becomes unboundedly large, the oligopolistic equilibria converge to the perfectly competitive, price-taking equilibrium. Some strong regularity conditions are required for the proof of this limit theorem and, in an important paper, Roberts (1980) provided a counter-example. Roberts (1980) shows that, under certain conditions, the market demand curve is not invertible. A *selection* from the demand correspondence may be inverted, but the resulting inverse demand curve will not be continuous. Specifically, at some point, an increase in the aggregate quantity supplied may cause a sharp (discontinuous) fall in the market price. The effect of this discontinuity is to prevent the increasing competitive pressure from expanding aggregate output beyond the discontinuity point. When the market is poised at a discontinuity point, producing an extra unit of output causes a loss on inframarginal units that is a higher order of magnitude than the revenue from selling an extra unit. No matter how many firms are in the market, the aggregate output may not increase beyond this discontinuity point.

Another way of looking at the problem is to say that, no matter how many firms and consumers are in the market, each firm continues to have a non-negligible effect on the market, since the slightest increase in output by one firm pushes the market over the precipice and leads to a sharp fall in the market price.

The Roberts (1980) example illustrates a more general problem. Unless some restrictions are placed on the payoff functions to ensure continuity of the payoffs as functions of the strategy profiles, there is no hope of achieving a limit theorem characterizing the behavior of sequences of Nash equilibria as the number of players increases without bound. This problem was studied in Green's (1984) work on limits of Nash equilibria in games. The problem posed by Roberts (1980) and studied by Green (1984) may appear to be a purely technical problem, one that can be remedied by assuming that games are sufficiently well behaved. However, a more robust form of discontinuity arises quite naturally in repeated games.

One weakness of the static Cournot model is that it does not capture the possibilities for collusion in a realistic way. In most industries, the competition among firms continues over many periods. This repeated interaction is naturally represented by a repeated game in which the stage game at each period is the static Cournot oligopoly game. Once we allow for repeated interaction, the set of (subgame-perfect) equilibria becomes much larger. According to the Folk Theorem for repeated games (see, for example, Fudenberg and Tirole, 1992), any profile of individually rational pay-offs can be supported by an SPE, as long as the rate of time preference is sufficiently low. In particular, there will be an equilibrium in which firms collude to share the monopoly profits.

One way of supporting the collusive outcome is by using the "Nash reversion" strategies. Suppose there are n firms in the market, operating under constant returns to scale. If y^m is the monopolistic level of output, then each firm is assigned an output of y^m/n and receives a fraction π^m/n of the monopoly profits π^m each period. However, if any firm deviates from the output level y^m/n, then every firm reverts in the next period to the Nash–Cournot equilibrium of the one-shot game, that is, to the level y^c. Playing an equilibrium strategy of the one-shot game in every period is an SPE strategy, and since the profits in every period will be lower under this strategy, the punishment on the deviating firm will be large enough to deter the deviation, as long as the discount rate is sufficiently low.

If we replicate this market by increasing the number of firms and consumers, it actually becomes easier to support the monopoly outcome. The monopoly outcome does not change, but the Nash–Cournot equilibrium of the one-shot game converges to the price-taking equilibrium, so the threat of reverting to the Nash–Cournot equilibrium becomes larger and more effective. Thus, increasing the number of firms does nothing to undermine the possibilities for collusive behavior.

This problem was studied by Edward Green in a prescient paper (Green, 1980). The focus of Green's study was again the Cournot model of oligopoly. Like Roberts, Green was interested in what he called the *Limit Principle*, under which the equilibria of the static Cournot oligopoly game converge to a price-taking competitive equilibrium when the number of firms becomes very large. As we have seen, the Limit Principle fails to hold in the repeated game.

Another way of thinking about the failure of the Limit Principle is as a failure of continuity in the limit: even though the number of firms becomes unboundedly large, so that the single firm becomes negligible relative to the entire market, the actions of a firm are still significant, because the entire market reverts to the Nash strategies when a single firm deviates.

It is also worth noting that the equilibrium strategies do not satisfy the Markov property, because the punishments are based on the history of the game.

This behavior of sequences of replica economies is in marked contrast to the limit economy with a non-atomic continuum of firms. Suppose that instead of replicating the economy we had assumed the existence of a continuum of firms with the same cross-sectional distribution of characteristics as the finite market. (Previously we assumed identical firms with constant returns to scale; now firms are allowed to be heterogeneous.) One way of doing this is to replace each firm in the finite market with a non-atomic continuum of firms having identical cost functions. Suppose further that the market game is *anonymous*, in the sense that firms cannot observe the output decisions of other firms; they can observe only the price in the market at each date. Now a single firm in this continuum model has literally no effect on price, because its output has no effect on the total quantity produced. (Each firm has measure zero and so cannot affect aggregate output.) As a result, each firm will take the price as given and it is easy to see that the equilibrium at each date will be the standard price-taking or perfectly competitive equilibrium of the static market. The firm does not have to worry about threats of retaliation. It can do whatever it likes without any fear that its deviation will be detected. In fact, this is just the Anti-Folk Theorem for repeated anonymous games (see Jovanovic and Rosenthal, 1988; Masso and Rosenthal, 1989).

This points to the crucial difference between the continuum model and the large-but-finite model. In the continuum model, the firm has no impact on the equilibrium price. In the large but finite model, no matter how many times the market has been replicated, a single deviation will lead to some change in price and this price change can trigger the punishment phase in which every firm reverts to the Nash–Cournot equilibrium. A single firm has a small direct impact on price, because the firm's output is small relative to the size of the market. However, that small price change has a large strategic impact on the future play of the game and hence on the future market price.

Green's insight is that the collusive equilibrium is unlikely to be robust. In practice, many random and unobservable factors would influence the price in addition to the actions of the firms. It is unlikely that firms in general will have enough information to infer from an observation of the price whether or not some firm has deviated from the collusive equilibrium. If enough noise enters the information channel, firms can cheat on the collusive agreement without fear of detection. In that case, the Limit Principle might be reinstated.

Green (1980) contains a detailed study of the limiting properties of sequences of replicated, anonymous, repeated games in which players can observe noisy public signals that depend on individual actions. Although the market studied is very specific, the framework developed in the paper is very general and applies to other repeated games. Green's results are generalized by Sabourian (1990), which makes use of the same framework and extends the analysis in several directions. Green considers only equilibria supported by Nash reversion strategies and also allows only strategies in which agents' actions depend on public signals. Sabourian's analysis applies to general equilibria, not just equilibria with Nash reversion strategies, and allows strategies to depend on past signals as well as the agent's own past actions.

The next four sections of this chapter are devoted to reinterpreting the analysis of Green and Sabourian in the context of repeated games with limited memory. The objective is to prove a limit theorem analogue of the Anti-Folk Theorem. This theory will apply not just to market games, but to repeated games in general. This treatment is more limited than Green (1980) and Sabourian (1990) – I do not attempt to characterize the limiting continuum game and the arguments are developed slightly differently – and the arguments are more direct and less abstract. The underlying ideas are the same, however. For an elegant treatment, the reader is referred to Sabourian (1990).

Sections 3.4 and 3.5 describe the general framework. I then in section 3.6 derive a limit theorem and consider the implications for the analysis of dynamic games.

3.4 Repeated games

A finite, normal-form game is denoted by $\Gamma = (N, X, u)$, where

- $N = \{1, \ldots, n\}$ is the set of players;
- X_i is the (finite) strategy set of player i and $X \equiv \times_{i=1}^{n} X_i$ is the set of strategy profiles;
- $u_i : X \to \mathbf{R}$ is the payoff function for player i and $u \equiv (u_1, \ldots, u_n)$ is the payoff function for the game.

The game is extended to allow for mixed strategies in the usual way. Let

$$\Delta(X_i) \equiv \left\{ p_i : X_i \to \mathbf{R}_+ | \sum_{x_i \in X_i} p(x_i) = 1 \right\}$$

denote the set of mixed strategies and $\Delta(X) \equiv \times_{i=1}^{n} \Delta(X_i)$. Then define $u_i : \Delta(X) \to \mathbf{R}$ by putting

$$u_i(p) = \sum_{x \in X} P(x) u_i(x)$$

where $p \equiv (p_1, \ldots, p_n)$ and $P(x) \equiv \times_{i=1}^{n} p_i(x_i)$.

A Nash equilibrium of Γ is a strategy profile p^* such that for any player i

$$u_i(p^*) \geq u_i(p^*_{-i}, p_i), \forall p_i \in \Delta(X_i),$$

where p^*_{-i} denotes the profile of strategies of players other than i and $(p^*_{-i}, p_i) \equiv (p_1^*, \ldots, p_{i-1}^*, p_i, p_{i+1}^*, \ldots, p_n^*)$. The set of Nash equilibria is denoted by $NE(\Gamma)$.

Continuity and anonymity

A repeated game consists of an infinite number of plays of a finite game, with play of the game occurring at a sequence of dates $t = 1, 2, 3, \ldots$ At each date the players can observe the play of the game in all of the preceding stages and condition their play in the current stage on that information. The payoff in the repeated game is the present value of the payoffs from the sequence of stage games.

Let Γ^∞ denote the countable repetition of the finite stage game Γ. The set of dates at which play occurs is denoted by $T = \{1, 2, \ldots\}$. The history of the game at date t is a finite sequence of (pure) strategy profiles, $\{x_s\}_{s=1}^{t}$ in X. Let H denote the set of histories of the game, including the null history $\emptyset$. Then a strategy for player i is a function $f_i : H \to \Delta(X_i)$, with the interpretation that $f_i(h) \in \Delta(X_i)$ is player i's mixed strategy in the stage game Γ at the information set h. A profile for the repeated game is a function $f : H \to \Delta(X)$. Let F_i denote the set of strategies for player i and let $F = \times_{i=1}^{n} F_i$ denote the set of strategy profiles. For each strategy profile f there is a unique path $\xi(f) = \{\xi_t(f)\}$. This path is random if the players choose mixed (behavioral) strategies and has a probability distribution μ_f. We can define the payoff function by putting

$$U(f) = E\left[\sum_{t=1}^{\infty} \delta^{t-1} u(\xi_t(f))\right] \tag{2.8}$$

for every f, where $\delta \in (0, 1)$ is the common discount factor for all players, and the expectations operator $E[\cdot]$ is with respect to μ_f.

A Nash equilibrium of Γ^∞ is a strategy profile f^* such that for each i and any strategy f_i

$$U_i(f^*) \geq U(f^*_{-i}, f_i).$$

For a fixed history h and a strategy f, we define a new strategy $f|h$ by putting

$$(f|h)(h') = f(h, h').$$

Then we say that f^* is a subgame-perfect equilibrium (SPE) if $f^*|h$ is a Nash equilibrium for every h.

3.5 Limited memory

In this section, I extend the framework of the repeated game to allow for the possibility that players cannot condition their behavior on the precise history of the game. This might be the result of bounded rationality, limited memory, or some other departure from the assumptions of the standard model.

Let S be a set of states of the game. These states represent what the players can remember about the history of the game. The states do not have any direct impact on the agents' strategies or their payoffs. The only function of the states is to allow players to condition their actions on some limited information about the past play of the game. S is assumed to be a metric space. The measure space $(S, \mathcal{B}(S), \lambda)$ is formed by endowing S with the σ–field $\mathcal{B}(S)$ consisting of the Borel sets of S and a σ-additive, positive measure λ. (For definitions and standard results, see any text on probability and measure theory, for example, Billingsley, 1985).

The evolution of the state is determined by the play of the game through a probability transition function. For each action profile x and state s, the probability distribution of the state in the next period is denoted by $\psi(x, s)$. Then ψ satisfies the following properties:

- $\psi : X \times S \to \Delta(S)$, where $\Delta(S)$ is the set of probability measures on $(S, \mathcal{B}(S))$.
- For any measurable set $A \in \mathcal{B}(S)$, $\psi(A|x, s)$ is a measurable function of (x, s).

The initial state of the game s_1 is assumed to be fixed.

A repeated game with limited memory $\Gamma_L^\infty(s_1)$ is defined by the repeated game Γ^∞ together with the measure space of states $(S, \mathcal{B}(S), \lambda)$, the transition probability function ψ, and the initial state s_1. Formally, this game is a stochastic game, but it is a degenerate kind of stochastic game because the states do not affect the payoffs or the set of strategies available. They are akin to the "sunspots" in models of correlated equilibria.

By definition, all strategies in a game of limited memory have the strong Markov property: a strategy profile for the stochastic game is a measurable function $f : S \to \Delta(X)$. In other words, the strategy profile chosen in the stage game Γ is a function of the current state of the game only. Together with the transition function ψ the strategy f defines a stochastic process $\xi(f) = \{\xi_t(f)\}_{t=1}^{\infty}$ and the payoff function U can be defined in the same way as before by (3.8). A Markov perfect equilibrium (MPE) for the stochastic game Γ_L^{∞} is a Markov strategy profile f^* such that for any date and state s, the strategy f^* is a Nash equilibrium of the game $\Gamma_L^{\infty}(s)$.

Markov perfect equilibria

It may appear that the MPE of the stochastic game are special, but in fact there is no essential loss of generality in focusing on MPE as long as the state space S and the transition probability ψ are suitably defined. Recall that the states do not affect anything of substance in the stage game Γ. They are merely "sunspots." So we can use them to carry information about the past. If this is done appropriately, then any SPE of the repeated game can be replicated as an MPE of the stochastic game.

Theorem 7 *Suppose that f^* is an SPE of the repeated game Γ^{∞} and consider the stochastic game $\Gamma_L^{\infty}(s_1)$ such that $S \equiv H$, $s_1 = \emptyset$ and F is the "deterministic" transition probability function defined by putting*

$$\psi(h'|x, h) = \begin{cases} 1 & \text{if } h' = (h, x) \\ 0 & \text{otherwise,} \end{cases}$$

for any (h', x, h). Then we can define an MPE g^* of $\Gamma_L^{\infty}(s_1)$ by putting $g^*(h) = f^*(h)$ for every $h \in H$.

Proof The statement of Theorem 7 is almost a proof. It is enough to note that for every state h the payoff associated with g^* will be the same as the payoff in the repeated game after the history h. ∎

Strategic foundations of general equilibrium

Note that the particular state space and transition probability used for the theorem are not essential. As long as S is (at least) countably infinite and the transition probability is an invertible function, Theorem 7 continues to hold. The essential thing is that the structure of the game allows us to encode the history in the set of states.

Theorem 7 shows that the Markov assumption loses its power to reduce the set of equilibria if the state space is appropriately expanded. The point of this result is simply to show that there is no loss of generality in making the Markov assumption in this context.

While Theorem 7 shows that we can replicate the SPE of a repeated game as the MPE of a game with limited memory, the replication requires a huge state space. The fact that these strategies are Markov does not mean that they are simple strategies when the state space is so large. In practice, it may seem unlikely that individuals could implement strategies that condition on such a complex memory space. Even if they had the ability to implement such strategies, how would they calculate the equilibrium strategies? Restricting the state space is a natural and attractive way to capture the notion that agents have some bounds on their rationality (ability to perform complex computations).

One way of representing "bounded rationality" is to assume that S is finite. This assumption includes as special cases a number of well known models of bounded rationality. An example introduced by Green (1982) and Rubinstein (1986) is the *finite automaton*, that is, a finite-state machine. The machine representing player i has a finite number of states, denoted by the set S_i, and his strategy (output) is a function $f_i : S_i \to X_i$. The player's state evolves according to a rule (transition function) $g_i : S_i \times X \to S_i$. In words, if his state at date t is s_i and the action profile is x then player i's state at date $t+1$ will be $s_i' = g_i(s_i, x)$. Both f_i and g_i are considered endogenous – in other words, both are chosen to satisfy the equilibrium conditions. In practice, the set of states is kept as small as possible. The interest of this kind of analysis lies

Continuity and anonymity

in seeing what kind of equilibria can be supported by very simple strategies.

To see that the finite automaton is a special case of the present framework, simply define the memory states as n-tuples of individual (machine) states, that is, put $s = (s_1, \ldots, s_n)$ and use the function $g = (g_1, \ldots, g_n)$ to define the (deterministic) transition probability ψ,

$$\psi(s'|x, s) = \begin{cases} 1 & \text{if } s' = g(s, x) \\ 0 & \text{otherwise.} \end{cases}$$

The strategy f_i can be treated as a function of s as long as we remember that it should depend only on the component s_i.

Another model of bounded rationality assumes that players have finite memories. The assumption of finite memory is more restrictive than the assumption of a finite memory space S. An agent with finite memory can remember only what has happened in a finite number of recent periods. This implies that strategies can depend only on the history of a finite number of periods. For example, the strategy of player i at date t would be a function $f_i(x_{t-T}, \ldots, x_{t-1})$ of the history of play in the last T periods. In that case, we put $S = X \times \ldots \times X$ and define the transition probability by putting

$$\psi(s'|x, s) = \begin{cases} 1 & \text{if } s' = (x_{t-T+1}, \ldots, x_{t-1}, x) \\ & \text{and } s = (x_{t-T}, \ldots, x_{t-1}) \\ 0 & \text{otherwise} \end{cases}$$

This is clearly just a variant of the framework described earlier, where we put $S = H$. An example of finite memory is found in Aumann and Sorin (1989), which studies cooperation in two-player coordination games. The players' actions are assumed to depend on a finite history of their opponent's actions. This means that any deviation from equilibrium play is eventually forgotten by the opponent and this allows players to experiment without fear of permanent punishment. It is important in the Aumann–Sorin setup that players do not condition their actions on the history of their own play. If they did condition on their own past play, they could use the fact that they had punished last period as a signal to punish again this period. In this way, their own past actions could act as a permanent reminder of an opponent's deviation and this would undermine the effect of the finite memory assumption.

These two examples show that the present framework can accommodate familiar models of bounded rationality, but it is more general than these models of individual behavior. A finite memory space is less restrictive than Aumman and Sorin's use of finite memory, because it allows for infinite punishment. A finite memory space is less restrictive than the finite automaton model because it allows for correlation of strategies and randomness.

3.6 Large anonymous games

Let Γ denote a finite n-player game. We say that the game Γ is *anonymous* if it satisfies the following conditions. First, the players have identical strategy sets

$$X_i = X \text{ for all } i = 1, 2, \ldots, n$$

and, secondly, a player's payoff depends only on his own strategy and the distribution of the strategies chosen by other players

$$u_i : X \times \Delta(X) \to \mathbf{R} \text{ for all } i = 1, 2, \ldots, n.$$

If player i chooses x_i and the strategies of players $j \neq i$ are represented by μ_{-i}, then player i's payoff is $u_i(x_i, \mu_{-i})$. In other words, it does not matter which players choose which strategies. It matters only how many of the players $j \neq i$ choose a particular strategy. Note that with only n players, not all the distributions in the set $\Delta(X)$ correspond to feasible choices for the other players. It is convenient to assume that the payoff function u_i is defined on all of $\Delta(X)$ because later we shall want to treat the number of players n as large and variable.

The corresponding repeated game with limited memory $\Gamma_L^\infty(s_1)$ will also be anonymous if the transition probability function is anonymous in the sense that it depends only on the distribution of the strategies chosen and not on the profile of strategies:

$$\psi : S \times \Delta(X) \to \Delta(S).$$

The objective of introducing anonymity is to provide a simple framework in which we can analyze the impact of a single player's actions on the subsequent course of a game as the number of players becomes very large. Note that the memory space S will be held fixed as the number of players n increases without bound. If the memory space S is bounded in an appropriate sense and the number of players is very large, then there is not enough information in the collective memory to make most players pivotal. This is a theme that we shall return to at the end of the chapter (p. 153).

Eventually, we shall want to apply this analysis to repeated games with limited memory, but first we consider a special case, which turns out to encompass all that we need to know about repeated games with limited memory.

The main lemma

Suppose that a finite symmetric game Γ is followed by another game that yields a payoff depending only on the state determined by the play of the first game. If the following state is s then the payoff to player i is denoted by $v_i(s)$ and the payoff function is denoted by $v = (v_1, \ldots, v_n)$. If the play of the first game generates the action profile x (with distribution μ) then the payoff from the convolution of the two games is given by

$$u_i(x_i, \mu_{-i}) + \delta \int v_i(s) d\psi(\mu, s_1).$$

Of course, player i does not know the value of μ when he chooses x_i unless all players are choosing pure strategies. To allow for mixed strategies, we assume that F_i is the probability distribution of μ when i chooses x_i. Then the payoff to player i from the continuation game can be written as

$$\pi_i = \int \int v_i(s) d\psi(\mu, s_1) dF_i.$$

We want to show that, under certain conditions, the payoff from the continuation game is independent of player i's current choice x_i when the number of players becomes unboundedly large. To do this, we first have to define a sequence of games and equilibria with increasing numbers of players. An *increasing sequence of games* is defined by

- a finite strategy set X;
- a sequence of players $i = 1, 2, \ldots$;
- a sequence of individual payoff functions $u_i : X \times \Delta(X) \to \mathbf{R}$, one for each $i = 1, 2, \ldots$;
- a symmetric probability transition function $\psi : \Delta(X) \times S \to \Delta(S)$;
- a sequence of measurable continuation-payoff functions $v^n : S \to \mathbf{R}^n$.

For each n, the game under consideration consists of the players $\{1, \ldots, n\}$ with the payoff function

$$U_i^n(x_i, \mu_{-i}) = u_i(x_i, \mu_{-i}) + \delta \int v_i^n(s) d\psi(\mu, s_1).$$

We impose the following assumptions on the sequence of games:

- The sequence of functions $\{v_i^n\}$ is uniformly bounded, that is, for some B and all n, $|v_i^n| \leq B$.
- The transition probability function ψ is assumed to be noisy, in the sense that $\psi(s, \mu)$ is uniformly absolutely continuous for any (s, μ). To be more precise, if λ is the measure on S then for some constant K and any $(s, \mu) \in S \times \Delta(X)$,

$$\psi(s, \mu)(A) \leq K\lambda(A)$$

  for any measurable set A contained in S.
- ψ is weakly continuous, that is, for any sequence $\{(s^n, \mu^n)\}$ converging to (s^0, μ^0), $\psi(s^n, \mu^n)$ converges weakly to $\psi(s^0, \mu^0)$ (see Billingsley, 1985, pp. 335 *et seq.*).

Fix an arbitrary player i and consider two possible pure strategies x_{i0} and x_{i1}. For each n, the equilibrium strategies

Continuity and anonymity

of the other players determine a probability distribution over the action profiles. Let $F_{ij}^n \in \Delta(X)$ denote the probability distribution over action profiles corresponding to player i's choice x_{ij} for $j = 0, 1$ respectively. Let π_{ij}^n denote the continuation payoff corresponding to the choice of x_{ij} in the nth game, that is,

$$\pi_{ij}^n = \int \int v_i^n(s) d\psi(\mu, s_1) dF_{ij}^n.$$

We want to characterize the limiting difference $\pi_{i0}^n - \pi_{i1}^n$ as $n \to \infty$.

To define a limiting equilibrium we must assume that

- $v_i^n \to v_i^0$ a.e. $[\lambda]$
- $F_{ij}^n \to F_i^0$ for $j = 0, 1$.

Notice that the second statement implies that in the limit, the distributions are independent of the strategies chosen by player 1. This is obvious, since there is an infinite number of players in the limit. So the only real force of this assumption is to require that the distributions F_{ij}^n converge to "something."

With these assumptions, we are finally ready to show that the action of agent i has a negligible impact on his payoff in the continuation game. Hence, he should choose a best response in the current stage game. The following lemma formalizes this claim.

Lemma 8 *Under the maintained assumptions, $(\pi_{i0}^n - \pi_{i1}^n)$* $\to 0$ *as* $n \to \infty$.

Proof Now

$$\int \int v_i^n(s)\psi(ds|s_1, \mu)F_{ij}^n(d\mu) - \int \int v_i^0(s)\psi(ds|s_1, \mu)F_i^0(d\mu)$$

$$= \int \int (v_i^n(s) - v_i^0(s))\psi(ds|s_1, \mu)F_{ij}^n(d\mu) -$$

$$\int \int v_i^0(s)\psi(ds|s_1, \mu)(F_{ij}^n(d\mu) - F_i^0(d\mu))$$

so that

141

$$\left| \int \int v_i^n(s)\psi(ds|s_1, \mu)F_{ij}^n(d\mu) - \int \int v_i^0(s)\psi(ds|s_1, \mu)F_i^0(d\mu) \right|$$

$$\leq \int \int |v_i^n(s) - v_i^0(s)|\psi(ds|s_1, \mu)F_{ij}^n(d\mu) +$$

$$\left| \int \int v_i^0(s)\psi(ds|s_1, \mu)(F_{ij}^n(d\mu) - F_i^0(d\mu)) \right|.$$

By Egoroff's Theorem (Royden, 1988, p. 73, exercise 30), we know that v_i^n converges almost uniformly to v_i^0, that is, for any $\varepsilon > 0$ there exists a set $A \subset S$ such that $\lambda(A) \leq \varepsilon$ and v_i^n converges uniformly to v_i^0 on $S \backslash A$. Choose N_1 so that

$$|v_i^n(s) - v_i^0(s)| \leq \varepsilon$$

for all $n \geq N_1$ and $s \in S \backslash A$. For $s \in A$ we know that $|v_i^n(s) - v_i^0(s)| \leq B$ for all n, so

$$\int \int |v_i^n(s) - v_i^0(s)|\psi(ds|s_1, \mu)F_{ij}^n(d\mu) \leq \varepsilon + BK\varepsilon$$

for $n \geq N_1$. By Lusin's Theorem (Halmos, 1974, p. 242), v_i^0 is almost continuous, that is, there exists a compact set $C \subset S$ such that $\lambda(S \backslash C) \leq \varepsilon$ and v_i^0 is continuous on C. Therefore, from the definition of weak convergence and from the fact that F_{ij}^n converges weakly to F_i^0, there exists a number N_2 such that

$$\left| \int \int v_i^0(s)\psi(ds|s_1, \mu)(F_{ij}^n(d\mu) - F_i^0(d\mu)) \right|$$

$$\leq \left| \int \int_C v_i^0(s)\psi(ds|s_1, \mu)(F_{ij}^n(d\mu) - F_i^0(d\mu)) \right| +$$

$$\left| \int \int_{S \backslash C} v_i^0(s)\psi(ds|s_1, \mu)(F_{ij}^n(d\mu) - F_i^0(d\mu)) \right|$$

$$\leq \varepsilon + BK\varepsilon$$

for all $n \geq N_2$. Putting the two inequalities together, we have

$$\left| \int \int v_i^n(s)\psi(ds|s_1, \mu)F_{ij}^n(d\mu) - \int \int v_i^0(s)\psi(ds|s_1, \mu)F_i^0(d\mu) \right|$$

$$\leq 2(\varepsilon + BK\varepsilon)$$

for $n \geq N = \max\{N_1, N_2\}$. Since ε is arbitrary, it follows that $\pi_{ij}^n \to \pi_i^0 \equiv \int \int v_i^0(s)\psi(ds|s_1, \mu)F_i^0(d\mu)$ as $n \to \infty$ for both $j = 0, 1$. ∎

The proof of Lemma 8 is intended to be heuristic rather than efficient. In particular, it is interesting to see how two of the three principles of functional analysis, Egoroff's Theorem and Lusin's Theorem, come into play in the proof. Needless to say, the whole argument could be replaced as a single continuity assumption, but that would have been very unilluminating.

Sabourian (1990) summarizes his central technical proof as follows:

> The proof is based on
> (a) showing that in any finite-player repeated game, the maximum gain a player can make, in any period, by deviating from any Nash equilibrium path of the repeated game, is bounded above by a product term consisting of a fixed number and the (metric) distance (when total variation norm is used) between the distribution of the random outcome when a deviation takes place, and that when the deviation does not take place;
> (b) showing that anonymity and continuity imply that the above distance between the two distributions approaches zero as the number of players becomes large;
> (c) constructing a sequence of finite player games that converge to a continuum, using Skorohod's embedding theorem (often used in core theory). (Sabourian, 1990, pp. 95–96)

Lemma 8 corresponds to parts (a) and (b) of this proof strategy. Without going further to carry out part (c), we cannot define a limit game or say in what exact sense the Limit Principle holds in this framework. However, it is intuitively clear that "in the limit" each player will choose an action, contingent on any memory state s, that is a best response in the current stage game. In this sense, what we should expect to observe is a profile of actions that forms a Nash equilibrium of the stage game at every date t and in every memory state s. This implies several different features of the equilibrium (in the limit) that are relevant to our enquiry:

- In choosing his action at any date t and in any memory state s, an agent does not take into account the effect that his action may have on the future play of the game. This is because, asymptotically, his action has a negligible effect on the next memory state and hence a negligible effect on the future play of the game.
- Although the equilibrium does not have the Markov property (the agents' strategies depend on the entire history of public signals as well, possibly, as their own actions), it does share the crucial feature of Markov equilibria, namely that punishment strategies based on an individual player's deviation are ruled out. Markov strategies rule out punishment strategies by preventing any dependence on memory; here we achieve the same end by restricting the dependence to aggregate signals and making sure that this dependence is continuous as an individual player becomes vanishingly small.
- This does not mean, however, that the memory states do not matter. The memory states can serve as a correlation device and random evolution of the memory states, independently of the actions of the agents, can generate "sunspot phenomena." What we observe over time is equivalent to a correlated equilibrium in the sense of Aumann (1974).

What might be called the Continuity Principle, the property that a single agent's action has a vanishingly small effect on the play of the game when the number of agents is unboundedly large, has been justified by introducing (a) a small amount of noise and (b) a sufficiently small memory space. These are the kind of assumptions that we need to justify the conditions used in chapter 2.

3.7 Non-anonymous games

While anonymity seems a natural assumption in the context of many models of markets, it is also restrictive. First, 'anonymity' is one of the properties that we would like to obtain endogenously from a study of the structure of the market game, rather than imposing it by assumption on the market game. Second, anonymity also reduces the dimensionality of the memory space by aggregating the actions of the agents into a distribution that determines the evolution of the state of the game. Expanding the dimensionality of the state space may change the results. A third restriction of the preceding analysis does not follow from anonymity *per se*, but is associated with it: in order to derive the Limit Principle we have to assume that the transition probability is *uniformly* absolutely continuous. What this means in more accessible terms is that the noise introduced into memory becomes large relative to the size of an individual agent's impact on the economy. While this does not immediately imply that the individual agent's action is not pivotal, it might be suspected of having something to do with it. In particular, it would be interesting to see whether smaller amounts of uncertainty would do the job.

In this section, another approach is adopted to test the robustness of the results based on anonymous games. The essential ideas are drawn from a related problem in the literature on mechanism design and the provision of public goods.

Continuity in the provision of public goods

Suppose there are n individuals $i = 1, \ldots, n$ in a community which has to decide whether to undertake a project to provide a public good. The project is indivisible, so without loss of generality we can assume that the amount of the public good is either 0 or 1. Preferences are linear in money. Then we can normalize the utility function so that each individual gets a payoff of $v - p$ if the good is provided, where v is the value of one unit of the good and p is the individual's contribution to the provision of the public good. If the good is not provided, each individual receives a payoff of 0.

There are two types of individuals, depending on the value assigned to the public good. Some get utility v_H

from the good and some get utility v_L, where $0 < v_L < v_H$. Individuals are *ex ante* identical and have independently distributed types, with probability $0 < \alpha < 1$ that the value of the public good is high. The total cost of the good is nc, where

$$v_L < c < (1 - \alpha)v_L + \alpha v_H.$$

In other words, the average cost of the public good is greater than the low valuation, so an agent with a low valuation will not want the good if he has to pay the average cost; but the expected value of the good to a typical agent is greater than the average cost, so *ex ante* it is efficient to provide the good.

We assume that individuals can opt out of the project: if they are asked to contribute more than the good is worth to them, they can refuse to participate.

Let v_i denote the valuation of agent i, let p_i denote the contribution of agent i, and let x denote the quantity of the public good provided. A mechanism for providing the good is a function that maps a profile of messages $(v_1, \ldots, v_n)$ into a decision about the provision of the good $x = 0, 1$ and a profile of contributions $(p_1, \ldots, p_n)$ such that $\sum_{i=1}^{n} p_i \geq xnc$. The individual rationality constraint requires that $v_i - p_i \geq 0$ for all i where v_i is the actual valuation of agent i. By the Revelation Principle (see, for example, Myerson, 1991, p. 260) we can restrict attention to truth-telling equilibria. The problem faced by the mechanism designer is that, given the individual rationality constraint, individuals are likely to want to misrepresent their preferences, claiming to have a low valuation in order to be assigned a low contribution. Why would anyone would want to participate in the provision of the public good if by opting out they can avoid paying anything? The answer is that the individual may regard himself as pivotal in determining whether the public good is provided or not. We can see this point through a simple example.

Suppose there are only two individuals, $i = 1, 2$. If both have low valuations it is not worth providing the good; if both have high valuations it is worth providing the good;

and if one has a high valuation and one has a low valuation it is worth providing the good if

$$2c < v_L + v_H,$$

which I assume to hold in what follows. Consider the following mechanism:

- if both announce low valuations, the good is not provided and no contributions are paid;
- if both announce high valuations, the good is provided and both pay $c < v_H$;
- if one announces the high valuation and one announces the low valuation, the good is provided, the agent with the low valuation pays v_L and the agent with the high valuation pays $2c - v_L$.

By making the low-valuation agent pay the maximum consistent with his individual rationality constraint, we relax the incentive constraint on truth-telling as much as possible. This mechanism is clearly feasible, individually rational, and efficient if agents tell the truth. Now consider the incentives for the agents to tell the truth.

If an agent has the low valuation, it cannot be in his interest to report the high valuation. At best this will raise his contribution without changing the provision of the public good; at worst it will raise his contribution and cause inefficient provision of the public good. So suppose that the agent has the high valuation and considers reporting the low valuation. If the other agent announces the high valuation, reporting the low valuation does not change the provision but reduces the contribution. If the other agent announces the low valuation, announcing the low valuation ensures that the good is not provided, and this reduces the agent's payoff. So there is a tradeoff between reducing one's contribution and reducing the probability of providing the good. The agent knows that in some states he is pivotal in determining the provision of the public good and this disciplines him against misreporting his valuation.

The payoff from mis-reporting when the true valuation is v_H is

$$\alpha(v_H - v_L)$$

and the payoff from truth-telling is

$$v_H - (1 - \alpha)(2c - v_L) - \alpha c.$$

The incentive constraint then is

$$\alpha(v_H - v_L) \le v_H - (1 - \alpha)(2c - v_L) - \alpha c$$

or

$$(1 - \alpha)v_H + v_L \ge (2 - \alpha)c.$$

This constraint is satisfied if the surplus is high and the value of α is not too high. For example, if $\alpha = 1$ then the constraint is clearly incompatible with the assumption that $v_L < c$.

What is true for small numbers of agents may not be true for large numbers, however. As the number of players gets larger, providing the public good is efficient as long as the fraction of agents with a high valuation is at least α. A single agent's signal will not change the distribution of signals reported very much and so the chance of the agent being pivotal seems intuitively to become small. When the number of agents is very large, the law of large numbers ensures that the fraction of agents with the high valuation will be very close to α with high probability, so the good will be produced with probability close to one if agents tell the truth. The temptation for an agent with a high valuation to mis-report his signal becomes very strong. In fact, it is easy to see that the public good will not be provided with probability one as efficiency requires. Beyond this obvious statement, however, it is hard to say exactly what will happen. As long as an agent thinks that he is pivotal, he may have an incentive to tell the truth. Furthermore, for any large but finite number n, some agents can be pivotal. What is not obvious is how many agents can be made pivotal and how much of the public good can be provided.

This problem was studied by Mailath and Postlewaite (1990) who showed that as the number n becomes unboundedly large, the probability that the public good is provided converges to zero for any individually rational and

Continuity and anonymity

incentive compatible mechanism. The main step in proving this result is a lemma that shows that, as n grows
unboundedly large, almost all agents become non-pivotal.
A particularly elegant proof of this principle is contained in
an appendix to Mailath and Postlewaite (1990) and is
attributed by them to a referee of the paper. In what follows, I am going to adapt the referee's argument to a game-
theoretic environment to show that even in games that are
not symmetric (anonymous), the Continuity Principle
holds for almost all players as the number of players
becomes unboundedly large.

The Referee's Lemma

Suppose that there is a countable sequence of players $i =
1, 2, \ldots$ and that each player has a finite action set X_i. For
any n we define the game Γ^n to consist of the first n players
$i = 1, \ldots, n$. Without the assumption of anonymity, the
payoff function of a given player changes as the number
of players varies. Let u_i^n be a real valued function defined
on $X^n \equiv X_1 \times \ldots \times X_n$ and let $u^n \equiv (u_1^n, \ldots, u_n^n)$ be the payoff function for Γ^n.

As before, the payoff from the continuation game is
represented by the payoff functions $v_i^n : S \to \mathbf{R}$ for every
$i \leq n$ and $n = 1, 2, \ldots$.

The evolution of the state is determined by the transition probability function $\psi^n : X^n \to \Delta(S)$, where reference
to the initial state is suppressed because it is held fixed in
what follows. We assume that S is (contained in) a Banach
space. (See Royden, 1988, p. 217.)

For each n the equilibrium strategies have the distribution $F^n \in \Delta(X^n)$.

Now consider a sequence of games and the corresponding equilibria satisfying the following conditions:

- v_i^n is a measurable function and for each i, the pointwise
  limit $\lim_{n\to\infty} v_i^n = v_i^0$ is a measurable function;
- for each n the function ψ^n is continuous when $\Delta(S)$
  is endowed with the topology of weak convergence;
  furthermore, $\lim_{n\to\infty} \psi^n = \psi^0$ in the sense that for any

149

sequence $\{x^n\}$ converging to x^0, $\psi^n(x^n)$ converges weakly to $\psi^0(x^0)$;

- there exists a distribution F^0 on $X^0 = X_1 \times X_2 \times \ldots$ such that the marginal distributions of F^n converge to the marginal distributions of F^0.

Our interest is first with the limiting "equilibrium" represented by F^0. The independence of the strategies used by the players implies that for each n

$$F^n = \times_{i=1}^n F_i^n$$

so in the limit we have

$$F^0 = \times_{i=1}^\infty F_i^0,$$

where we can interpret the marginal distribution F_i^0 as the distribution of player i's mixed strategy. Let $(\Omega, \mathcal{B}(\Omega), P)$ be a probability measure space and for each i let x_i be a random variable defined on $(\Omega, \mathcal{B}(\Omega), P)$ with values in X_i and with marginal distribution F_i^0. Similarly, let y be the random variable on $(\Omega, \mathcal{B}(\Omega), P)$ with values in S and having a distribution given by $\psi^0 \circ F^0$. Then define the random variable y_i to be the expectation of the state y conditional on player i's mixed strategy x_i:

$$y_i = E[y|x_i]$$

and normalize the random variables y_i by putting

$$\bar{y}_i = \frac{y_i}{E[(y_i)^2]}$$

so that $E[(\bar{y}_i)^2] = 1$ and $E[y_i] = E[y]$. Without loss of generality we can normalize y so that $E[y] = 0$ in what follows so that $E[y_i] = 0$ for each i.

Now, it is important for what we are going to do that each of the random variables y_i be distinct. For this to be true, the random variables must be non-degenerate. There are two ways that this may happen. First, if x_i is degenerate then, of course, y_i will be degenerate too. So we must assume that x_i is not degenerate. However, even if x_i is non-degenerate it may still be the case that $y_i = 0$ if x_i does not influence y. However, since we want to prove that x_i has no influence on y, there is no loss of generality in assuming that this case does not arise. Equivalently, disregard the agents for whom this is true. So the critical assumption is that x_i is non-degenerate, i.e. not a pure strategy.

It is easy to see why pure strategies need to be ruled out. Suppose that

$$X_i = \{0, 1\}, \forall i,$$

$$S = \{0, 1\},$$

$$\psi^0(x) = \max_i\{x_i\}, \forall x \in X^\infty$$

and

$$v_i^0(s) = -sM$$

for some large number M. Then it will be easy to support the choice of $x_i^* = 0$ for all i by choosing M sufficiently large. Any deviation from $x_i^* = 0$ by a single player will subject the player to a large punishment that offsets any short-run gain. Despite the fact that there is an unboundedly large number of players, each player regards himself as pivotal and it is this perception that supports the choice of $x_i^* = 0$ as an equilibrium.

Note that even a small amount of uncertainty will upset this equilibrium. For example, suppose that we appeal to the "trembling hand" argument of Selten (1975) to test the robustness of this equilibrium. We introduce a small "tremble" by requiring each agent to place a probability weight of at least $\varepsilon > 0$ on each pure strategy. However small ε is, the number of agents choosing $x_i = 1$ will be infinite with probability one. To make each player pivotal in this way requires each player to be standing on the edge of a precipice so that a small amount of uncertainty will push some of them over. Likewise, if players choose a mixed strategy, then $\max\{x_i\} = 1$ with probability one so again the action of an individual player has no effect.

Note also that in a anonymous game it is only the distribution of the players' actions that counts and the effect of the "trembling hand" disappears in the limit. The fraction of agents choosing each strategy will be almost surely constant by the strong law of large numbers. So the uncertainty introduced by the "trembling hand" would not have been sufficient to produce the desired result in the preceding section. However, it is sufficient in what follows. I assume therefore that for some $\varepsilon > 0$ and all i the probability placed on each strategy by F_i^0 is at least ε:

$$P[x_i = \xi] \geq \varepsilon, \forall \xi \in X_i.$$

Since the strategy of player i puts positive probability on each action (pure strategy), there is a well defined expectation of the state conditional on any choice of action by player i. This allows us to see the effect that any choice of action by player i would have on the continuation payoff and determine whether player i is pivotal or not.

Since the random variables x_i are independent, the random variables y_i are also. If we assume that y_i is nondegenerate – i.e. not identically 0 – then it follows that all the elements of $\{\bar{y}_i\}$ are distinct.

Consider the random variables $\{\bar{y}_i\}$ and y as elements of $L^2((\Omega, \mathcal{B}(\Omega), P), S)$, that is, the linear space of square integrable functions from $(\Omega, \mathcal{B}(\Omega), P)$ to S (the mathematical basis for the following is found in Royden, 1998,   p. 245 *et seq.*). With the inner product defined by

$$x \cdot y = \int xy \, dP,$$

L^2 is a Hilbert space and $\{\bar{y}_i\}$ is an orthonormal system, that is, the elements are orthogonal

$$\bar{y}_i \cdot \bar{y}_j = 0 \text{ for all } i \neq j;$$

they are distinct

$$y_i \neq y_j \text{ for all } i \neq j;$$

and they have unit norms

$$\|\bar{y}_i\| \equiv \int (\bar{y}_i)^2 \, dP = 1 \text{ for all } i.$$

Define the Fourier coefficients $\{a_i\}$ by putting

$$a_i = E[y\bar{y}_i]$$

for each i. Then Bessell's Inequality (Royden, 1980, p. 246) tells us that

$$\sum_{i=1}^{\infty} a_i^2 \leq \|y\| = E[y^2] < \infty.$$

In other words, $a_i \to 0$ as $i \to \infty$. This means that for any $\varepsilon > 0$, $|a_i| < \varepsilon$ for all except a finite number of players i. Now a_i measures the impact of x_i on the memory state y. More precisely, a_i measures the correlation between the state y and the conditional expectation of the state y_i. When a_i is small, the action chosen by agent i has little value in predicting the outcome y.

A more general treatment of these problems has been provided by Al-Najjar and Smorodinsky (1998a) and Lehrer and Neeman (1998) in the context of mechanism design problems. Al-Najjar and Smorodinsky (1998b) have extended the earlier results of Green (1980) and Sabourian (1990) to allow for games in which the aggregate outcome is not necessarily an anonymous function of players' actions and where players' strategies may depend non-anonymously on signals of other players' actions.

Pivotal players in games

Speaking loosely, the Referee's Theorem tells us that all but a finite number of agents will have little effect on the outcome of the game, so almost every player will be choosing an action that maximizes his payoff in the stage game, independently of what happens in the continuation game. This is a very powerful and general result, but it is important to see what it does and does not mean. The following example will be useful.

Consider the following two-stage game. There is a large but finite number of sellers S and a large but finite number of buyers $B > S$. Every seller has one unit of an indivisible good, whose value to the seller is zero, and every buyer wants to purchase one unit of the good, whose value to the buyer is one. All agents have quasi-linear utility functions. In the first stage of the game, the buyers and sellers are randomly matched and the seller makes a proposal to the buyer (unmatched buyers must remain passive). The seller can offer one of two prices $0 < p_L < p_H < 1$. The buyer accepts or rejects the offer. If the offer is accepted, the trade is carried out at the proposed price; the buyer gets a payoff of $1 - p$ and the seller gets a payoff of p. The agents who have traded leave the game and take no further part. The rest of the players, whether they were matched or not, proceed to the second stage of the game. At the second stage, the matching of the remaining buyers and sellers and the prices at which the goods are exchanged between each pair are determined by an exogenous mechanism. Again, if a buyer and seller trade the good at the price p, the buyer's payoff is $1 - p$ and the seller's payoff is p. Agents who do not trade get 0.

The mechanism that comes into play at the second stage is, of course, intended to represent the continuation of the game without forcing us to analyze a (potentially) infinite-horizon game. By choosing an appropriate mechanism at the second stage, we can easily manipulate the agents' pay-offs in any way we like. Suppose, for example, that we wanted the goods to trade at the price p_L. If a seller demands a price p_H then the buyer rejects and next period gets the good at a price of zero. If the seller demands p_L and the buyer rejects, then the buyer gets the good in the next period for a price of one. In the same way, we could support any mixture of high and low prices by appropriately punishing individual buyers and sellers for their deviations at the first stage. It does not matter how many agents there are in the game, each agent perceives that his actions are going to have a marked effect on the future of the game. In what ways does this example violate the conditions of the Referee's Theorem?

First of all, we have considered only pure strategies, whereas the Referee's Theorem requires us to have completely mixed strategies. The example is easily adapted to allow for mixtures by introducing a "trembling hand." Suppose that with probability ε the price offered is the opposite of the one chosen by the seller. For $\varepsilon > 0$ small enough, this will have no effect on the equilibrium described above. If the "trembling hand" forces the seller to offer the wrong price, he will be punished at the second date, but this will not alter his best response because the probability of punishment is small and exogenous. Similarly, if there is a small probability that the buyer will accept when he should reject or reject when he should accept, that will not change the seller's best response if the probability of the "tremble" is sufficiently small. So the absence of mixed strategies does not by itself explain the existence of multiple equilibria here.

The second point to note is that the space of outcomes from the first stage of the game includes, for each pair consisting of a buyer and a seller, the price offered and the response. The dimension of the memory space required to describe this outcome is proportional to the number of agents. As the number of agents increases, the dimension of the memory space increases. With more buyers and sellers, there are more goods to trade, more prices to choose, and more payoffs to determine. In the framework used to describe the Referee's Theorem, there is a fixed memory space. As the number of agents increases, the dimension of the space of action profiles increases, but the range of the function that maps action profiles into memory states or outcomes remains the same. So a larger and larger action space is being mapped into a fixed memory space. To do this in a reasonably orderly way, one has to ignore most of the information in the larger space, that is, most of the components of the action profile do not matter very much in determining the outcome.

In a public good provision problem, the outcome that agents care about, the provision of the public good, does not change as the number of agents increases. So it is natural to work with a fixed outcome space. This is not true in a market with private goods, where the dimension of the allocation increases with the number of agents. In the bargaining game above, two things are happening as the number of buyers and sellers increases. First, the dimension of the memory space increases, allowing the actions of more agents to be recorded in the memory state. Secondly, the part of the memory state that a single agent cares about is

Strategic foundations of general equilibrium

getting smaller relative to the outcome or memory state. A typical buyer, for example, does not care about the entire allocation; he cares only about getting one unit of the good for himself and the price he has to pay for it. An individual agent's action has little effect on the outcome of the first stage, in the sense that his trade and the corresponding price are a negligible part of the resulting description in the memory state; but the agent's action has a big effect on his payoff in the continuation game. This is why the seller does not maximize his short-term payoff in the example.

To rule out this kind of equilibrium, in which a seller's first-stage action has a large effect on his second-stage payoff, it is not enough to hold the memory space constant as the number of agents increases. One could always achieve the same effect by assuming the memory space S is so large that it accommodates a complete description of the first-stage outcome for any number of players. So in addition one needs to assume that S is not "too large" and that in turn requires some structure in terms of the continuity properties of the payoffs v_i^0 and the topology on S. One needs both the assumption that a single agent's action has a small effect on s and the assumption that a small change in s has a small effect on v_i^0. The second assumption is violated in the example, because the action of the seller has a small effect on the state but a large effect on v_i^0. To rule this out, we could assume that the payoff functions $\{v_i^0\}$ are in some sense equi-continuous. This again is a form of anonymity, a restriction on the extent to which individual actions can be remembered and used to condition the future payoffs of individual agents. In the end we are assuming that an agent's future payoff is dependent on an aggregate state which the agent's current action can only effect marginally.

What this example makes clear is that, even in a non-anonymous game, some form of the anonymity assumption is required.

CHAPTER 4

BOUNDED RATIONALITY

In chapter 3, we appealed to a variety of notions of bounded rationality and simplicity to try to justify the special assumptions needed for the competitive limit theorem in chapter 2. These included the Markov property of equilibria used to characterize the equilibria of finite economies and the Continuity Principle imposed on the competitive sequences of equilibria.

If we take the idea of bounded rationality seriously, however, the complexity of these games is still very demanding. Furthermore, the assumption that the agents know not only their own equilibrium strategies but those of the other agents, is very demanding. Where do they get this information? Sometimes the common knowledge of equilibrium strategies is interpreted as the outcome of a process of introspective reasoning (Binmore, 1990, calls this *eductive* reasoning). Sometimes it is treated as the outcome of a process of learning by trial and error. Clearly, the eductive approach does not reduce the computational ability required of the agents. The trial-and-error approach may do so. Adaptive, rule-of-thumb behavior is less demanding both informationally and computationally. If it leads to equilibrium behavior, it may provide some support for the notion that boundedly rational individuals can acquire strategies that are close to equilibrium strategies.

In this chapter, I present an example of this kind of rule-of-thumb or adaptive behavior that leads not very bright agents to a competitive equilibrium. There are many examples of rule-of-thumb or adaptive behavior in the economics literature and it is not my intention to review them all here; a few relevant papers are mentioned in section 4.1.

One of the problems with this kind of model of boundedly rational behavior is that there are so many possibilities and so few accepted modeling principles. This is why the charge of "*ad hocery*" is so often and so justifiably aimed at this kind of theorizing. There is no *a priori* defense against these charges: the proof of the pudding is in the eating. If this attempt provides some insight or some surprises, then it may not have been a waste of time.

4.1 Imitation and experimentation

The model that is the focus of this chapter is based on ideas that were first explored in a paper I wrote with Robert Rosenthal. Before describing the model, I begin with a brief summary of the model and results from Gale and Rosenthal (1998, hereafter GR). GR studies the "learning" behavior of boundedly rational agents who play a strategic game repeatedly over time. The broad objective of this line of research is to see whether boundedly rational agents can learn to play the equilibrium strategies of the game. The answer to this question turns out to be complex and subtle. Much of the interest of the paper lies in the complex dynamics that are generated by apparently simple behavioral rules.

The GR model can be seen as an application of bounded rationality to social learning. The process of learning to play this game is "social" in two senses. First, because of strategic interaction through the game, one agent's learning (adaptation) affects the learning of the others. Secondly, agents can learn from each other by imitating the behavior that they observe in the rest of the population.

The social aspect of learning raises a number of well known efficiency issues. One of these is the *free-rider problem* associated with informational externalities (Caplin and Leahy, 1994; Chamley and Gale, 1994). In models of asymmetric information, an agent's actions reveal his private information. Because the agent is concerned only with his own payoff, he ignores the value of this information to other agents. This externality typically leads to inefficient decisions: in equilibrium, either too little information is revealed or it is revealed too slowly.

Another aspect of social learning that has attracted a lot of attention is the phenomenon of *herd behavior*. In some models of herd behavior (for example, Banerjee, 1992; Bikhchandani, Hirshleifer and Welch, 1992), agents ignore their own information and base their decisions on the public information revealed by the actions of their predecessors. This information may be incorrect, in which case the decisions based on it will be inefficient. More importantly, the agents who decide to join the herd are suppressing their own information. Because their actions are independent of their own information, they do not reveal their private information. The result may be that only a small fraction of the information available to the agents as a group ever becomes common knowledge. Even in models where agents never ignore their own information completely, it can be shown that under certain circumstances there is always a positive probability that agents herd on the incorrect choice (Smith and Sorensen, 1996). In models with endogenous timing (Chamley and Gale, 1994; Gul and Lundholm, 1995), the inefficiency of social learning can take the form of delay rather than herd behavior.

The literature on social learning and herd behavior is firmly in the tradition of rational, Bayesian, maximizing behavior (with some exceptions, for example, Ellison and Fudenberg, 1993, 1995). In a model of bounded rationality, there is no explicit decision to be a free rider or to join a herd. The behavior rules of the agents are assigned exogenously. However, free riding and herd behavior do have an anolog in the imitative behavior that is crucial to the dynamics of the GR model.

The GR model focuses on two types of behavior, imitation and experimentation. Imititators copy what they see other agents doing. Experimenters try new strategies randomly and persist with the strategies that do best. While a sensible agent might engage in both experimentation and imitation, GR simplifies by assuming that each agent specializes in exactly one of these activities. In a further simplification, GR assumes that there is only one experimenter and that the rest of the agents are imitators.

There is a large literature dealing with optimal experimentation. Some, such as Banks and Sundaram (1992) and Bolton and Harris (1999), are models of rational learning, rather than rule-of-thumb learning, and they assume that the underlying environment is stationary. Others, such as Aghion, Bolton and Harris (1991), are closer in spirit to the random experimenter in the GR model. The motivation given by GR for assuming random search is that agents have very little information about the environment in which they are operating and have very limited ability to process the information they do have. In that situation, the least demanding strategy is to search randomly. The fact that search is random turns out to have important implications for the dynamics of the model, as we shall see.

Another important feature of the model is that the search for a better strategy goes on indefinitely. In most models of learning, there is a single fixed parameter that agents try to estimate. As time passes, the agents' beliefs converge to the true value of this parameter, their estimates become insensitive to new information, and experimentation dies out. This is true of the literature on learning in games, for example, including models of fictitious play and Bayesian learning (Fudenberg and Kreps, 1993; Jordan, 1993; Kalai and Lehrer, 1993a, 1993b; Krishna and Sjostrom, 1995; Marimon, 1995; Benaim and Hirsch, 1996). The GR model, by contrast, assumes that experimentation continues indefinitely.

The interest in the case of permanent experimentation comes from the observation that we live in a non-stationary environment. When the environment is constantly changing, one can never assume that one is close to the equilibrium or that experimentation can stop. Models of fictitious play, Bayesian learning, and adaptive learning assume both a stationary environment and that agents place less and less weight on recent experience as time passes. Such increasing inertia is essential to guarantee convergence. It makes sense in a stationary environment, where individual behavior can in principle converge to an equilibrium and beliefs can converge to the truth. In a world that is constantly changing, agents have no reason to assume that they have reached a permanent state of equilibrium. Consequently, they do have reason to continue to experiment and to give significant weight to recent experience. Although GR studies a stationary environment in order to obtain clean and transparent results, the model is motivated by the assumption that agents always have something to learn.

In each period, the imitators observe their own actions and the actions of the other agents. Then they adjust their actions a constant fraction λ of the distance between their previous actions and the average action of the other agents. Since it is only the average of the imitators' actions that matters and their decision rule is linear, there is no loss of generality in replacing them with a representative agent.

At each date $t = 1, 2, \ldots$ the agents play a symmetric normal-form game. They are all assumed to have the same payoff function, but only the experimenter makes use of the payoff to update his action. If q is the action chosen by the experimenter and $\bar{q}$ is the average action of the imitators, then the experimenter's payoff is

$$-(q - B\bar{q})^2,$$

B is the slope of each player's best-response line. When $B < 0$, agents' actions are strategic substitutes, as in the standard Cournot model; when $B > 0$, actions are strategic complements. When $B \neq 1$, the game has a unique symmetric equilibrium, in which all agents choose $q = 0$.

Clearly, if the imitators choose $\bar{q}$, the best response is $B\bar{q}$. Because of the quadratic form of the payoff function, a strategy is better for the experimenter if and only if it is closer to the best response $B\bar{q}$ than his current strategy q. The experimenter searches randomly for a better strategy. If the experimenter chose a strategy q_{t-1} last period, then he "tests" a new strategy that is uniformly distributed on the interval $[q_{t-1} - 1, q_{t-1} + 1]$. Note that this interval is centered on last period's action and that its size does not change over time. If the randomly drawn strategy falls in the better-response set then he adopts it as q_t. Otherwise, he puts $q_t = q_{t-1}$.

Denote by X_t the experimenter's action at t and by Y_t the average of the imitators' actions at t. Then, under the behavioral rules specified above, for any initial condition (x_0, y_0) these behavioral rules define a Markov chain $\{(X_t, Y_t)\}$ having state space $\mathbf{R}^2$.

This model has a number of interesting dynamic properties:

- First, assuming $B < 1$, it is *stable in the large*. This means that from any initial state (x_0, y_0) the chain converges with probability one to a compact neighborhood of the origin.
- Secondly, for the case of strategic substitutes (B negative and sufficiently large in absolute value) the symmetric equilibrium is *unstable in the small*. This means that for any sufficiently small neighborhood of the origin and any initial condition (x_0, y_0) in that neighborhood ($x_0 \neq 0$), the chain leaves the neighborhood with probability one.
- Finally, for the case of strategic substitutes (B negative and sufficiently large in absolute value), it is *not too unstable*. This means that, for any neighborhood of the equilibrium, however small, the probability of the chain being in the given neighborhood at date t converges to one as t approaches ∞.

At the macroscopic level, stability in the large tells us that these adaptive rules do work, by bringing the agents' actions to a compact neighborhood of the equilibrium where they are approximately optimal. On the other hand, at the microscopic level, instability in the small tells us that the agents can never learn the equilibrium strategies exactly. Their actions fluctuate permanently around the equilibrium levels. How large these fluctuations are depends on the parameters λ and B and the size of the search window (here normalized to two).

The third result is puzzling, since it appears to contradict the second. The two results can be reconciled, but the explanation depends on another feature of the model, namely, that the chain $\{(X_t, Y_t)\}$ is *null recurrent*.

Although the chain leaves sufficiently small neighborhoods of the origin with probability one, the expected time this takes is infinite. The reason is that for states (x, y) very close to the origin the better-response set is very small. It is hard to find a better response and, as a result, the chain changes very slowly. If an econometrician looked at the cross-sectional frequency distribution of a set of sample paths, he might conclude that the process was converging. This is a result of the fact that almost every path occasionally comes close to the origin and then takes a very long time to get away. If the same observer looked at a single sample path, he might come to a very different conclusion.

Null recurrence is a strange property: it seems to lie between convergence and instability. It depends on the fact that close to the equilibrium nothing much happens most of the time, although when something does happen the result is "unstable." To test the robustness of the null recurrence result, GR studies a version of the game with small random perturbations to the payoffs. The payoff function of the experimenter in the perturbed game is

$$-(q_t - B\overline{q}_t - \varepsilon_t)^2$$

for every t, where $\{\varepsilon_t\}$ is an i.i.d. sequence that takes the values ε and $-\varepsilon$ with probability $1/2$ each. The shock ε_t simply shifts the best-response function up or down by a small amount. For small values of ε the behavior of the resulting chain is similar to that of the unperturbed chain. Stability in the large and instability in the small continue to hold in the perturbed model, but the not-too-unstable result changes. The long-run behavior of the chain is described by a non-degenerate invariant probability measure and the probability distribution of states at date t converges to the invariant distribution as $t \to \infty$.

Two properties of the model are crucial for these results: the presence of strategic substitutes and the non-vanishing size of the search window. To get a better sense of the importance of strategic substitutes, GR also studies the (unperturbed) model under the assumption that the game exhibits strategic complements. More precisely, they assume that $0 < B < 1$, so the strategic complements are "not too strong." Under this assumption the symmetric equilibrium is shown to be stable in a strong sense: for any initial condition (x_0, y_0) the chain converges to the origin with probability one.

To examine the role of the non-vanishing window size, GR extends the base-case model to allow for exogenously shrinking search windows. Formally, it assumes that the experimenter chooses a strategy randomly from the interval $[x_{t-1} - d_t, x_{t-1} + d_t]$, where $d_t > 0$, for every t. Here again GR finds that the equilibrium is stable in the same strong sense when the size of the search window converges to 0 as long as it does not converge too fast. More precisely, if

$$\lim_{t \to \infty} d_t = 0 \text{ and } \lim_{T \to \infty} \sum_{t=1}^{T} d_t = \infty$$

then for any initial condition (x_0, y_0) the chain converges to 0 with probability one. This result holds whenever $B < 1$.

What have we learned from these exercises?

- The first lesson is that the interaction of two simple types of behavioral adaptation can produce *endogenous cycles*. This may turn out to be a useful way of looking at certain kinds of macroeconomic fluctuations.
- A second lesson concerns the roles of *strategic complements and substitutes*. There has been a lot of interest in using models with strategic complements to explain the severity of macroeconomic fluctuations. In such models if individual activity levels are strategic complements, each agent's best response is an increasing function of the activity levels of the others. If an agent increases his activity because of an exogenous shock, the others will increase their actions too. In this way, strategic complementarity magnifies the effect of the inital shock to the economy. One of the interesting features of our model is that strategic substitutes are necessary for local instability, whereas with strategic complements the model is very stable.

- A third lesson is that the cycles in the models with strategic substitutes have a *highly structured complexity* that does not appear in other models in the literature. For example, in simulations we find that the amplitude of these cycles varies over time, sometimes being very damped and then growing again; but these variations are regular in the sense that the average amplitude of successive cycles is positively correlated.
- A fourth lesson concerns the *role of experimentation*. The randomness in the experimenter's behavior is essential to generate the changing relative rates of adaptation (between experimenters and imitators) that drive the dynamics. When the chain is close to the equilibrium, the experimenter rarely finds a better strategy than the one that he is currently using. When the chain is far from the equilibrium, he finds a better strategy relatively frequently. Thus, adaptation is faster or slower for the experimenter depending on the degree of disequilibrium in the system. The imitators, on the other hand, are constantly adjusting their actions toward the average action (hence, on average, toward the experimenter's action) at a constant proportionate rate. This means that the relative speeds of adjustment for experimenter and imitators vary, depending on the distance from equilibrium; and that explains how the model can be stable in the large but unstable in the small. It also accounts for the fact that the system can spend long periods close to the equilibrium, then cycle away in an increasing orbit for a long period, and then approach the equilibrium again.

In the rest of this chapter, I present a simple model of boundedly rational behavior in the context of a market for a single good. The essential idea is to assume that agents search at random for a better strategy, where a strategy is a limit price at which the agent is willing to trade the good. The motivation for random search is the same as in the GR paper: in the first place, if agents knew exactly where to look for a better strategy, they would not be learning at all; secondly, boundedly rational agents cannot master the computational complexity of Bayesian learning. So, we are left with the assumption that they search randomly for better strategies. In this version of the model, there is no role for imitative behavior, though imitative behavior can easily be introduced.

4.2 A behavioral model of competition

The market

There is a single indivisible commodity, called "the good," that can be exchanged in integer amounts and there is a divisible numeraire commodity, called "money." Traders are divided into buyers and sellers. There are N sellers indexed by $i = 1, ..., N$ and N buyers indexed by $j = 1, ..., N$. There is no loss of generality in assuming equal numbers of buyers and sellers, since an agent with an extreme valuation is effectively not a participant in the market.

Preferences are quasi-linear and each agent wants to buy or sell at most one unit of the good. This means that each agents' preferences can be parameterized in terms of their valuation of one unit of the good. The valuation of seller i is denoted by u_i and the valuation of buyer j is denoted by v_j. If a seller i has x_i units of the good and m_i units of money, his utility is

$$U_i(x_i, m_i) = u_i x_i + m_i.$$

Similarly, the utility of a buyer with y_j of the good and m_j units of money is

$$U_j(y_j, m_j) = v_j y_j + m_j.$$

In practice, the quasi-linearity of the utility function allows us to normalize initial holdings of the good and money to zero and henceforth conduct the analysis in terms of surplus or "gains from trade." (For analytical simplicity we ignore the non-negativity constraints on quantities of the good and money.) If seller i exchanges one unit of the good for p units of money, his surplus is $p - u_i$. Similarly, if buyer j obtains one unit of the good for p

Bounded rationality

units of money, his gain from trade is $v_j - p$. In this notation, we can put

$$U_i(-x_i, p) = (p - u_i)x_i$$

and

$$U_j(y_j, -p) = (v_j - p)y_j,$$

where $x_i, y_j \in \{0, 1\}$.

The primitive data of the market, then, are the size of the market, N, and the valuations $u = (u_1, \ldots, u_N)$ and $v = (v_1, \ldots, v_N)$ of the sellers and buyers, respectively. The agents are ordered so that $0 < u_1 < u_2 < \ldots < u_N$ and $v_1 > v_2 > \ldots > v_N > 0$. We also assume that no buyer and no seller have the same valuation:

$$u_i \neq v_j, \forall i, j = 1, \ldots, N.$$

The assumption that no two agents have the same valuation simply rules out inconvenient ties. The assumption is satisfied generically in the sense that if the market data (N, u, v) were chosen at random, the probability of violating these assumptions would be zero.

Market-clearing prices

For any market data, (N, u, v), we have to distinguish four possible configurations of valuations. The *marginal seller* (resp. *marginal buyer*) is the highest valuation seller (resp. lowest valuation buyer) who gets to trade in a competitive equilibrium. The index of the marginal agent, which is the same for sellers and for buyers, of course, is denoted by m and defined by the conditions that

$$u_m < v_m \text{ and } u_{m+1} > v_{m+1}.$$

The sellers $i = 1, \ldots, m$ (resp. buyers $j = 1, \ldots, m$) who trade in a competitive equilibrium are called *inframarginal*.

Because of the discreteness of demand and supply (each agent wants to trade zero or one units), there exists a nondegenerate interval of market-clearing prices that equate demand and supply. For any market data (N, u, v), exactly

167

one of the following four configurations is (generically) possible:

$$
\begin{array}{ll}
(A - B) & u_m < v_{m+1} < u_{m+1} < v_m \\
(A' - B') & v_{m+1} < u_m < v_m < u_{m+1} \\
(A' - B) & v_{m+1} < u_m < u_{m+1} < v_m \\
(A - B') & u_m < v_{m+1} < v_m < u_{m+1}.
\end{array}
$$

In each case, there is a different set of market-clearing prices. Only the first m agents on each side of the market can trade so the price must be less than or equal to u_{m+1} to exclude seller $m + 1$ and greater than or equal to v_{m+1} to exclude buyer $m + 1$. In Case $(A - B)$, for any price in this interval, precisely the first m agents on each side of the market want to trade, so the set of market-clearing prices is the interval $[v_{m+1}, u_{m+1}]$. By similar reasoning, we can calculate the interval of market-clearing prices in each case:

$$
\begin{array}{ll}
(A - B) & [v_{m+1}, u_{m+1}] \\
(A' - B') & [u_m, v_m] \\
(A' - B) & [u_m, u_{m+1}] \\
(A - B') & [v_{m+1}, v_m].
\end{array}
$$

The interval of market-clearing prices can be more compactly denoted by $[c_0, c_1]$, where $c_0 = \max\{u_m, v_{m+1}\}$ and $c_1 = \min\{u_{m+1}, v_m\}$. A situation in which all inframarginal agents trade at a single price belonging to this interval will be referred to as a *perfectly competitive outcome*.

The market game

The trading process is represented by a normal-form stage game in which agents submit limit orders to a profit-maximizing market-maker, who then arranges trades between pairs of buyers and sellers.

The agents' strategies are the limit prices at which they are willing to trade one unit. Each seller i chooses an asking price a_i and each buyer j chooses a *bid price* b_j. The asking price a_i signifies that the seller is willing to supply a single unit of the good at any price equal to a_i or higher. Similarly, the bid price b_j signifies that the buyer is willing to purchase one unit of the good at any price up to and including b_j.

For simplicity, the agents' strategies are restricted to a compact interval. Seller i's asking price a_i is restricted to be at least as great as his private valuation u_i and no greater than some large finite number M. By restricting the sellers' strategies in this way, we are assuming that no agent is so unintelligent as to choose a dominated strategy. This seems reasonable and is not particularly important in what follows. Buyer j's bid price b_j is restricted to be non-negative and no greater than his valuation v_j. Let

$$\mathbf{X} = \{(a, b) \in \mathbf{R}_+^N \times \mathbf{R}_+^N \mid u_i \le a_i \le M, 0 \le b_j \le v_j, \forall i, j\}$$

denote the set of strategy profiles for the buyers and sellers and denote a typical strategy profile by $x = (a, b)$ where $a = (a_1, \ldots, a_N)$ and $b = (b_1, \ldots, b_N)$ are the strategy profiles for sellers and buyers, respectively.

Suppose that the agents submit the limit orders (a, b). The market-maker arranges matching trades to maximize his profits. By submitting limit orders, the agents have committed themselves to trading at any price that does not violate their limits. In order to maximize his profit, the market-maker will execute the trades at the limit prices, that is, he will pay seller i the tendered ask price a_i and charge buyer j the tendered bid price b_j. Denote seller i's trade by ξ_i, where $\xi_i = 0$ means that i does not trade and $\xi_i = 1$ means that i sells one unit, and denote buyer j's trade by ζ_j, where $\zeta_j = 0$ means that j does not trade and $\zeta_j = 1$ means that j buys one unit. Then the market maker's profit will be

$$\Pi(\xi, \zeta, a, b) = \left\{ \sum_{j=1}^N b_j \zeta_j - \sum_{i=1}^N a_i \xi_i \right\},$$

where $\xi = (\xi_1, \ldots, \xi_N)$ and $\zeta = (\zeta_1, \ldots, \zeta_N)$. Formally, the market-maker's problem is to choose $(\xi, \zeta) \in \{0, 1\}^{2N}$ to solve

$$\Pi^*(a, b) = \max_{(\xi, \zeta)} \Pi(\xi, \zeta, a, b)$$

subject to the usual feasibility constraint

$$\sum_{j=1}^{N} \zeta_j \leq \sum_{i=1}^{N} \xi_i.$$

A generic profile $(a, b) \in \mathbf{X}$ is one in which no two agents, whether both buyers or both sellers or one buyer and one seller, choose the same limit price. For any generic profile (a, b), there is a unique profit-maximizing assignment of trades (ξ, ζ) defined by the conditions that $\sum_{i=1}^{N} \xi_i = \sum_{j=1}^{N} \zeta_j$, $\xi_{i_0} > \xi_{i_1}$ implies that $a_{i_0} < a_{i_1}$, $\zeta_{j_0} > \zeta_{j_1}$ implies that $b_{j_0} > b_{j_1}$, and $\xi_i = \zeta_j = 1$ implies that $a_i < b_j$. Hence, for any generic profile (a, b) in $\mathbf{X}$, this trading mechanism defines a unique payoff $\pi_i^s(a, b)$ for seller i and $\pi_j^b(a, b)$ for buyer j. (When the context makes it clear whether the trader is a buyer or seller, the superscripts s and b are dispensed with.)

To ensure a unique outcome (ξ, ζ) for each strategy profile (a, b), I assume that where the market-maker is indifferent between two offers, bids or asks, he randomizes between the agents with equal probabilities. Where he is indifferent between executing a trade and not executing it, I assume that he executes it. These assumptions simply serve to define a unique trading mechanism and are not crucial in what follows.

In what follows, there is no loss of generality in restricting the discussion to generic profiles. The reason is that buyers and sellers choose their strategies randomly, so the probability of observing a non-generic profile is zero. This completes the definition of the normal-form game $\Gamma = (N, \mathbf{X}, \pi)$.

Several aspects of this matching and trading procedure are noteworthy:

- the market-maker executes the trades at the bid and ask prices, keeping the difference as his profit,
- the procedure maximizes the volume of trade, subject to the constraint that each trade be voluntary,
- the procedure is efficient in the sense that trades go to the buyers who offer the most and the sellers who demand the least.

The fact that there is a maximizing agent at the center of the market is significant. For example, if we had adopted an alternative approach, matching pairs of buyers and sellers in each period and letting them bargain over the terms of trade, none of the three features above would necessarily hold. The use of a market-maker thus introduces by design an element of efficiency that is not characteristic of all trading mechanisms.

The second and third properties are implications of the market-maker's maximizing behavior. Since the market-maker can choose the price at which to execute a trade, subject to the limits of the traders' orders, he will want to arrange as many trades as possible as long as he makes a non-negative profit on each one. Similarly, profit maximization implies that the buyers with the highest bids and the sellers with the lowest asks will get to trade. A more decentralized procedure, such as random matching and bargaining, would not necessarily have these very useful properties.

Behavioral rules

In this section, I describe the behavior of the individual traders. Rather than assigning beliefs to agents and assuming that each agent maximizes his long-run payoff relative to these beliefs, I define behavioral rules directly for the agents. The motivation for this approach is the realization that maximization is too demanding in many contexts. It is interesting to see whether "simpler" behavioral rules can lead agents to use equilibrium strategies. Of course, the environment we are studying is itself very simple, a reflection of our own bounded rationality. So in order to capture the notion that agents have limited ability to understand complex systems, that is, agents are simple relative to their environment, we shall have to assume that they are very stupid indeed.

There are many ways of specifying boundedly rational behavior – as was pointed out in section 4.1, this is one of the weaknesses of the approach – and the behavioral rules specified here are not the only ones that might recommend themselves for study. But they are simple and provide a vehicle for discussing a number of interesting issues. The basic idea is that agents of very limited intelligence search at random for good strategies and abandon their current strategies when they encounter a better one. Random search presumes no knowledge of the environment (the structure of the model) apart from the appropriate strategy set. It requires no memory apart from the knowledge of the agent's current strategy. And it requires no foresight – in fact, it assumes complete myopia on the part of the agents. This is about the simplest kind of behavior one could imagine and for that reason it is a natural place to start.

Before getting down to the details of the search procedure, one aspect deserves some discussion. The idea of random search employed here involves choice (between the current strategy and a randomly selected alternative) and that implies that the agent "knows" the payoff from both strategies. How does the agent learn the payoffs? The eductive approach assumes that the agent knows the payoff functions, so that he can calculate the payoffs from any strategy; but then there is nothing to stop him from calculating the best response rather than searching at random. I do not want to assume that the agent knows the payoff function because it assumes a degree of sophistication and "computing power" that is incompatible with random search.

A less demanding interpretation is that the agent learns the payoff by experimenting with different strategies. Imagine that every so often a single agent gets a chance to search for a better strategy. This involves selecting a strategy at random, trying it for a short period of time, noting the payoff flow, comparing that flow to the flow from the previous strategy and then choosing between the new and the previous strategy based on the payoff comparison. While all this is going on, the other agents continue to use the same strategy. This procedure does not demand too much "brain power" on the part of the agent, but it is rather cumbersome to describe and makes the dynamics rather complicated. So instead I assume that agents can conduct "virtual experiments," in which they discover the payoff to a new strategy instantaneously and adopt it only if the payoff is greater than or equal to that of their current strategies. This is an approximation to a real experiment with a new strategy, which lasts for a short but finite interval. Nothing of importance seems to hang on this simplification.

Another point to note about the search procedure is that only one agent at a time is allowed to search. If two or more agents were experimenting at the same time, the result of their experiments with new strategies might be misleading. For example, a strategy that appeared to be better for seller i when buyer j was experimenting with a new strategy might actually turn out to be worse when buyer j decides to return to his previous strategy. These kinds of errors are ruled out by assuming that only one agent at a time can experiment with a new strategy. If search is a costly and hence discrete event, the probability of two agents searching at the same time is likely to be small. Here we take the probability to the limit and assume it is zero. This does not mean that search is slow, since the time scale is arbitrary. However, it does mean that there is an element of inertia in the system. A related assumption of inertia is found in the evolutionary game literature, where it is sometimes assumed that only a fraction of a population is allowed to change strategies in any period (for example, Kandori, Mailath and Rob, 1993; Young, 1993).

Trade takes place at a sequence of dates $t = 1, 2, \ldots$ At each date, one of the $2N$ agents is chosen at random to alter his strategy. If seller i is chosen, he randomly chooses a new strategy from his strategy set X_i. If this price gives a (weakly) higher payoff than his current ask price, he adopts the new price as his strategy. If not, he retains his previous strategy. Similarly, if a buyer j is chosen he randomly chooses a new strategy from his strategy set X_j. If this price gives a (weakly) higher payoff, he adopts the new bid price as his strategy. Otherwise, he retains the existing strategy.

These simple rules define a stochastic process. The state vector at any date is the current profile of limit order strategies. Suppose that $x = (a, b)$ is the state at date $t - 1$ and

$x' = (a', b')$ is the state at the next date t. If seller i is chosen to move at date t, a new ask price ω_i is chosen according to the uniform distribution on $[u_i, M]$. Then $b' = b$ and

$$a' = \begin{cases} (\omega_i, a_{-i}) & \text{if } \pi_i((\omega_i, a_{-i}), b) \geq \pi_i(a, b) \\ a & \text{if } \pi_i((\omega_i, a_{-i}), b) < \pi_i(a, b). \end{cases}$$

Similarly, if buyer j is chosen to move at date t, then ω_j is drawn from a uniform distribution on $[0, v_j]$ and the new state satisfies $a' = a$ and

$$b' = \begin{cases} (\omega_j, b_{-j}) & \text{if } \pi_j(a, (\omega_j, b_{-j})) \geq \pi_j(a, b) \\ b & \text{if } \pi_j(a, (\omega_j, b_{-i})) < \pi_j(a, b). \end{cases}$$

Note that in the event that agents are indifferent between the new strategy and the existing strategy, they switch to the new. In particular, if the initial state $x = (a, b)$ is one in which seller i cannot trade, so that $\pi_i(a, b) = 0$, then any price in X_i is weakly preferable and so the new price is drawn randomly from X_i. This assumption is important because it eliminates the possibility of getting stuck in situations where no trade is possible. For example, suppose that $a_i = M$ for every seller i and $b_j = 0$ for every buyer j. This is a possible state and one in which no trade is possible. Moreover, no deviation by any single buyer or seller will make trade possible. So if agents switch only to *strictly* better strategies, the original position will be a rest point for the system and there is no possibility of convergence to a competitive outcome. For this reason, it is essential to allow agents to switch to *weakly* better strategies.

The Markov chain $\{X_t\}$

(The material in this subsection is rather technical and the reader who is not interested in this detail may wish to skip ahead to section 3.3, noting only Lemma 1 and its corollary, which are used in the sequel.)

A stochastic process is a family $\{X_t\}$ of random elements, defined on an underlying probability space $(\Omega, \mathcal{F}, P)$. A *Markov chain* $\{X_t\}$ is a particular type of stochastic process, with a countable parameter set $T = \{1, 2, \ldots\}$, a sequence of random elements X_t taking values in the state space **X**, and a probability distribution P_x that satisfies:

$$P_x(X_t \in A|X_{t_1} = x_{t_1}, \ldots, X_{t_k} = x_{t_k}) = P_x(X_t \in A|X_{t_k} = x_{t_k})$$

for any initial state x and for any times $t_1 < \ldots < t_k < t$.

The behavioral rules described in the preceding section define a Markov chain. In fact, the evolution of the stochastic process can be represented by a (time-invariant) transition probability $P(x, A)$ which tells us, for any current state x, the probability that the state of the system at the next date belongs to the set A. The purpose of this section is to translate the behavioral rules defined above into a formal definition of the transition probabilty $P(x, A)$.

The set of admissible strategy profiles **X** is endowed with the Borel σ-field $\mathcal{B}(\mathbf{X})$ of measurable sets (the σ-field generated by the open sets of **X**). Using the rules outlined above, for any given initial position, $x = (a, b)$ and any measurable set $A \in \mathcal{B}(\mathbf{X})$, we can define a Markov transition probability $P(x, A)$. For any agent k and any state x, let $B_k(x)$ denote the *better than set*, that is,

$$B_k(x) = \{x'_k|\pi_k(x'_k, x_{-k}) \geq \pi_k(x)\}.$$

Since the agent searches randomly for a better strategy, if he finds a better strategy it will be uniformly distributed on the better than set. Then let $U_k(x, \cdot)$ denote a probability distribution on **X** such that the support of $U_k(x, \cdot)$ is $[B_k(x) \times \{x_{-k}\}]$ and the restriction of $U_k(x, \cdot)$ to the set $[B_k(x) \times \{x_{-k}\}]$ is the uniform distribution. For practical purposes we can think of $U_k(x, \cdot)$ as the uniform distribution on $[B_k(x) \times \{x_{-k}\}]$ but it is important to remember that it is defined for every measurable subset of **X**. Let $D(x, \cdot)$ denote the Dirac distribution concentrated on x and let $\delta_k(x)$ denote the ratio of the diameter of the better response set to the strategy set of agent k:

$$\delta_k(x) = \begin{cases} \text{diam}B_k(x)/(M - u_k) & \text{if } k \text{ is a seller} \\ \text{diam}B_k(x)/v_k & \text{if } k \text{ is a buyer}. \end{cases}$$

Then, conditional on the current state x and agent k being chosen to move, the distribution of the new state is given by

$$G_k(x, \cdot) = \delta_k(x)U_k(x, \cdot) + (1 - \delta_k(x))D(x, \cdot).$$

With probability $\delta_k(x)$ agent k finds a better strategy and, given that he finds a better strategy, his strategy is uniformly distributed on $B_k(x)$; with probability $1 - \delta_k(x)$ he does not find a better strategy and, if he does not find a better strategy, the new state will be the same as the old. Since each of the agents is chosen to move with equal probability, the transition probability can be defined by putting

$$P(x, A) = (2N)^{-1} \sum_{i=1}^{N} G_i(x, A) + (2N)^{-1} \sum_{j=1}^{N} G_j(x, A),$$

for each state x and measurable set A. In other words, we take $G_k(x, A)$ to be the transition probability conditional on k being chosen to search for a better strategy; and then the (unconditional) transition probability $P(x, A)$ is just the expected value of the conditional transition probabilities $\{G_k(x, A)\}$, where the weights $(2N)^{-1}$ are the probabilities of choosing each agent as the experimenter.

If $P : \mathbf{X} \times \mathcal{B}(\mathbf{X}) \to \mathbf{R}_+$ is the transition probability function for a Markov chain then by definition it satisfies the following two conditions:

(1) for each $A \in \mathcal{B}(\mathbf{X})$, $P(\cdot, A)$ is a non-negative, measurable function on $\mathbf{X}$;
(2) for each $x \in \mathbf{X}$, $P(x, \cdot)$ is a probability measure on $\mathcal{B}(\mathbf{X})$.

From the definition of the function P it is clear that property (2) is satisfied. To show that property (1) is satisfied, we need only to note that for any measurable subset $A \subset \mathbf{X}$, the probability $G_k(A, \cdot)$ is a measurable function of x.

For any initial state x, the transition probability $P(x, A)$ defines a Markov chain $\{X_t\}$ on the probability space $(\Omega, \mathcal{F}, P_x)$. In this case, we take the set Ω to be $\mathbf{X}^\infty$, the countable product of copies of $\mathbf{X}$, $\mathcal{F}$ to be the σ-field generated by the cylinder sets $A_1 \times \ldots \times A_t \in \mathcal{B}(\mathbf{X}) \times \ldots \times \mathcal{B}(\mathbf{X})$, and P_x to be the unique extension of the set functions defined inductively on the cylinder sets $A_1 \times \ldots \times A_t$ by the transition kernel P:

176

Bounded rationality

$$P_x^1(x, A_1) = P(x, A_1)$$

$$P^2(A_1 \times A_2) = \int_{A_1} P(x, dy_1)P(y_1, A_2)$$

$$\vdots$$

$$P^n(A_1 \times \ldots \times A_t) = \int_{A_1} P(x, dy_1) \int_{A_2} P(y_1, dy_2) \ldots P(y_{t-1}, A_t).$$

(See Meyn and Tweedie, 1993, section 3.4, for the details of the procedure and a proof.) This Markov chain has the property that for any initial condition x and any cylinder set $A_1 \times \ldots \times A_t$

$$P_x(X_1 \in A_1, \ldots, X_t \in A_t)$$
$$= \int_{A_1} P(x, dy_1) \int_{A_2} P(y_1, dy_2) \ldots P(y_{t-1}, A_t).$$

A stochastic process with finite dimensional distributions satisfying this property for every t is called a *time-homogeneous Markov chain* with transition probability kernel $P(x, A)$ and initial condition x.

There are a couple of technical results that will be used repeatedly in the sequel and which it will be convenient to state here.

For any set $A \in \mathcal{B}(\mathbf{X})$ and initial condition x, let $L(x, A)$ denote the probability that the Markov chain $X = \{X_t\}$ enters the set A at some date t, that is,

$$L(x, A) = P_x[X \in A],$$

where $[X \in A]$ denotes the event $\{\omega | X_t(\omega) \in A, \exists t\}$. Let $Q(x, A)$ denote the probability that it enters A infinitely often, that is,

$$Q(x, A) = P_x[X \in A, \text{ i.o.}],$$

where $[X \in A, \text{ i.o.}]$ denotes the event $\{\omega | X_t(\omega) \in A, \text{ for infinitely many } t\}$. We say that a set $B \in \mathcal{B}(\mathbf{X})$ is *accessible* from a set $A \in \mathcal{B}(\mathbf{X})$ if $L(x, B) > 0$ for every initial condition $x \in A$ and we say that B is *uniformly accessible* from A if there exists a $\delta > 0$ such that

$$\inf_{x \in A} L(x, B) \geq \delta.$$

If B is uniformly accessible from A we write $A \leadsto B$. A set $A \in \mathcal{B}(\mathbf{X})$ is called Harris recurrent if $Q(x, A) = 1$ for any $x \in A$. The next result tells us that if A is uniformly accessible, then the chain visits A infinitely often with probability one. Intuitively, if the probability of going from A^c to A is at least δ then the probability of staying out of A forever must be $(1 - \delta)^\infty = 0$. The second part tells us that if B is uniformly accessible from A then if A is visited infinitely often, so is B.

Lemma 1 *(i) For any $A \in \mathcal{B}(\mathbf{X})$, if $\mathbf{X} \leadsto A$ then A is Harris recurrent; in fact, $Q(x, A) = 1$ for any $x \in \mathbf{X}$; (ii) For any sets $A, B \in \mathcal{B}(\mathbf{X})$, if $A \leadsto B$ then $\{X \in A \text{ i.o.}\} \subset \{X \in B \text{ i.o.}\}$ a.s.*

(Meyn and Tweedie, 1993, theorem 9.1.3.) A set $A \in \mathcal{B}(\mathbf{X})$ is called *absorbing* if $P(x, A) = 1$ for all $x \in A$. In other words, once in A the system stays there forever with probability one. The next result tells us that if B is absorbing and B is uniformly accessible from a disjoint set A, then the probability of visiting A infinitely often is zero; because once the system enters B it never returns and if it visits A infinitely often it must visit B infinitely often, contradicting the Lemma.

Corollary 2 *For any sets $A, B \in \mathcal{B}(\mathbf{X})$ satisfying $A \cap B = \emptyset$, if B is absorbing and $A \leadsto B$ then $Q(x, A) = 0$ for any x.*

Proof Let E_t be the event $\{X_t \in B, X_s \in A, \exists s > t\}$. Since B is absorbing, $P_x(E_t) = 0$ for all t and since the probability measure P_x is σ-additive, $P_x(\cup_{t=1}^\infty E_t) = 0$. From conclusion (ii) of Lemma 1, $\{X \in A \text{ i.o.}\} \subset \{X \in B \text{ i.o.}\}$, so

$$\{X \in A \text{ i.o.}\} \subset \cup_{t=1}^\infty E_t.$$

Hence, $Q(x, A) = P_x\{X \in A \text{ i.o.}\} = 0$ as required. ∎

We are now ready to study the convergence properties of the Markov chain $\{X_t\}$.

Bounded rationality

4.3 Convergence to competitive prices

Volume-maximizing trade

The main objective is to show that, in some sense, the Markov chain described above converges to a competitive outcome, that is, to a situation in which all trade takes place at competitive prices. The analysis of convergence can be conveniently broken down into two steps. The first step involves showing that, with probability one, the volume of trade is maximized in finite time and, from that point onwards, the volume of trade remains constant. The next step is to show that, asymptotically, all trade takes place at market-clearing prices.

To analyze the volume of trade, we first need some additional notation. For any state $x \in X$ and any measurable set $A \in \mathcal{B}(X)$, define $P^n(x, A)$ to be the probability that the system belongs to A exactly n periods later, given that it started at x, that is, $P^n(x, A) = P_x(X_n \in A)$. Then $P^n(x, A)$ can be defined recursively by putting

$$P^n(x, A) = \int P(x, dy) P^{n-1}(y, A).$$

Let A be the set of (generic) states such that m units of the good are traded whenever the state of the system belongs to A. Let A' denote the subset of A in which it is the inframarginal agents $i = 1, \ldots, m$ and $k = 1, \ldots, m$ who get to trade. Then we show that A' is accessible from any state in X. In mathematical notation this is written $X \rightsquigarrow A'$. Although the proof is rather lengthy, accessibility simply requires one to show that, from any starting point, there is a positive probability (bounded away from zero) that random search will lead the traders to a configuration of strategies (prices) that is consistent with maximal trade.

Lemma 3 $X \rightsquigarrow A'$.

Proof In fact, we can show that for any initial condition x there exists an integer $n > 0$ and a number $\alpha > 0$ such that $P^n(x, A') \geq \alpha$.

First, let $x = (a, b)$ and take the infra-marginal sellers $i = 1, \ldots, m$ and arrange them in decreasing order according to their asking prices. That is, let $\{i_1, \ldots, i_m\}$ be an ordered m-tuple of the first m sellers such that $1 \leq i_h \leq m$ for any h and

$$a_{i_h} > a_{i_{h+1}}, \forall h = 1, \ldots, m - 1.$$

There is a probability $(2N)^{-m}$ that the sellers are chosen to move in precisely this sequence in the periods $t = 1, \ldots, m$.

Suppose that the sellers are chosen in just this sequence to choose new strategies. When seller i_h has a chance to move, he draws a new price according to the uniform distribution from the interval $[u_{i_h}, M]$ and with probability $(\bar{a} - c_0)/(M - u_{i_h})$ the new asking price a'_{i_h} lies in the interval $[c_0, \bar{a})$, where $\bar{a} = (c_0 + c_1)/2$. The probability of this sequence of events is at least

$$(2N)^{-m}\left(\frac{(\bar{a} - c_0)}{(M - u_1)}\right)^m$$

since seller 1 has the smallest probability of picking a price in the interval. According to our behavioral rules, if seller i_h weakly prefers the new price he has chosen, he adopts it. Otherwise, he sticks with the old price.

Notice that once we have gone through the sequence of infra-marginal sellers and determined a new N-tuple of asking prices $a' = (a'_1, \ldots, a'_m, a_{m+1}, \ldots, a_N)$, it must be the case that for each $i = 1, \ldots, m$ either seller i can trade at the new prices (a', b) or $a'_i \in [c_0, \bar{a})$. To see this, note that $a'_i \notin [c_0, \bar{a})$ only if a_i is weakly preferred to the prices in $[c_0, \bar{a})$, that is, i can already trade when he has the opportunity to change his strategy and $a_i > \bar{a}$. Since asking prices are decreasing in this sequence, it follows that all the sellers in $\{i_{h+1}, \ldots, i_m\}$ can trade when their turn to move comes. Since these sellers can already trade, a change in their prices will not affect the ability to trade of seller i.

Now go through an exactly similar argument with the buyers. Arrange the m infra-marginal buyers in order of increasing bid prices. Then the set $\{j_1, \ldots, j_m\}$ satisfies $1 \leq j_h \leq m$ for all h and

$$b_{j_h} < b_{j_{h+1}}, \forall h = 1, \ldots, m - 1.$$

With probability $(2N)^{-m}$ the m buyers are chosen in precisely this order and, when it is buyer j_h's turn to move, with probability $(\bar{a}, c_1]/v_{j_h}$ he chooses a new price in the interval $(\bar{a}, c_1]$. Of course, he picks the new price as his strategy if and only if it is weakly preferred to b_{j_h}, given the choices of the other agents. The probability of this sequence of events is at least

$$(2N)^{-m}\left(\frac{(c_1 - \bar{a})}{v_1}\right)^m$$

since buyer 1 has the smallest probability of choosing a price in the interval $(\bar{a}, c_1]$.

Once we have allowed all the infra-marginal buyers to choose a new strategy, we note that for every buyer $j = 1, \ldots, m$ either $a'_j \in (\bar{a}, c_1]$ or buyer j can trade at the state $x' = (a', b')$. Again, this follows from the fact that if $b'_j \in (\bar{a}, c_1]$ then $b_j < \bar{a}$ and buyer j was able to trade at b_j when he had the opportunity to move. Since all the other buyers were offering higher prices, a change in their prices cannot affect buyer j.

I claim now that all infra-marginal buyers and sellers must trade at (a', b'). The sellers who were able to trade at the original prices can still do so, since changes in the buyers' prices will not affect the sellers' ability to trade. Likewise, buyers who were able to sell at their original prices can still do so. The rest of the infra-marginal sellers $i = 1, \ldots, m$ (resp. buyers $j = 1, \ldots, m$) are charging prices $a'_i \in [c_0, \bar{a})$ (resp. $b'_j \in (\bar{a}, c_1]$). It is clear that all the extra-marginal sellers $i = m + 1, \ldots, N$ (resp. buyers $j = m + 1, \ldots, N$) must charge prices $a_i < c_0$ (resp. $b_j > c_1$), so the market-maker will maximize profits by arranging trades among the rest of the infra-marginal buyers and sellers.

Thus, after $n = 2N$ periods, with probability at least

$$\alpha = (2N)^{-2m}\left(\frac{(\bar{a} - c_0)}{(M - u_1)}\right)^m\left(\frac{(c_1 - \bar{a})}{v_1}\right)^m,$$

$X_n \in A'$. ∎

Since $A' \subset A$, Lemma 3 implies that A is accessible from **X**. Then Lemma 1 implies that from any initial condition x, the system almost certainly reaches a state in which the volume of trade is maximal, in finite time.

Lemma 4 *For any initial state x, X reaches A in finite time with probability one, that is, $L(x, A) = 1$ for any $x \in$* **X**.

In fact, Lemma 1 tells us something stronger, namely that $Q(x, A) = 1$ for any x, but we do not need this result since we can show that the set A is absorbing: once X reaches A it remains there with probability one.

Lemma 5 *The set A is absorbing.*

Proof Suppose that $x = (a, b) \in A$ is a generic initial state and let x' denote the immediately following state along some realization. If the agent who is chosen to move at date 1 is an agent who is already trading, then the same set of agents are trading in the new state x'. This follows because the moving agent will never change his price unless it is (weakly) better for him to do so and this requires that he trade. The identities of the other trading agents are unaffected, because the moving agent is merely moving his price within the trading range.

If the agent who is chosen to move is a non-trading agent, then either his new choice does not fall in the trading range, in which case the set of trading agents is unchanged, or it does fall into the trading range, in which case he replaces one of the trading agents on his side of the market. However, the total number of trading agents cannot be changed. Since we are already at the maximum number of trades, the number of trades could only fall and this will not happen because all the existing trades continue to be profitable. ∎

Bounded rationality

Convergence to a competitive outcome

Now that we have established the inevitability of maximal trade, we can show that the chain converges almost surely to a competitive outcome. The analysis can be restricted to the set A of generic states in which m units of the good are traded. Again, however, this requires us to examine a number of different cases. We characterize these cases in terms of the *bid–ask* spread. First, at any state $x \in A$, define the *marginal ask* $\alpha(x)$ and the *marginal bid* $\beta(x)$ by putting

$$\alpha(x) = a_{i_m} \text{ and } \beta(x) = b_{j_m},$$

where the sellers $i_1, \ldots, i_m, \ldots, i_N$ are ordered by increasing asking prices and the buyers $j_1, \ldots, j_m, \ldots, j_N$ are ordered by decreasing bid prices. The marginal ask is the highest price demanded by a seller that is accepted in state x; similarly, the marginal bid is the lowest price offered by a buyer that is accepted in state x. These are just mth-order statistics for the ask and bid prices, arranged in increasing and decreasing order, respectively. Clearly, $\alpha(x) < \beta(x)$ for any (generic) state $x \in A$.

For any initial state x in A, put

$$(\alpha_t, \beta_t) \equiv (\alpha(X_t), \beta(X_t)), \forall t = 1, 2, \ldots$$

The sequences $\{\alpha_t\}_{t=1}^{\infty}$ and $\{\beta_t\}_{t=1}^{\infty}$ are stochastic processes that have some useful properties. As noted above, $\alpha_t < \beta_t$ for all t with probability one. Furthermore,

$$\alpha_t < u_{m+1} \Longrightarrow \alpha_t \leq \alpha_{t+1}$$

and

$$\beta_t > v_{m+1} \Longrightarrow \beta_t \geq \beta_{t+1}.$$

To see this, consider the position of the sellers when $\alpha_t < u_{m+1}$. Since there are m trading sellers and α_t is the highest accepted asking price, the sellers who manage to trade must be $i = 1, \ldots, m$. At date $t + 1$ either none of these sellers changes his price, in which case $\alpha_{t+1} = \alpha_t$, or one of them is chosen to move and finds a better price, which must be a higher one. This price change either leaves the marginal ask unchanged or raises it, so in either case $\alpha_{t+1} \geq \alpha_t$. The explanation of the second implication is similar. These monotonicity properties are used to prove the following convergence theorem. Let B denote the set of states such that both marginal prices are contained in the competitive interval $[c_0, c_1]$, that is,

$$B = \{x \in A \mid c_0 < \alpha(x) < \beta(x) < c_1\}.$$

Theorem 6 *Suppose that the initial state* $x \in B$. *Then there exists a random variable* X_∞ *such that*

$$\lim_{t \to \infty} \alpha_t = \lim_{t \to \infty} \beta_t = X_\infty \in (c_0, c_1), P_x-a.s.$$

and, for any seller $i = 1, \ldots, m$, $X_{it} \to X_\infty$ *almost surely (resp. for any buyer* $j = 1, \ldots, m$, $X_{jt} \to X_\infty$ *almost surely).*

Proof By the monotonicity properties of $\{\alpha_t\}$ and $\{\beta_t\}$, $\lim_{t \to \infty} \alpha_t$ and $\lim_{t \to \infty} \beta_t$ both exist and are measurable and $\lim_{t \to \infty} \alpha_t \leq \lim_{t \to \infty} \beta_t$. Furthermore, we can show that for any $\varepsilon > 0$ there is a $\delta > 0$ such that $|\alpha_t - \beta_t| > \varepsilon$ implies that with probability at least δ, $|\alpha_{t+1} - \beta_{t+1}| < \varepsilon/2$. To see this, note that with probability $m(2N)^{-1}$ one of the sellers $i = 1, \ldots, m$ is chosen to move and with probability $\varepsilon/2(M - u_i)$ he chooses a price in the interval (α_t, β_t). Then it is clear that the probability that $|\alpha_t - \beta_t| > \varepsilon$ for all t is zero, for any fixed but arbitrary $\varepsilon > 0$. Hence, $\lim_{t \to \infty} \alpha_t = \lim_{t \to \infty} \beta_t = X_\infty \in (c_0, c_1)$ as required.

To show that the prices of the individual buyers and sellers also converge to c, one uses similar arguments. For example, if $|X_{it} - \alpha_t| > \varepsilon$ for all t, for any fixed $\varepsilon > 0$, then we can find a fixed $\delta > 0$ such that with probability δ, $|X_{it+1} - \alpha_{t+1}| < \varepsilon/2$. Hence the probability that $|X_{it} - \alpha_t| > \varepsilon$ for all t and any fixed $\varepsilon > 0$ must be zero, and this, together with the monotonicity of $\{X_{it}\}$ implies that $X_{it} \to X_\infty$ almost surely. The proof for buyers is exactly similar. ∎

This convergence theorem gives us the essential argument for establishing the competitive outcome, for in the limit we have all infra-marginal agents charging the same (random) price X_∞ which belongs to the competitive interval $[c_0, c_1]$. However, the assumption that the initial state is such that both marginal prices belong to the interval

$[c_0, c_1]$ leaves something to be done. How do we know that such a situation will eventually arise? In fact, in some cases, the marginal bid and ask prices may only approach the competitive interval asymptotically. For this reason the competitive convergence theorem takes the following form.

Theorem 7 *For any initial condition x, with probability one, either (i) X reaches B in finite time, in which case Theorem 6 tells us that the chain converges to a competitive outcome, or (ii) X does not reach B in finite time, but α_t and β_t converge to a common limit belonging to the set $\{c_0, c_1\}$.*

Establishing part (ii) turns out to be rather tedious and involves ruling out a number of other possible cases. In each case, the key fact is again the monotonicity of $\{\alpha_t\}$ and $\{\beta_t\}$.

Case 1
The first case to consider is the possibility that the interval $[\alpha_t, \beta_t]$ contains the competitive interval in its interior infinitely often. Let C denote the set of states such that $[c_0, c_1] \subset [\alpha(x), \beta(x)]$, that is,

$$C = \{x \in A \mid \alpha(x) < c_0 < c_1 < \beta(x)\}.$$

The next result shows that $\{X_t\}$ belongs to C infinitely often with probability 0. The idea of Lemma 8 is to show that B is an absorbing state and that B is uniformly accessible from C.

Lemma 8 *For any initial condition x, $Q(x, C) = 0$.*

Proof Theorem 6 implies that B is an absorbing set, so it is sufficient to note that $C \rightsquigarrow B$ and then apply Corollary 2. To see that B is uniformly accessible from C, note that with probability $(2N)^{-1}$ the seller $i = 1$ is chosen at date $t + 1$ and with probability $(c_0 + c_1)/2(M - u_1)$ he chooses a price in the interval $(c_0, (c_0 + c_1)/2)$; similarly, with probability $(2N)^{-1}$ the buyer $j = 1$ is chosen at date $t + 1$ and with probability $(c_0 + c_1)/2v_1$ he chooses a price in the interval $((c_0 + c_1)/2, c_1)$. ■

Case 2

Using the result from Case 1, we can show that α_t (resp. β_t) must be greater than c_0 (resp. less than c_1) infinitely often. If not then one of the marginal prices α_t and β_t lies outside the competitive interval $[c_0, c_1]$ for all sufficiently large values of t and then Lemma 8 implies that the other price must lie inside.

Lemma 9 *For any initial condition x, with probability one, one of the following must occur:*

> *(i)* $c_0 < \alpha_t < \beta_t < c_1$ *for some t;*
> *(ii)* $\alpha_t < c_0$ *for all t sufficiently large;*
> *(iii)* $\beta_t > c_1$ *for all t sufficiently large.*

Proof Suppose that case (i) does not occur. Then since $\alpha_t < \beta_t$ for all t, it must be the case that $\alpha_t < c_0$ infinitely often or $\beta_t > c_1$ infinitely often. Since the marginal prices do not straddle the competitive interval infinitely often, except for a finite number of dates $\alpha_t < c_0$ implies that $\beta_t < c_1$ and $\beta_t > c_1$ implies that $\alpha_t > c_0$. Then having ruled out case (i), $\alpha_t < c_0$ (resp. $\beta_t > c_1$) implies that $\alpha_{t+1} < c_0$ (resp. $\beta_{t+1} > c_1$) except for a finite number of dates. Thus, (ii) and (iii) are the only alternatives to (i). ■

Case 3

If case (i) of Lemma 9 holds, then we are done. It remains to show that cases (ii) and (iii) do not rule out the competitive outcome. If one of these Cases does occur, the marginal price converges to the appropriate endpoint, c_0 or c_1, without ever entering the interval $[c_0, c_1]$. Then the prices at which trade occurs will be competitive in the limit, but the marginal trade can oscillate indefinitely between the marginal trader and an extra-marginal trader. For example, along some realization (sample path) of the Markov chain, we may have $\alpha_t < c_0$ for all t sufficiently large; then $\alpha_t \to c_0$ as $t \to \infty$. Unfortunately, we cannot analyze individual sample paths because they occur with probability zero. Instead we have to reformulate the claim in terms of a set of states.

For any $\varepsilon > 0$ let A_ε denote the set of states $x = (a, b)$ such that

$$a_i \leq \min\{v_m, u_{m+1}\} + \varepsilon \text{ for } i = 1, \ldots, m$$

and

$$b_j \geq \max\{u_m, v_{m+1}\} - \varepsilon \text{ for } j = 1, \ldots, m.$$

Lemma 10 says that, starting from any initial condition x and for any ε, A_ε is uniformly accessible from any point in the state space $\mathbf{X}$. Unfortunately, while the proof of the lemma is straightforward, it is rather tedious. It consists of considering arbitrary initial states and showing inductively that with positive probability, price-cutting by sellers and price-raising by buyers will lead the infra-marginal traders to choose prices close to the competitive interval.

Lemma 10 *For any $\varepsilon > 0$, $\mathbf{X} \leadsto A_\varepsilon$.*

Proof More precisely, we shall show that for any x and $\varepsilon > 0$, there exists an integer $n > 0$ (independent of ε and x) and a number $\gamma > 0$ such that $P^n(x, A_\varepsilon) \geq \gamma$. We begin with the sellers and then repeat the argument for the buyers. We need to distinguish two different cases, depending on whether $v_m > u_{m+1}$ or $u_{m+1} > v_m$. ∎

Case A $v_m > u_{m+1}$
In this case, let $x = (a, b)$ be the initial condition and consider the first $m + 1$ sellers, $i = 1, \ldots, m + 1$. Arrange them in descending order according to their asking prices: $i = i_1 , \ldots, i_{m+1}$ so that $a_{i_h} > a_{i_{h+1}}$ for $h = 1, \ldots, m$. Note that we only consider generic initial states, in which there are no ties. Since ties occur with probability zero, this does not entail any loss of generality in what follows. Now suppose that these agents are chosen to make changes in their strategies in precisely this order. This will happen with probability $(2N)^{-(m+1)} > 0$. Consider first seller i_1. If $a_{i_1} \leq u_{m+1} + \varepsilon$ there is nothing more to prove so suppose that

$a_{i_1} > u_{m+1} + \varepsilon$. At this price, the agent is unable to trade, since at most m sellers can trade, the market-maker always assigns trades to the sellers with the lowest asking prices, and there are m sellers with lower prices. Therefore this seller, when given the chance, will randomize on the interval $[u_{i_1}, M]$ and has a positive probability $(u_{m+1} + \varepsilon - u_{i_1})/(M - u_{i_1}) > 0$ of choosing a price $a'_{i_1} \leq u_{m+1} + \varepsilon$.

Now move to the second seller. If this seller is choosing a price $a_{i_2} \leq u_{m+1} + \varepsilon$, there is nothing more to prove. If $a_{i_2} > u_{m+1} + \varepsilon$ then seller i_2 has the highest price and cannot trade. Then he will randomize on the interval $[u_{i_2}, M]$ and there is a probability $(u_{m+1} + \varepsilon - u_{i_2})/(M - u_{i_2}) > 0$ of choosing a price satisfying $a'_{i_2} \leq u_{m+1} + \varepsilon$.

To complete the proof by induction, suppose that $a'_i \leq u_{m+1} + \varepsilon$ for $i = i_1, \ldots, i_h$ and consider i_{h+1}. If $a_{i_{h+1}} \leq u_{m+1} + \varepsilon$ there is nothing to prove so suppose that $a_{i_{h+1}} > u_{m+1} + \varepsilon$. Then i_{h+1} cannot trade at this price (since there are m lower prices), so when given the chance seller i_{h+1} will randomize on the interval $[u_{i_{h+1}}, M]$ and with probability $(v_{m+1} + \varepsilon - u_{i_{h+1}})/u_{i_{h+1}}$ the new price will satisfy $a'_{i_{h+1}} \leq u_{m+1} + \varepsilon$. By induction we have shown that for all $i = i_1, \ldots, i_{m+1}$ there is a positive probability that $a_i \leq u_{m+1} + \varepsilon$ within exactly $m + 1$ periods. In fact, the probability of this happening is at least

$$\frac{(2N)^{-(m+1)} \varepsilon^{m+1}}{(M - u_{m+1})^{m+1}}$$

since seller $m + 1$ has the smallest probability of choosing a price in the acceptable interval.

Case A' $u_{m+1} > v_m$

In this case, arrange the first m sellers $i = 1, \ldots, m$ in decreasing order according to their asking prices: $i_1, \ldots, i_m$ satisfy $a_{i_h} > a_{i_{h+1}}$ for $h = 1, \ldots, m - 1$. Then there is a probability $(2N)^{-m}$ that these sellers will be chosen in precisely this order to change their asking prices. If $a_{i_1} > u_{m+1}$ he cannot trade since there are $m - 1$ sellers with lower prices and there are only $m - 1$ buyers who are willing to buy at prices as high as a_{i_1}. Consequently, this seller will randomize on the interval $[u_{i_1}, M]$ and choose a price satisfying $a'_{i_2} \leq v_m$ with probability $(v_m - u_{i_1})/(M - u_{1_1})$. Suppose that all sellers $i = i_1, \ldots, i_h$ have chosen a price $a'_i \leq v_m$ and that $a_{i_{h+1}} > v_m$. Then i_{h+1} cannot trade at his current price. When he gets a chance to change his strategy he will randomize over the interval $[u_{i_{h+1}}, M]$ and choose a price $a_{i_{h+1}} \leq v_m$ with probability $(v_m - u_{i_{h+1}})/u_{i_{h+1}}$. By induction, we have shown that all sellers $i = 1, \ldots, m$ will choose a price less than or equal to v_m in exactly m periods with a probability greater than or equal to

$$\frac{(2N)^{-m}(v_m - u_m)^m}{(M - u_{m+1})^m}.$$

We proceed in an exactly similar way with the buyers, this time distinguishing the cases $v_{m+1} > u_m$ and $v_{m+1} < u_m$.

Case B $v_{m+1} > u_m$

In this case, buyer $m + 1$ can sometimes compete with buyer m for trade. Take the first $m + 1$ buyers $j = 1, \ldots, m + 1$ and arrange them in increasing order of bid prices $j_1, \ldots, j_{m+1}$ so that $b_{j_h} < b_{j_{h+1}}$ for all $h = 1, \ldots, m$. There is a probability $(2N)^{-(m+1)}$ that the buyers will be chosen in precisely this order to change their strategies. Consider the decision of buyer j_1. Since he is offering the lowest price of $m + 1$ buyers, he cannot possibly trade. Therefore his new strategy will be a random draw from the interval $[0, v_{j_1}]$. With probability $(v_{j_1} - v_{m+1} + \varepsilon)/v_{j_1}$ the new price will satisfy $b'_{j_1} \geq v_{m+1} - \varepsilon$. Suppose that $b'_j \geq v_{m+1} - \varepsilon$ for $j = j_1, \ldots, j_h$ and consider j_{h+1}. If $b_{j_{h+1}} \geq v_{m+1} - \varepsilon$ there is nothing to prove so suppose that $b_{j_{h+1}} < v_{m+1} - \varepsilon$. Then j_{h+1} cannot trade at this price (since there are m higher prices), so when given the chance buyer j_{h+1} will randomize on the interval $[0, v_{j_{h+1}}]$ and with probability $(v_{j_{h+1}} - v_{m+1} + \varepsilon)/v_{j_{h+1}}$ the new price will satisfy $b'_{j_{h+1}} \geq v_{m+1} - \varepsilon$. By induction we have shown that for all $j = j_1, \ldots, j_{m+1}$ there is a positive probability that $b_j \geq v_{m+1} - \varepsilon$ within $m + 1$ periods. In fact, the probability of this event will be at least

$$\frac{(2N)^{-m+1}\varepsilon^{m+1}}{v_{m+1}{}^{m+1}},$$

since buyer $j = m + 1$ has the smallest probability of choosing an acceptable price.

Case B′ $v_{m+1} < u_m$

Arrange the first m buyers in increasing order according to their bid prices: $j_1, \ldots, j_m$ satisfy $b_{j_h} < b_{j_{h+1}}$ for $h = 1, \ldots, m - 1$. Then there is a probability $(2N)^{-m}$ that these sellers will be chosen in precisely this order to change their asking prices. If $b_{j_1} < u_m$ he cannot trade since there are $m - 1$ sellers with lower prices and there are only $m - 1$ sellers who are willing to accept a price as low as b_{j_1}. Consequently, this seller will randomize on the interval $[0, u_{j_1}]$ and choose a price satisfying $b'_{j_1} \ge u_m$ with probability $(u_m - v_{j_1})/v_{j_1}$. Suppose that all buyers $j = j_1, \ldots, j_h$ have chosen a price $b'_j \ge u_m$. Then j_{h+1} cannnot trade at his current price. When he gets a chance to change his strategy he will randomize over the interval $[0, v_{j_{h+1}}]$ and choose a price $b_{j_{h+1}} \ge u_m$ with probability $(u_m - v_{j_{h+1}})/v_{j_{h+1}}$. By induction, we have shown that all buyers $j = 1, \ldots, m$ will choose a price $b'_j \ge u_m$ in m periods with probability greater than or equal to

$$\frac{(2N)^{-m}(u_m - v_m)^m}{v_m{}^m}.$$

The concatenation of these two arguments, for sellers and buyers, respectively, obviously establishes the desired result. Note however that in Cases A and B, for sellers or buyers, the probability of reaching the set A_ε depends on the value of ε. This follows from the fact that we use the extra-marginal seller or buyer $m + 1$ to discipline the infra-marginal sellers and buyers, respectively, and his chance of choosing an acceptable price is proportional to ε. ∎

Because Lemma 10 holds for arbitrary $\varepsilon > 0$, we conclude that even in Cases (ii) and (iii) the limit points of *one* of the marginal prices, $\{\alpha_t\}$ or $\{\beta_t\}$, are contained in the competitive interval $[c_0, c_1]$.

Lemma 11 *Suppose that $\alpha_t < c_0$ (resp. $\beta_t > c_1$) for all t sufficiently large; then $\lim_{t\to\infty} \alpha_t = c_0$ (resp. $\lim_{t\to\infty} \beta_t = c_1$).*

Proof Let A_n be the set A_ε with $\varepsilon = 1/n$ and let

$$\Omega_n = \{\omega \in \Omega | X_t \in A_n \text{ i.o.}\},$$

where "i.o." means for all but a finite number of t. Since $P_x(\Omega \backslash \Omega_n) = 0$,

$$P_x(\cap_{n=1}^{\infty} \Omega_n) = P_x(\Omega \backslash \cup_{n-1}^{\infty} (\Omega \backslash \Omega_n))$$
$$\geq 1 - P_x(\cup_{n-1}^{\infty}(\Omega \backslash \Omega_n))$$
$$\geq 1 - \sum_{n=1}^{\infty} P_x(\Omega \backslash \Omega_n) = 1.$$

Let $\Omega' = \cap_{n=1}^{\infty} \Omega_n$ and let

$$\Omega_0' = \{\omega \in \Omega' | \alpha_t < c_0 \text{ i.o.}\}$$

and

$$\Omega_1' = \{\omega \in \Omega' | \beta_t > c_1 \text{ i.o.}\}.$$

Then by construction we know that for any $\omega \in \Omega_0'$ (resp. any $\omega \in \Omega_1'$), $\alpha_t(\omega) \nearrow c_0$ (resp. $\beta_t(\omega) \searrow c_1$), as required. ∎

By a similar argument, we can show that in both Cases (ii) and (iii), both marginal prices converge.

Lemma 12 *Suppose that $\alpha_t < c_0$ (resp. $\beta_t > c_1$) for all t sufficiently large; then $\lim_{t\to\infty} \beta_t = c_0$ (resp. $\lim_{t\to\infty} \alpha_t = c_1$) where as usual the limits hold almost surely.*

Proof For any $\varepsilon > 0$ let B_ε denote the set of states such that $\alpha(x) < c_1 - \varepsilon$ and $\beta(x) > c_1$, that is,

$$B_\varepsilon = \{x \in A | c_0 < \alpha(x) < c_1 - \varepsilon < c_1 < \beta(x)\},$$

where A is the set of states consistent with maximum trade. For any state $x \in B_\varepsilon$ there is a positive probability, bounded away from zero, of entering the set $B = \{x \in A | c_0 < \alpha(x) < \beta(x) < c_1\}$. For example, with probability $m/2N$, an infra-marginal buyer is chosen to move and with probability at least ε/v_1 chooses a price in the

191

interval $[c_1 - \varepsilon, c_1]$. Once in the set B, the system never leaves, so we can use a previous argument to show that the system cannot be in the set B_ε infinitely often: for any initial state x and any fixed but arbitrary $\varepsilon > 0$,

$$P_x(X_t \in B_\varepsilon \text{ i.o.}) = 0.$$

Since we have also shown already that the system cannot be in a straddling position infinitely often, it follows that, defining $B'_\varepsilon = \{x \in A \mid \alpha(x) < c_1 - \varepsilon < c_1 < \beta(x)\}$, we have

$$P_x(X_t \in B'_\varepsilon \text{ i.o.}) = 0.$$

From this it is immediate that, on a subset of Ω having full measure, if case (iii) occurs then $\alpha_t \to c_1$.

By an exactly similar argument, show that in Case (ii) $\beta_t \to c_0$. ∎

So, in both Cases (ii) and (iii), we have shown that the marginal prices converge to elements of the competitive interval $[c_0, c_1]$. Because the marginal prices only approach the competitive interval asymptotically, it is possible that the extra-marginal agents $i = m + 1$ and $j = m + 1$ are able to trade infinitely often. However, this trade will be infrequent because the probability that an extra-marginal agent is able to trade in any period goes to zero as the marginal prices converge to c_0 or c_1.

4.4 Extensions

Finite strategy sets

Although we have been analyzing a simple model, the analysis turns out to be complicated. Some of the complexity of the analysis in this chapter is associated with the fact that the state space $\mathbf{X}$ is an infinite set. It is natural to ask if the analysis could be simplified by replacing $\mathbf{X}$ with a finite subset.

For example, if the agents were restricted to choosing from a finite number of bid and ask prices, the set of admissible strategy profiles would be finite. The behavior of the system could then be represented by a finite Markov chain and this would eliminate some of the technical complications.

There is a certain realism in the assumption that admissible prices must belong to a finite set. In practice, the price of an indivisible good will be an integral multiple of the smallest monetary unit (cents, lire, etc.) and since the price is naturally bounded in this context, this implies that only a finite number of prices needs to be considered.

Assuming a finite number of prices simplifies the analysis in some ways and makes it more complicated in others. With a continuum of prices, the probability of two agents quoting the same price is zero, so we do not have to worry about ties. If prices have to be an integral number of monetary units, then it is natural to assume that each agent can choose from the same set of prices and this makes ties a probable event. The treatment of ties may be important for the evolution of the system. For example, if goods are allocated randomly in the event of a tie, it may make it difficult for the system to settle down unless one agent can undercut the other. Suppose that two buyers have very similar reservation values and that there is no price that lies between the two values. Then both could end up offering the same price and the trade would bounce between them until one of them raised his bid.

One way to avoid ties is to assume that different agents have different sets of admissible prices. This seems a little contrived, given the motivation for finiteness in terms of a minimal currency unit, but it would work. The assumption that no two agents have the same reservation value plays a similar role in the preceding model.

There is another problem that arises even if the set of admissible prices is fine enough so that there exists an admissible price between any two reservation values. An example will make this clear. Suppose that there is a single buyer with a reservation price of 3 and two sellers, one with a reservation price of 1 and the other with a reservation price of 2. Call these agents 1, 2, and 3. Then a competitive equilibrium price must lie in the closed interval $[1, 2]$. Suppose that the smallest admissible price greater than 2 is 2.1. If 2.1 belongs to the price set of seller 1, then seller 1 can hold the marginal price and there is nothing seller 2 can do about it. On the other hand, if 2.1 belongs to the price set of seller 2, then at some point seller 1 will have to choose an ask price less than two in order to trade and in that case the marginal price will eventually get inside the competitive interval. Whether convergence occurs or not depends on exactly how we choose the admissible prices.

If the grid of admissible prices were sufficiently fine, one might hope the outcome would be approximately competitive. In other words, we can prove a limit theorem characterizing the asymptotic prices as $t \to \infty$ and then prove another limit theorem characterizing these prices as the grid becomes finer and finer until it approximates the continuous state space $\mathbf{X}$. The fact that, for some choices of the grid, the asymptotic prices (as $t \to \infty$) remain outside the competitive interval echoes Case (ii) of Theorem 7.

Taking limits provides us with an analog of Theorem 7 but is unlikely to be any easier and in some ways could be more complicated than dealing directly with the continuous state space $\mathbf{X}$.

Trading multiple units

One of the important simplifications of the theory developed in this chapter is the assumption that each agent wants to trade a single unit of the good. There are markets where this is a reasonable simplification (think of the labor market or the market for consumer durables, for example) and there are many examples in the literature on economic theory where substantial progress has been made with the aid of this assumption. Nonetheless, it is a restrictive assumption and it limits the applicability of the theory.

There is one particular feature of the assumption that should worry us, given our interest in perfect competition. As long as an agent wants to trade at most one unit of the good, there is absolutely no incentive for the agent to distort his demand or supply in order to influence the price. The agent only has two alternatives, to trade or not to trade. If he does not trade his payoff is zero and the price is irrelevant. So an agent must trade to get a positive payoff. He will try to trade at the best possible price but there is no useable tradeoff between the amount traded and the price.

The fact that we get a competitive outcome for any finite number of agents in the market is surprising. One might suspect that the assumption that each agent trades only one unit has something to do with it. For this reason it is important to examine the case of a market in which agents can trade multiple units of the good.

When an agent wants to trade more than one unit, he immediately faces the possibility of a tradeoff between price and quantity. This is most clearly apparent if the agent is forced to trade all units at the same bid or ask price. Then in order to trade an extra unit a seller will have to lower the price at which he offers all units and conversely a buyer will have to raise the price he bids for all units. But this is not the only way of extending the model, and, in fact, there are many ways that one could go about it, with different results.

Perhaps the simplest way of extending the model is to adapt the behavioral rules used in this chapter by representing each agent as a collection of behavioral rules, one for each unit of the good traded. Suppose, for simplicity, that there is a single seller and a single buyer. The seller is assumed to have N different units of the good and the buyer is assumed to have N different uses for the good. Then the seller's preferences are represented by a sequence of valuations $u = (u_1, \ldots, u_N)$, where $0 < u_1 < u_2 < \ldots < u_N$ and the buyer's preferences are represented by a sequence of valuations $v = (v_1, \ldots, v_N)$, where $v_1 > v_2 > \ldots > v_N > 0$. The interpretation here is that u_i is the valuation the seller places on unit i of the good and v_j is the valuation the buyer places on a unit of the good applied to use j. Notice that these are not marginal valuations, the value of the nth unit of the good bought and sold. Rather these are valuations that attach to identifiable units of the good or identifiable uses of the goods. This requires us to assume that the seller regards different units of the good as somehow distinct, independently of the number sold and that the buyer regards different units of the good as identical, but applicable to distinct uses in which they have different valuations, independently of the number of units purchased.

The seller chooses a sequence of ask prices $a = (a_1, \ldots, a_N)$ where a_i denotes the price asked for unit i and the buyer chooses a sequence of bid prices $b = (b_1, \ldots, b_N)$, where b_j denotes the price bid for a unit that will be applied to use j. The bids and asks are then matched by the profit-maximizing market-maker.

The crucial question is how the bids and asks are chosen. Because of the special assumptions we have placed on preferences, it is possible to assign bid and ask prices to goods independently of the number of goods bought and sold. This means that the prices for different units/uses can be varied independently. In fact, it is possible to regard the seller as a collection of N sellers, each with a different valuation, and the buyer as a collection of N buyers, each with a different valuation. So one way to model the behavior of a buyer or seller is to adopt the behavioral rule used previously by choosing each price to maximize the surplus realized on that unit of the good. Then the previous analysis applies and we get a convergence theorem even with two agents in the market.

As a thought experiment, to see how one might use the results developed in this chapter to understand the behavior of a market in which individuals trade multiple units, this exercise has some value. However, it is not entirely convincing for a number of reasons.

First, an agent is not necessarily choosing a better strategy when he adjusts the ask price for unit i or the bid price for unit j. The reason is that he is competing with himself and increasing the surplus earned on one unit of the good may decrease the surplus earned on another. In fact, he may end up worse off as a result of changing his strategy in this way.

There are two possible responses to this criticism. One response is that, if the object is to model bounded rationality, it may not be such a bad thing that the behavioral rules are somewhat incoherent. Building in more rational-ity does not necessarily make the model more realistic. Another response is that, if there were many buyers and sellers in the market, the probability that a change in an agent's price for one unit would affect his surplus on another unit would be small and hence might pass unno-ticed.

Another, possibly more serious, criticism is that by assuming agents choose the prices for different units inde-pendently, we are building into the model an unrealistic amount of competition. There is no possibility for the agent to discover that by varying the prices of different units simultaneously he can exert market power and improve his welfare as a result. In fact, by using the surplus earned on a single unit as the criterion for changing the strategy, we are not even allowing the agent to take into account how his utility changes as a result of a change in strategy.

Finally, the specification of the preferences is artificial. It does not allow for the usual, natural interpretation that u_i is the seller's valuation of the ith unit sold and that v_j is the buyer's valuation of the jth unit bought. If utility is a function of the number of units bought or sold, we cannot specify a strategy for unit i or unit j independently of the other units.

Suppose then that we take the more normal interpreta-tion where each additional unit sold has a higher marginal disutility (cost) and each additional unit bought has a smal-ler marginal utility. As before, we can illustrate the model by assuming a single buyer and a single seller who choose ask prices $a = (a_1, \ldots, a_N)$ and bid prices $b = (b_1, \ldots, b_N)$, respectively. We may want to restrict strategies so that obviously dominated strategies are ruled out, but that is not important as long as the set of admissible strategies is bounded and contains the usual strategies.

The market-maker is, as usual, assumed to choose trades to maximize profits, but here his allocation will have to respect the buyer's and seller's ordering of the bids. If he chooses to trade n units, the profit will be

$$\sum_{j=1}^{n} b_j - \sum_{i=1}^{n} a_i.$$

This is because a seller cannot trade the nth unit unless he is also trading the first, second, . . . and $(n-1)$th units as well.

At each date, one of the agents is chosen at random to change his strategy. He randomly selects one from the admissible set. If it is better than the current strategy, he adopts it; otherwise he stays with the current strategy.

There are various ways in which the search for a better strategy could be structured. An agent could vary the price of one unit at a time or simultaneously change the prices of all units. These modeling choices have important effects on the behavior of the system. Consider first the case where agents vary one price at a time. Suppose that strategies are limited so that $u_i \le a_i \le M$ and $0 \le b_j \le v_j$. Then the surplus from trade is always non-negative and the agent will never want to restrict his trade, as opposed to carrying on the same trade at more favorable prices. If agents adjust the price for one unit at a time, the model will have the property that once the maximum volume of trade is achieved, it stays the same forever. The reason is that, on the one hand, an agent will never choose to reduce his trade and, on the other, he can increase his trade only by stealing a unit from an agent on the same side of the market. This suggests that the analysis of the model in this chapter could be extended to show convergence if prices are changed one unit at a time.

Would the equilibrium prices converge to the competitive interval? That is not so clear, but the similarity to Bertrand competition suggests that it might be possible to prove a competitive limit theorem, even with a finite number of agents.

The property that the maximum volume of trade, once achieved, is maintained forever depends on the assumption that agents change one price at a time. If agents can change several prices simultaneously the model does not have this property. For example, it may well be advantageous for an agent to reduce his trade if at the same time he gains enough by changing the prices of infra-marginal units. The maximum volume property played an important role in the analysis of convergence in this chapter. If it no longer holds when multiple units are traded and prices on different units are changed simultaneously, this suggests that the analysis of this case will be much more difficult.

If convergence to something holds, will that "something" be perfectly competitive? The fact that agents recognize the price–quantity tradeoff suggests that simultaneous price changing will lead to imperfect competition. In that case, large numbers of buyers and sellers will be needed to achieve a perfectly competitive outcome.

An important special case of simultaneous price changing is one in which the agents must quote a single price for all units traded, possibly accompanied by a limit on the number of units to be traded. A limit on trades is needed because otherwise the agent runs the risk of cornering the market at a disadvantageous price. The interest of this case is that it makes the link between the price quoted and the quantity traded quite tight and so emphasizes the role of imperfect competition. Again, large numbers may be needed to achieve the perfectly competitive outcome.

Multiple goods

The restriction of the analysis to a single market (i.e. the market for a single good) is just as limiting as the restriction to trading a single unit of the good. If each buyer and seller operates in only one market, then the extension to multiple goods adds nothing to the story developed so far: an economy with many markets is just a collection of single-market economies that do not interact in any meaningful way. So to make the extension interesting, one wants agents to buy and sell in more than one market (buy and sell more than one good).

It is not difficult to extend the definition of the model to allow for more than one good, especially if we retain the assumption of quasi-linear utility. For simplicity, suppose that agents can trade at most one unit of each good, but there is a finite number of goods indexed by $h = 1, \ldots, \ell$ in

Strategic foundations of general equilibrium

addition to the numeraire (money). There is a finite number of sellers $i = 1, \ldots, N$ each of whom sells a vector $x_i \in \{0, 1\}^N$ of goods at the ask prices $a_i \in \mathbf{R}_+^N$ and receives a payoff $a_i \cdot x_i - u_i(x_i)$, where $-u_i(x_i)$ is the disutility of giving up x_i. Similarly, there is a finite number of buyers $j = 1, \ldots, N$ each of whom purchases a vector of goods $x_j \in \{0, 1\}^N$ at the bid prices $b_j \in \mathbf{R}_+^N$ and receives a payoff of $v_j(x_j) - b_j \cdot x_j$.

There is no difficulty in adapting the behavioral rules to the multi-good case, because there is a price for each different good and the matching of demands and supplies can be carried out for each market independently of the others. Thus, one could choose an agent at random to change his strategy and assume that he randomly chooses a good and randomly chooses a new bid–ask price for that good. If the new price increases the agent's payoff it would be adopted; otherwise the current price would be maintained. This specification has the advantage of simplicity and allows us to extend the analysis of the single-good model in a straightforward way. However, it has the unattractive feature that certain improvements that can be achieved only by changing two prices at once are ruled out.

An example will make this clear. Suppose there are two goods, A and B, and three buyers A, B, and C. Buyer A likes good A, buyer B likes good B, and buyer C likes goods A and B. More precisely, assume that $v_j(0) = 0$ for all j and that

$$v_A(0, 1) = 0; v_A(1, 0) = v_A(1, 1) = 2;$$
$$v_B(1, 0) = 0; v_B(0, 1) = v_B(1, 1) = 2;$$
$$v_C(1, 0) = v_C(0, 1) = 1; v_C(1, 1) = 6.$$

So buyer A will pay up to 2 for one unit of A; buyer B will pay up to 2 for one unit of B; and buyer C will pay up to 1 for a unit of either A or B and will pay up to 6 for a bundle consisting of a unit of both A and B. Thus, C has potentially the highest valuation for both goods, but only if he can buy one unit of each. If he can get only one good, buyers A and B each have higher valuations in their respective markets.

200

Bounded rationality

For simplicity, assume that there is a single seller with one unit of each good that he values at 0.

Now consider a situation in which A and B are both buying one unit of the good at a price of $1 < p < 2$ and C is bidding less than p for both goods. If C has the chance to change his bid for one of the goods, he will not find it profitable to bid more than p so there is no way that he can become a purchaser. If the seller is asking p then we have an equilibrium. On the other hand, if C could alter both bid prices simultaneously, he could capture the marginal bid on both goods from buyers A and B.

This suggests that agents should be allowed to search for better prices of all goods simultaneously. The analysis of this model will not be so easy, however. Because the marginal valuation of a good depends on the other goods being traded, an agent may well find himself engaged in unrewarding trade. As a result, the process defined by this rule does not have the property of maximizing the volume of trade. An example will make this clear. Suppose that C has the marginal bid for both goods, say, $b_C = (1, 1.5)$. Then buyer A gets a chance to change his strategy and by bidding 1.5 for good A he takes the marginal bid away from C. Then C finds himself paying 1.5 for a unit of good B which is not individually rational. So if C next gets a chance to change his strategy, he may end up choosing not to trade, that is, offering a price below the marginal bid for good B. If the other buyers are also offering low prices for good B there may be no trade in good B. Thus, with multiple goods the volume of trade can fall, unlike the single-good case.

The multi-good model has a tradeoff between price and quantity, in the sense that a trade in one market may influence the price that has to be paid in other. In the example above, buyer C's marginal willingness to pay increases when he consumes a unit of the other good. The opposite could be the case. Suppose that C's preferences satisfy:

$$v_C(1, 0) = v_C(0, 1) = 1; v_C(1, 1) = 1.5.$$

Then C is willing to pay up to 1 for a unit of good A if he consumes no B but would only pay $1.5 - b$ if he were already purchasing one unit of B at a price of b. If buyers A and B trade both goods, they might discover by trial and error that by letting C have a unit of good B they reduce his competition for good A, thus reducing the price they have to pay for it.

An interesting question is whether the interaction of the two markets leads to a kind of imperfect competition, as did the price–quantity tradeoff in the multi-unit, single-good case.

From partial equilibrium to general equilibrium

I have been writing about models with multiple goods as if they were models with multiple markets; but the "markets" in these models are not really separate and distinct. We can say that there is a market for each good, but this is just a figure or speech. Agents simultaneously trade and quote prices for all of the goods. Since every agent is simultaneously participating in every one of these "markets," we could equally well say that there is a single market in which all the goods are traded.

Likewise, the models discussed in the preceding chapters sometimes assume a single good (plus money) and sometimes a finite but arbitrary number of goods. We could interpret the former as models of a single market (partial equilibrium models) and the latter as models of an economy with many markets (general equilibrium models), but there is no fundamental difference between them. The specification of behavior and equilibrium are essentially the same. Thus, in the model studied in chapter 2, all the agents are being matched with each other, presumably in a single location, and when they are matched they offer to trade bundles of commodities rather than individual commodities. There is no sense in which different commodities are being traded on different markets.

If the only difference between a model of a single market and a model of an economy with many markets is the dimension of the commodity space, then it follows that equilibrium in an economy is achieved in the same way as in a single market. This contradicts a long-standing tradition in economic thought, beginning with Keynes if not earlier, that holds the determination of equilibrium in an economy is fundamentally different from the determination of equilibrum in a Marshallian market.

I would argue that although the theory developed here pretends to be a theory of general equilibrium, it does not take seriously the distinction between partial and general equilibrium. A more convincing model of general equilibrium might differ from this one in many ways. One important way in which it ought to differ is in recognizing that markets are distinct and that not all individuals participate in all markets at a given time. This in turn implies that the problem of achieving an efficient allocation of resources is more difficult than the models developed here suggest.

CHAPTER 5

AFTERTHOUGHTS

When Adam Smith wrote about the working of the invisible hand, how it led self-interested individuals to act in a way that furthered the efficient allocation of resources, he had in mind an economy that was already decentralized and complex. In this economy, each individual was a small part and had little knowledge of the whole. These individuals pursued their own narrow interests with little thought for the rest of the complex process that constituted the life of the economy. That order could come from the uncoordinated decisions of these agents is still an amazing insight.

The theory of competitive general equilibrium that culminated in the the Arrow–Debreu–McKenzie (ADM) model is a beautiful formalization of Smith's insight. It remains the best rationalization we have of the viability of the market system. It also provides an analytical model that is still the workhorse of many areas of economics. But in spite of its subtlety and power, the ADM model hardly does justice to the richness of Smith's vision. The decision-making framework represented by the ADM model, which we take to be the paradigm of perfect competition, reduces the whole economy to a single auction market. Although the ADM model can be interpreted as a theory of general equilibrium in a complete economy, it does not take seriously the distinction between partial and general equilibrium. It allows for any number of commodities, even an infinite number, and this is often interpreted as meaning that there is a large number of markets. It would be more accurate to say that there is a single market in which any number of commodities can be simultaneously traded. In any case, the qualitative properties of the model are essentially the same regardless of the number of commodities/markets, so this is not a theory in which the number of markets matters much.

It was suggested at the end of chapter 4 that the models we have been discussing, like the ADM model, do not take seriously the distinction between partial and general equilibrium. There are many ways in which these models could be made more realistic. Two I want to emphasize are incompleteness of markets and incomplete participation in markets.

It has long been recognized that markets are *incomplete*. The ADM model distinguishes commodities by physical characteristics, time and place of delivery, and the state of nature on which delivery is contingent, and then assumes that a market exists at the beginning of time in which all these commodities can be traded. Clearly, it is literally impossible to trade all of these commodities at a single place and at a single point in time and in that sense markets are "incomplete." Models of general equilibrium with incomplete markets (GEI) have been developed to deal with the intertemporal issues that arise when it is impossible to trade all commodities simultaneously. Since every commodity can be traded at some point in time, trade has to continue through time. Incompleteness of this kind is important because it restricts agents' ability to share risks and smooth consumption and production flows efficiently.

There are special conditions under which markets that are not literally complete, as in the ADM model, are nonetheless effectively complete because they allow an efficient allocation of resources to be achieved through dynamic trading of a small set of commodities and securities. This is an important extension of the classical theory and one that has found extremely important applications in finance, but the more interesting possibilities from the point of view of understanding the economic coordination problem arise when markets are effectively incomplete and the resulting allocation of resources is not necessarily efficient.

Another kind of incompleteness takes the form of *incomplete participation*. In the classical theory, even with incomplete markets, every agent participates in all the markets that exist at any point in time. As a result, a large part of the coordination function that Smith ascribed to the invisible hand is here rendered more or less automatic by the assumption that all agents are interacting in all active markets at the same time. A more realistic and more challenging vision would recognize that most economic agents do not trade most goods and do not therefore participate in most markets. Furthermore, if we look only at the restricted set of markets that an individual agent does participate in, we would see that he is not active in all of those markets simultaneously. These observations have important consequences for the operation of markets.

There are special conditions under which markets with incomplete participation will behave like markets with complete participation, just as there are conditions under which incomplete markets will perform like complete markets. For example, middlemen and arbitrageurs can eliminate gains from trade between different markets and ensure an efficient allocation of resources in the absence of complete participation. But these conditions are restrictive and in any case that is not the most interesting use of this theory. The more interesting possibility is to see under what conditions we get different results.

Extending the theory to take account of these two kinds of incompleteness will not be easy. Allowing for incomplete markets will not be easy because it requires one to introduce time in a very different way. In the preceding chapters, time has been used as an opportunity for trading to reach an efficient allocation in a stationary environment or it has been used as an opportunity for learning about or adapting to a stationary environment. We start with an essentially static model and study how the equilibrium of the static model is achieved as the outcome of a pseudo-dynamic process. Models with incomplete markets are dynamic. They presuppose time in which things happen and the world changes. Mixing up these two uses of time is not likely to be easy.

Allowing for incomplete participation raises different problems. First, there is no well developed counterpart to Walrasian equilibrium theory with incomplete participation, although there are some intriguing examples. Secondly, it is not clear what the relevant questions are. One suggestion is that incomplete participation has something to do with bounded rationality. One way that the economy responds to the complexity of the world is through the division of labor. Individuals specialize in different markets. In principle, this may lead to the same outcome as a model with complete participation. Roughly speaking, if arbitrageurs and middlemen ensure that all the local first-order conditions are satisfied, this may result in a global optimum (efficiency). But that outcome seems optimistic if the agents specialize in the first place because of bounded rationality. How do we know that agents operating in different markets will make the right decisions? Doesn't it require too much common knowledge, too much rationality in their expectations? That really is the question and just as the ADM model does not explain how we get to equilibrium or under what circumstances the Walrasian definition of equilibrium is appropriate, so it seems that modeling the coordination of markets as if they were a single market does not quite do the trick either. But that is another story and far beyond the scope of this book.

REFERENCES

Aghion, P., P. Bolton and C. Harris (1991). "Optimal Learning by Experimentation," *Review of Economic Studies*, 58, 621–54

Al-Najjar, N. and R. Smorodinsky (1998a). "Pivotal Players and the Characterization of Influence," *Center for Mathematical Studies in Economics and Management Science, Discussion Paper*, 1174R, Northwestern University

(1998b). "Large Non-anonymous Repeated Games," MEDS, Kellogg Graduate School of Management, Northwestern University, unpublished

Arrow, K. and G. Debreu (1954). "Existence of Equilibrium for a Competitive Economy," *Econometrica*, 22, 265–90

Arrow, K. and F. Hahn (1971). *General Competitive Analysis*, Amsterdam and New York: North-Holland

Aumann, R. (1974). "Subjectivity and Correlation in Randomized Strategies," *Journal of Mathematical Economics*, 1, 67–96

(1987). "Correlated Equilibrium as an Expression of Bayesian Rationality," *Econometrica*, 55, 1–18

Aumann, R. and L. Shapley (1974). *Values of Non-atomic Games*, Princeton, Princeton University Press

Aumann, R. and S. Sorin (1989). "Cooperation and Bounded Recall," *Games and Economic Behavior*, 1, 5–39

Banerjee, A. (1992). "A Simple Model of Herd Behavior," *Quarterly Journal of Economics*, 107, 797–817

Banks, J. and R. Sundaram (1992). "Denumerable-armed Bandits," *Econometrica*, 60, 1071–96

Benaim, M. and M. Hirsch (1996). "Learning Processes, Mixed Equilibria, and Dynamical Systems Arising from Repeated Games," unpublished

Bikhchandani, S., D. Hirshleifer and I. Welch (1992). "A Theory of Fads, Fashions, Custom, and Cultural Change as

References

Informational Cascades," *Journal of Political Economy*, *100*, 992–1026

Billingsley, P. (1985). *Probability and Measure*, 2nd edn., New York: John Wiley

Binmore, K. (1990). "Modeling Rational Players: Parts I and II," in K. Binmore, *Essays on the Foundations of Game Theory*, Oxford and Cambridge, MA: Blackwell, 151–85, 186–231

Binmore, K. and M. Herrero (1988a). "Matching and Bargaining in Dynamic Markets," *Review of Economic Studies*, *55*, 17–31

(1988b). "Security Equilibrium," *Review of Economic Studies*, *55*, 33–48

Binmore, K., A. Rubinstein and A. Wolinsky (1986). "The Nash Bargaining Solution in Economic Modelling," *Rand Journal of Economics*, *17*, 176–88

Bolton, P. and C. Harris (1999). "Strategic Experimentation," *Econometrica*, *67*, 349–74

Caplin, A. and J. Leahy (1994). "Miracle on Sixth Avenue: Information, Externalities, and Search," New York University, unpublished

Chamley, C. and D. Gale (1994). "Information Revelation and Strategic Delay in a Model of Investment," *Econometrica*, *62*, 1065–85

Chatterjee, K. and H. Sabourian (1998). "Multiperson Bargaining and Strategic Complexity," Pennsylvania State University and King's College, Cambridge, unpublished

Cournot, A. A. (1938). *Researches into the Mathematical Principles of the Theory of Wealth*, trans N. T. Bacon, with an essay on "Cournot and Mathematical Economics" and a bibliography of mathematical economics by Irving Fisher, New York: A. M. Kelley (1960)

Dagan, N., R. Serrano and O. Volij (forthcoming). "Bargaining, Coalitions and Competition," *Economic Theory*

Debreu, G. (1970). "Economies with a Finite Set of Equilibria," *Econometrica*, *38*, 387–92

Edgeworth, F. Y. (1881). *Mathematical Psychics: An Essay on the Application of Mathematics to the Moral Sciences*, London: Kegan Paul

Ellison, G. and D. Fudenberg (1993). "Rules of Thumb for Social Learning," *Journal of Political Economy*, *101*, 612–43

(1995). "Word-of-mouth Communication and Social Learning," *Quarterly Journal of Economics*, *110*, 93–125

References

Fudenberg, D. and D. Kreps (1993). "Learning Mixed Equilibria," *Games and Economic Behavior*, 5, 320–67

Fudenberg, D. and E. Maskin (1986). "The Folk Theorem in Repeated Games with Discounting or with Incomplete Information," *Econometrica*, 54, 533–54

Fudenberg, D. and J. Tirole (1992). *Game Theory*, Cambridge, MA: MIT Press

Gale, D. (1986a). "A Simple Characterization of Bargaining Equilibrium in a Large Market Without the Assumption of Dispersed Characteristics," University of Pennsylvania Center for Analytic Research in Economics and the Social Sciences (CARESS), Working Paper, 86–05

(1986b). "Bargaining and Competition Part I: Characterization," *Econometrica*, 54, 785–806

(1986c). "Bargaining and Competition Part II: Existence," *Econometrica*, 54, 807–18

(1987). "Limit Theorems for Markets with Sequential Bargaining," *Journal of Economic Theory*, 43, 20–54

Gale, D. and R. Rosenthal (1998). "Imitation, Experimentation, and Stochastic Stability," *Journal of Economic Theory*, 84

Goldman, S. and R. Starr (1982). "Pairwise, *t*-Wise, and Pareto Optimality," *Econometrica*, 50, 593–606

Green, E. (1980). "Noncooperative Price Taking in Large Dynamic Markets," *Journal of Economic Theory*, 22, 155–82

(1982). "Internal Costs and Equilibrium: The Case of Repeated Prisoner's Dilemma," unpublished

(1984). "Continuum and Finite-player Noncooperative Models of Competition," *Econometrica*, 52, 975–93

Gul, F. and R. Lundholm (1995). "On the Clustering of Agents' Decisions: Herd Behavior versus the Timing of Actions," *Jouirnal of Political Economy*, 103, 1039–66

Gul, F., H. Sonnenschein and R. Wilson (1986). "Foundations of Dynamic Monopoly and the Coase Conjecture," *Journal of Economic Theory*, 39, 155–90

Hahn, F. (1974). "On the Notion of Equilibrium in Economics," Inaugural Lecture, Cambridge University (1974); reprinted in F. Hahn, *Equilibrium and Macroeconomics*, Cambridge, MA: MIT Press (1984)

Halmos, P. (1988). *Measure Theory*, New York: Springer-Verlag

Hayek, F.A. (1945). "The Use of Knowledge in Society," *American Economic Review*, 35, 519–30

Hicks, J. (1967). *Critical Essays in Monetary Theory*, Oxford: Clarendon Press

References

Hildenbrand, W. (1974). *Core and Equilibria of a Large Economy*, Princeton: Princeton University Press

Jordan, J. (1993). "Three Problems in Learning Mixed-strategy Equilibria," *Games and Economic Behavior*, 5, 368–86

Jovanovic, B. and R. Rosenthal (1988). "Anonymous Sequential Games," *Journal of Mathematical Economics*, 17, 77–87

Kalai, E. and E. Lehrer (1993a). "Rational Learning Leads to Nash Equilibrium," *Econometrica*, 61, 1019–46

(1993b). "Subjective Equilibria in Repeated Games," *Econometrica*, 61, 1231–40

Kandori, M., G. Mailath and R. Rob (1993). "Learning, Mutation, and Long Run Equilibria in Games," *Econometrica*, 61, 29–56

Karlin, S. and P. Taylor (1975). *A First Course in Stochastic Processes*, San Diego: Academic Press

Krishna, V. and T. Sjostrom (1995). "On the Convergence of Fictitioius Play," Harvard Business School, unpublished

Lehrer, E. and Z. Neeman (1998). "The Scope of Anonymous Voluntary Bargaining under Asymmetric Information," Boston University, unpublished

Madden, P. (1976). "Theorem on Decentralized Exchange," *Econometrica*, 44, 787–91

Mailath, G. and A. Postlewaite (1990). "Asymmetric Information Bargaining Problems with Many Agents," *Review of Economic Studies*, 57, 351–67

Makowski, L. (1983). "Competitive Stock Markets," *Review of Economic Studies*, 50, 305–30

Marimon, R. (1995). "Learning from Learning in Economics," University of Minnesota, unpublished

Marshall, A. (1920). *Principles of Economics: An Introductory Volume*, 8th edn., London: Macmillan

Mas-Colell, A. (1989). "An Equivalence Theorem for a Bargaining Set," *Journal of Mathematical Economics*, 18, 129–39

Masso, J. and R. Rosenthal (1989). "More on the 'Anti-Folk Theorem'," *Journal of Mathematical Economics*, 18, 281–90

McKenzie, L. (1954). "On Equilibrium in Graham's Model of World Trade and Other Competitive Systems," *Econometrica*, 22, 147–61

McLennan, A. and H. Sonnenschein (1991). "Sequential Bargaining as a Noncooperative Foundation for Walrasian Equilibrium," *Econometrica*, 59, 1395–1424

References

Meyn, S. and R. Tweedie (1993). *Markov Chains and Stochastic Stability*, London and Berlin: Springer-Verlag

Moulin, H. (1986). *Game Theory for the Social Sciences*, 2nd and rev. edn., New York: New York University Press

Myerson, R. (1991). *Game Theory: Analysis of Conflict*, Cambridge, MA: Harvard University Press

Nash, J. (1951). "Noncooperative Games," *Annals of Mathematics*, 54, 289–95

(1953). "Two-person Cooperative Games," *Econometrica*, 21, 128–40

Negishi, T. (1962). "The Stability of a Competitive Economy: A Survey Article," *Econometrica*, 30, 635–69

Osborne, M. and A. Rubinstein (1990). *Bargaining and Markets*, San Diego, London, Sydney, and Toronto: Harcourt Brace Jovanovich and Academic Press

Ostroy, J. (1980). "The No-surplus Condition as a Characterization of Perfectly Competitive Equilibrium," *Journal of Economic Theory*, 22, 183–207

Roberts, K. (1980). "The Limit Points of Monopolistic Competition," *Journal of Economic Theory*, 22, 256–78

Royden, H. (1988). *Real Analysis*, 3rd edn., New York: Macmillan

Rubinstein, A. (1982). "Perfect Equilibrium in a Bargaining Model," *Econometrica*, 50, 97–109

(1986). "Finite Automata Play Repeated Prisoner's Dilemma," *Journal of Economic Theory*, 39, 83–96

Rubinstein, A. and A. Wolinsky (1985). "Equilibrium in a Market with Sequential Bargaining," *Econometrica*, 53, 1133–50

(1990). "Decentralized Trading, Strategic Behaviour and the Walrasian Outcome," *Review of Economic Studies*, 57, 63–78

Sabourian, H. (1990). "Anonymous Repeated Games with a Large Number of Players and Random Outcomes," *Journal of Economic Theory*, 51, 92–110

Schmeidler, D. and K. Vind (1972). "Fair Net Trades," *Econometrica*, 40, 637–42

Selten, R. (1965). "Spieltheoretische Behandlung eines Oligopolmodells mit Nachfrageträgheit," *Zeitschrift für die gesamte Staatwissenschaft*, 12, 301–24

(1975). "Reexamination of the Perfectness Concept for Equilibrium Points in Extensive Form Games," *International Journal of Game Theory*, 4, 25–55

References

Shaked, A. (1994). "Opting Out: Bazaars versus 'Hi Tech' Markets," *Investigaciones Economicas*, 18, 421–32

Shapley, L. and M. Shubik (1977). "Trade Using One Commodity as a Means of Payment," *Journal of Political Economy*, 85, 937–68

Shubik, M. (1959). "Edgeworth's Market Games," in R. D. Luce and A. W. Tucker (eds.), *Contributions to the Theory of Games IV*, Princeton: Princeton University Press

(1973). "Commodity Money, Oligopoly, Credit and Bankruptcy in a General Equilibrium Model," *Western Economic Journal*, 11, 24–38

Smith, A. (1976). *An Enquiry into the Nature and Causes of the Wealth of Nations*, general eds. R. H. Campbell and A. S. Skinner, textual ed. W. B. Todd, Oxford: Clarendon Press

Smith, L. and P. Sorensen (1996). "Pathological Outcomes of Observational Learning," MIT, unpublished

Stahl, I. (1972). *Bargaining Theory*, Stockholm: Economics Research Institute, Stockholm School of Economics

Stokey, N. and R. Lucas, with E. C. Prescott (1989). *Recursive Methods in Economic Dynamics*, Cambridge, MA: Harvard University Press

Uzawa, H. (1960). "Edgeworth's Barter Process and Walras' *Tâtonnement* Process," *Technical Report*, 83, Office of Naval Research, Contract Nonr-255 (50), NR-047-004, Department of Economics, Stanford University

Von Neumann, J. and O. Morgenstern (1980). *Theory of Games and Economic Behavior*, 3rd edn., Princeton: Princeton University Press

Walras, L. (1954). *Elements of Pure Economics*, London: Allen & Unwin

Weibull, J. (1995). *Evolutionary Game Theory*, Cambridge, MA: MIT Press

Young, P. (1993). "The Evolution of Conventions," *Econometrica*, 61, 57–84

INDEX

Index

Index

Index

Index

Index

Smorodinsky, R. 153
social norms 62
Sonnenschein, H. 23–4, 28
Sorensen, P. 159
Sorin, S. 137–8
Stahl, I. 13–14, 50, 86, 116
Starr, R. 48
Stokey, N. 36
strategies
  complementary and substitute
    164–5
  feasible 53–4
  finite 192–4
  Markov 58, 110, 121, 144
  profile 55–6
subgame-perfect equilibrium
    (SPE) 14, 23, 26, 28, 56–8, 78,
    106–7
  continuum of outcomes 117–19
  discounting 115–17
  with imperfect memory 125–6
  indeterminate 57
  quasi-stationary 16
  repeated games 133, 135–6
  seller's payoff 113
submartingale 101–2
substitution, limited 73–4
Sundaram, R. 160

Taylor, P. 95, 102
theory predictions 50
time 50–1
time-preference 86–7
Tirole, J. 129
trading
  multiple goods 199–202

multiple units 194–9
pairwise 61
rules 77, 80
volume-maximizing 179–82
"trembling hand" 151–2, 154–5
Tweedie, R. 177–8

uncertainty 145, 151
uniqueness 79, 83
utility 61
  and payoffs 54–5
utility function 62–3, 97
  Cobb–Douglas 46
  curvature 69–71, 73
  in pure exchange economies 44
Uzawa, H. 59

Vind, K. 8, 24
Volij, O. 24
von Neumann, J. 3, 16

Walras, L. 2, 35, 39
Walras allocation 8, 11, 28–9, 77,
    79–81, 104, 107
Walrasian equilibria 24, 207
Walrasian models 21–3
Walrasian outcomes 106–7
Weibull, J. 37
Welch, I. 159
Welfare Economics Theorems 41
Wilson, R. 28
Wolinsky, A. 13, 15–20, 22–6, 30,
    87, 110–19

Young, P. 37, 173

219